MOLIÈRE

LE BOURGEOIS GENTILHOMME

COMÉDIE–BALLET, 1670

Par MOLIÈRE

Edited, with Introduction, Notes, and
Vocabulary

by

THOMAS EDWARD OLIVER, Ph.D.

PROFESSOR OF ROMANCE LANGUAGES IN
THE UNIVERSITY OF ILLINOIS

INTER-
NATIONAL
MODERN
LANGUAGE
SERIES

GINN AND COMPANY

BOSTON · NEW YORK · CHICAGO · LONDON
ATLANTA · DALLAS · COLUMBUS · SAN FRANCISCO

The Athenæum Press
GINN AND COMPANY · PRO-
PRIETORS · BOSTON · U.S.A.

11696

TO
B. JOY JEFFRIES, M.D.
THE SKILLED OCULIST AND TRUE FRIEND
WHO RESTORED MY SIGHT, THUS MAKING POSSIBLE
THE TEACHER'S LIFE
THIS BOOK IS GRATEFULLY DEDICATED
BY THE EDITOR

PREFACE

The text of this edition of " Le Bourgeois gentilhomme " has been carefully collated with that of the standard edition found in Volume VIII of the " Œuvres de Molière " edited by Eugène Despois and Paul Mesnard. In the preparation of the Notes and Vocabulary the editor has consulted the important English and American editions, as well as many editions in French and several in German. Besides these editions a considerable amount of literature treating of Molière has been read, and such use made of it as seemed necessary for the present purpose.

Since this edition is intended for use in high schools as well as in colleges, the notes have been made rather full and a vocabulary has been added.

Grateful acknowledgment is given to Professor A. L. Owen of the University of Kansas and to Professor B. H. Bode of the University of Illinois for assistance in the case of several important notes. Professor Jean Beck of the University of Illinois also kindly aided in the preparation of several notes which involved a contrast of Molière's syntax with that of more modern French. The editor desires also to express his deep appreciation to Mr. Maurice W. Mather who watched the proof with great care, and to Mr. Steven T. Byington who gave valuable suggestions for the interpretation of the Arabic phrases in the Turkish ceremony.

Urbana, Illinois

CONTENTS

INTRODUCTION

MOLIÈRE

It is not intended to present here a biography of Molière of any length, but merely to emphasize the leading points in the genius of this greatest of French writers, and to suggest some interpretation of this genius. The serious student of Molière should consult for the details of his life and works any of the standard volumes upon that subject, chief among which should be mentioned Paul Mesnard's "Notice biographique sur Molière," which forms Volume X of the standard edition of Molière by Eugène Despois and Paul Mesnard. This edition is in the series known as "Les Grands Écrivains de la France." [1]

Molière was born in Paris on or before January 15, 1622, this being the date of his baptism, and died there February 17, 1673. If we reckon the time of his wanderings through France from about 1646 to 1658 as a portion of his education or preparation for his life work, as indeed it was, we are confronted by

---

[1] Other standard biographies are those by Voltaire, L. S. Auger, Louis Moland, Gustave Larroumet, Jules Claretie in French; L. H. Vincent, Henry M. Trollope, H. C. Chatfield-Taylor, Brander Matthews in English; also the English translation of Karl Mantzius' "Molière and his Times." Nor should the German work of Lotheissen or that of Mahrenholtz be omitted. The ever increasing body of literature on Molière, dealing with some phase of his life or with his plays in detail, cannot here be noted; the reader is referred for this literature prior to 1875 to Paul Lacroix's "Bibliographie Moliéresque"; for that subsequent to 1875 much is given in the tenth and eleventh volumes of the Despois-Mesnard edition, and in the "Catalogue of the Molière Collection in Harvard College Library." Contemporary additions to this literature may be found listed in the volumes of the important periodical *Revue d'histoire littéraire de la France* and in other similar periodicals. Mention should also be made of the introductory material to the other Molière plays issued in the International Modern Language Series by the publishers of the present volume.

the remarkable fact that Molière in less than fourteen years and in the midst of many and varied distractions, not to speak of his mental and physical anguish, wrote twenty-eight plays of great merit, and won that high place in the literature of the world which has never been, and never can be, denied him.

Truly nothing less than the flame of genius could have guided the young man of scarcely twenty-one when he turned his back on the quiet, respectable life which his father had destined for him, and began the despised career of an actor in a strolling company of players. It was then that he adopted the professional name of Molière to spare the feelings of his father and to save as far as possible the family name of Poquelin from disgrace. It is doubtful if this family would ever have been widely known, had not the stage name of its most distinguished member reflected on it the light of his great fame.

The fact that from this time on Molière was first and foremost an actor has seemed to many not sufficiently emphasized by his biographers. The wonderful knowledge of stagecraft which he possessed and displayed in all his dramas is a point of prime importance. He knew instinctively what was wanted and what was effective on the stage. It is inconceivable that he could have attained the summit of his genius without this knowledge, which came to him out of his own, and not merely out of other men's, experience. Hence the doubly great importance of those years of wandering, when he not only was the keen observer of men, but was learning to represent man to his fellow man. That he learned to do this latter is proved by the testimony of all trustworthy contemporaries, who declare that he was the greatest actor of comedy of his day and that he gathered about him the greatest group of actors that France had yet seen. When " Le Bourgeois gentilhomme " was first acted, the troupe of Molière consisted of twelve members in full standing, one pensioned member, and one apprentice. This troupe testifies to

Molière's ability as an organizer and as a leader; his devotion and loyalty to his fellow actors, and theirs to him, forms the chief bright and happy spot in his great career. The histrionic element in the genius of Molière died with him except in so far as the traditions of his method of acting have endured and been followed. For posterity, therefore, the actor has almost completely been absorbed by the author, but it is well to remember that Molière's genius and skill as an actor contributed in large measure to his success as a writer.

If France could choose but one representative in a group of the world's greatest literary men, that choice would unquestionably be Molière. What would be the chief reasons for such a choice? First and foremost it may be said that Molière completed in absolutely perfect form the task that he set himself to do. He said of his own work, " Le devoir de la comédie est de corriger les hommes en les divertissant." He chose to amuse as well as to correct, and for this double purpose he selected the best literary form, comedy. France has had many a moralist of the highest excellence, but no other nation ever had such a rare combination as the greatest moralist and the greatest entertainer in one person. Molière's greatness as a moralist does not rest on a mere passive depicting of vice and virtue, but on the fact that, in addition to the picture of life that we see, we find him as the ardent champion of the right, the good, the true. To him nature was truth, and hence he bitterly attacked and held up to ridicule all who deformed or distorted what was natural. Everything that was affected, artificial, hypocritical, selfish, extravagant, or merely conventional without other merit, was the aim of his satire. His belief that nature was the best guide led him to have faith in the innate goodness of man rather than in his corruption. Hence the antagonism of the strictly puritanical orthodox of the day, who saw in Molière, and perhaps rightly, an enemy of their formal dogma. To this antagonism, more than to the fact that Molière was an actor, was due the refusal of priests to come to his deathbed and the efforts of the established clergy to prevent his burial in consecrated ground. Yet how noble the death of this great apostle and teacher of mankind was in contrast with the pettiness and narrowness of his enemies !

Molière encompassed the wide field of comedy from the most boisterous and preposterous farce to the highest type of the comedy of character. This latter type, represented by his greater masterpieces, " L'Avare," " Don Juan," " Le Tartuffe," and " Le Misanthrope," closely approaches tragedy in the depth of questions discussed, as well as in the method of treatment. Indeed, the element of pathos frequently becomes of considerable importance, so much so that our interest in these higher comedies may be said to rest more in their seriousness than in their mirth-provoking elements. Beginning with an imitation of the conventional and loose-jointed Italian comedy known as the *commedia dell'arte*,[1] Molière rose by degrees, after exhausting the possibilities of his models, to the creation of new dramatic types and methods that have endured and shall ever endure. He discovered the great underlying and basic secret of true comedy, that of bringing his contemporaries on the stage as types of the humanity of all ages. For mere plot Molière cares little, but he is insistent that his characters be real, living human beings. In this application of true psychological analysis Molière is one of the greatest of realists, for he never makes the blunder of modern realism in its emphasis of vice alone and in its consequent distortion of the true picture of life. Nor does Molière thrust openly his own ideas before his audience ; rather does he cleverly veil them, either positively or negatively, in the humor

[1] The *commedia dell'arte* was a sort of comedy peculiar to the Italians. In this comedy only the skeleton or outline of the plot was written, the dialogue being improvised as the play progressed. This improvisation required actors of great skill and intelligence despite the fact that the plots and characters of the plays were of a conventional type.

or in the sincerity of a character or of a scene. Thus it may well be said that indirectly Molière is a great idealist; for, while he makes us laugh at the vagaries of men or makes us feel contempt for the meanness and selfishness of our fellows, we are unconsciously led to scorn the bad and to prefer the good in ourselves as well as in those about us. Molière's method in delineation of character is well summed up by Trollope in the words, " He did not try to draw men as they ought to be; his object was to show them as they are and very often as they ought not to be."

The enemies of Molière said of him that he was undermining the very bases of society, that he was attacking the institution of the family, and casting ridicule on religion and even on virtue. Nothing could be farther from the truth, for he never does either of these things. His plea is always for a purer family life, freed from parental selfishness and all other unnaturalness; for true love as the basis of marriage; for sincerity in religion; and for a sound, healthy, and sane morality instead of the affectation of virtue, so common in this world. He attacks humbug in every form. He shows the harm which comes from greed and dishonesty, from vanity and selfishness. He is the enemy of all that separates man from man. Hence in that most aristocratic age, the century of Louis XIV, he is the great commoner, the true democrat, revealing often more sense and more uprightness in the humble persons of his plays than in those who enjoy higher social advantages. He seeks a more rational, liberal, and sane education for both sexes, and womankind should see in him a true friend and a great champion, since, in the great essentials of life, he pleads for a real equality of man and woman. Especially true is this in the matter of love and marriage. There is scarcely a play of his in which he does not urge the right of girls to choose their life partners instead of being forced to assent to the choice of selfish parents.

Molière's style has often been criticized, but, while it is true that the hurry and worry of a busy life as actor, author, and manager undoubtedly prevented his giving that amount of attention to the style of his comedies which they deserved, yet his critics are apt to forget that a dramatist's style must vary objectively with the character represented. From this point of view Molière's style seems to many almost perfect, for it is always in harmony with the education and the social position, as well as with the temperament and the characteristic peculiarities, of the person speaking. Even could we conceive of Molière's independence surrendering to the rigidity of Vaugelas and the purists, the result would be disastrous, inasmuch as the great variety of his types could not be forced into the narrowness of Vaugelas and remain true types. Were all his characters to speak more or less alike, Molière would cease to be Molière. Moreover it must be remembered that Molière's plays were written primarily for the stage rather than for the library; they were written for listeners rather than for readers. In this connection it has been noted by competent critics that Molière's style is most effective in the theater, a further proof of the value of his having been an actor. In the *Avertissement* to the "Lexique de la langue de Molière," prepared by Messieurs Arthur and Paul Desfeuilles in 1900 and forming the twelfth and thirteenth volumes of the Despois-Mesnard edition, we find a short but excellent analysis of Molière's style. Here are emphasized the richness, the variety, the cleverness in use, the originality and the effectiveness for stage purposes of the language of the great actor-author. In regard to this effectiveness, we quote one passage from this *Avertissement*:

"Molière a gardé quelque chose du ton oratoire, du style classique de son époque. Les phrases sont construites de façon à porter jusqu'au fond de la salle de spectacle; elles sont très rhythmées, assez sonores pour dominer les rires du parterre, assez pleines pour qu'un détail mal entendu n'empêche pas de bien saisir l'ensemble du sens."

In this connection it is of great interest to read Molière's own instructions to his actors in the opening scenes of the " Impromptu de Versailles," where we see his solicitude that the speech of each character should conform in style and in delivery to the nature of that character.

As a man, Molière was a lover of his fellow man, notwith-standing the sorrows of his own life, which might well have made him a pessimist. His nobility of soul is revealed no better than on the last day of his life, when, despite the urgings of friends who realized how ill he was, he nevertheless went to the theater to play the title rôle in " Le Malade imaginaire," in order that his company and the stage hands might not lose their day's wage. And when he was borne away from the tragic irony of this last performance to his deathbed, his last hours were soothed by the ministrations of some sisters of charity to whom he had given shelter and hospitality. When he died, the anguish of his fellow actors, who loved him deeply, was most pathetic. They had lost their best friend.

It has been well said that if all the books printed about Molière were put into a room together, they would not be worth " Le Misanthrope." While this is true, yet it is not amiss to recall, in closing, the universal praise which has been given Molière by the critics of all nations. France has never had any difficulty in recognizing and appreciating the greatness of Molière, and he has been acclaimed as the greatest of comic poets by the comedy writers and critics of other lands. Many declare him the only rival of Shakespeare as a literary genius, and Sir Walter Scott even places him above the great English dramatist. In this connection the opinion of a recent critic, Mr. Chatfield-Taylor, is of interest: " Though Molière may be inferior to our own ' myriad-minded ' genius in his imagery and in the sublimity of his conceptions, as a creator he is, as M. Coquelin himself so happily expresses it, 'his equal in fecundity, his superior in truth.'" When Napoleon I took the great Talma and the other actors of the Comédie Française with him to Erfurt to play before the kings of Europe he would not allow Molière's dramas to be played, for, said he, "they are more capable of understanding the beauty and grandeur of French classic tragedy, than of penetrating the profoundness of Molière." And Goethe, whom the German nation would choose as worthy to sit beside Dante, Shakespeare, and Molière, said of him, "I have known and loved Molière from my youth up, and I have learned from him throughout my whole life."

Le Bourgeois Gentilhomme

It is difficult to translate the name of this comedy into concise English, and none of its several translations has rendered the title in a satisfactory manner. Ozell gives "The Gentleman Cit" as the title; Wall's "The Shopkeeper turned Gentleman" is unsatisfactory because it is inaccurate, for Monsieur Jourdain had never been a shopkeeper; Van Laun's "The Citizen who apes the Nobleman" is accurate but clumsy. More concise might be "The Parvenu" or "The Would-be Nobleman."

Although "Le Bourgeois gentilhomme" does not rank as one of the greatest of Molière's plays, yet it has long served as the best play with which to begin the study of classic French comedy for the twofold reason that its language is simple and its humor readily apparent. It has, therefore, been more widely read than any other of Molière's plays. Its appeal is universal and will endure as long as the frailty which it ridicules. While the vanity and folly of imitating one's social superiors is a failing common to all ages, in the seventeenth century this weakness of human nature was especially prevalent on account of the peculiar organization of society. The middle, or citizen, class was then, on account of the dominance of the aristocracy, relatively less important in the scale of society than it is now. This very domination, therefore, made the attainment of the advantages of the aristocracy the ambition of many more of the less favorably born than would be the case in the democratic organization of modern society. It was not uncommon for men of great wealth to purchase titles of nobility, and all who wished to be prominent socially imitated slavishly the dress and the manners of the noble class. This aping of the nobility in the age of Louis XIV even affected really great men like Colbert, Boileau, and Racine. It was the object of the satire of other authors than Molière. Many of La Fontaine's fables deal with this idea, and La Bruyère also in his " Caractères " found it an important theme. Molière himself had already recognized its dramatic possibilities in several of his earlier plays, notably in " Les Précieuses ridicules," " L'École des femmes," and " George Dandin."

As was the case with many of Molière's plays, " Le Bourgeois gentilhomme " was written at the command of Louis XIV and primarily for the entertainment of the court. The best evidence shows that the king merely wished some kind of a framework for the celebrated satire known as the Turkish ceremony. Louis had been displeased at the conduct of an embassy of the Turks, which apparently had not been as impressed with the greatness of the French king as that monarch had hoped. He therefore commanded the chevalier d'Arvieux, who had journeyed in Oriental countries, to assist Molière in the preparation of this Turkish burlesque. How much the chevalier collaborated with Molière will be discussed in a later paragraph. The chief point of importance is that Molière so modified the material that he was engaged upon that the Turkish burlesque, or " mamamouchi " ceremony, became the climax of the picture of Monsieur Jourdain's vanity. This vanity, however, remains still the central interest of the play and continues to be the pivot on which the whole action turns. Thus, despite the highly farcical nature of the fourth and fifth acts, the play retains that unity of action and interest which is essential to every work of art. We need not, therefore, sympathize with those critics who feel that the comedy proper of " Le Bourgeois gentilhomme " ends with the third act. The closing scenes, farcical as they may be, are necessary to raise the ridicule aimed at Jourdain's vanity to the highest degree. Moreover, farce is just as effective a weapon for a comedy of satire as anything else. Farce is, so to speak, the caricature of the comedy of manners, and character may be represented quite as accurately by the one as by the other. The means are different, but the purpose and the result are essentially the same. We believe, therefore, that the fourth and fifth acts are essential to the unity of interest, since they complete that unity and bring it to its climax. Not only is the unity of action kept, but it is noteworthy that the unities of time and place are also observed. The play takes place in Monsieur Jourdain's house, and in reality requires merely the time necessary to speak the lines, since at the beginning of each act the dialogue is resumed precisely where it left off. From every conventional standpoint, therefore, " Le Bourgeois gentilhomme " conforms to the model of classic drama.

The unity of interest, then, is upheld by the vanity of Monsieur Jourdain. It is of importance to observe how each character contributes to sustain that unity. The principle of foil, or contrast, is constantly used. As so often in Molière's plays the folly of one person is contrasted with the common sense of others. Thus Madame Jourdain, Cléonte, and Nicole, each in a different manner and in differing degree, stand out as foils to the follies of the master of the house. It is clear that Molière does not intend to ridicule the bourgeoisie as a class, since, aside from Jourdain himself, all the sensible persons belong to that group of society; nor does he sacrifice the bourgeoisie to the nobility, for the latter class is unfavorably represented in the tricky and contemptible Dorante and in the weak and colorless Dorimène. We have here, therefore, a striking instance of that independence of mind which is one of the great moral qualities of Molière. He flatters no class nor does he spare any class. All alike come under the aim of his ridicule if they deserve that ridicule. In a most aristocratic age, when the nobility were a privileged class and held by right of birth the highest places in the government, in the army, and at court, Molière did not fear to cast ridicule on their supposed superiority by showing them quite as capable of wickedness as other men. Thus Dorante in " Le Bourgeois gentilhomme " is a contemptible parasite, lacking all qualities of heart and devoid of conscience. " Don Juan " is a deeper and more developed study of this good-for-nothing, parasitic type of noble. It is not unlikely that the king rather enjoyed seeing his courtiers thus held up to scorn and took pleasure in forcing them to see themselves as others saw them. In any event it is clear that in this particular he never put any obstacles in Molière's way.

To the king and court the comedy proper of " Le Bourgeois gentilhomme " was undoubtedly less important than the *ballets*, or interludes of music, singing, and, above all, dancing, which terminated each act. It was here that the magnificence of costume and decoration was most in evidence, especially in the court performances. Some idea of the elaborate and costly nature of these costumes may be gained by reading merely the list of them in the expense account of these earlier performances.[1] It should be noted that the word *ballet* must not be translated in its present narrow signification, but rather in the meaning of a less artificial and more quiet dance of great beauty and dignity. Ballets in this sense had been popular

[1] See this document reprinted in part in Moland's " Molière et la comédie italienne," page 363 ; and more fully by Claretie in *Le Temps* for August 31, 1880 ; and by Livet in his edition of the comedy, pages xxix–xxxviii. The original document is in the *Archives nationales*, carton O, in Paris.

at the court of France since the reign of Louis XIII, and Louis XIV himself in his younger years had often danced in them in the performances at court. Molière cleverly incorporated the Turkish ceremony by making it the interlude at the end of the fourth act. The ballet at the end of the fifth act is the celebrated *Ballet des Nations*, which served as a grand finale to the whole entertainment. Since this was an integral part of the earlier performances and is usually reproduced at the more elaborate revivals of the play, we have felt that it ought not to be omitted from the present edition, despite the fact that its interest and its connection with the play itself are slight. The music of these interludes, as well as most of the intervening music of the play, was written by Jean-Baptiste Lulli, a composer of Italian birth, who attained great celebrity in the seventeenth century. Indeed, in the court performances Lulli took the part of the Muphty in the Turkish ceremony in such an acceptable manner as to add greatly to his laurels and to the favors which the king bestowed on him.

THE TURKISH CEREMONY

Of all the interludes the Turkish ceremony merits the most attention and the most praise. It is doubtful if anywhere in literature, outside of the similar ridiculous interlude in " Le Malade imaginaire," when Argan is created a doctor, there is any burlesque so ludicrous. When well presented the effect is contagious, and one must indeed be beyond hope, not to yield to the fun of the scene and to swell the volume of laughter. Much has been written and surmised regarding the origin and the purpose of this burlesque. As has already been stated, " Le Bourgeois gentilhomme " was apparently written in its present form for the sake of the Turkish ceremony, rather than the reverse. The latest writer on the subject is Pierre Martino, in the *Revue d'histoire littéraire de la France* for January–March, 1911, pages 37–60. He is of the opinion that the ceremony was introduced after the main lines of the comedy were laid down; and he accepts the tradition that the ceremony was designed for the king as a species of revenge because of the haughtiness and indifference to his grandeur of a Turkish embassy led by the Sultan's envoy, Suleïman Aga, who was in Paris in 1669–1670, only a few months before the first performances in October, 1670. Be that as it may, it is known that the chevalier d'Arvieux, who had lived twelve years in the Levant, had frequently entertained the court with stories of Eastern manners and customs, and that he was asked to help Molière regarding the words, the costumes, and the stage business of the ceremony. Mr. Martino, in the above-mentioned article, makes a careful study of the memoirs of d'Arvieux. We see from this study that d'Arvieux had been intrusted with the organization of the first reception by M. de Lionne of the Turkish ambassador. This took place before the official reception by the king. This preliminary reception, at which d'Arvieux had acted as interpreter, had been arranged in imitation of Turkish receptions of foreign ministers, and had greatly interested and amused the court. It was therefore natural that d'Arvieux should be designated by the king to help Molière in the insertion of a satire on the Turks, once the king had made his request for such a satire. That the king appreciated his collaboration is seen in the fact that in 1671 d'Arvieux was appointed envoy extraordinary to Turkey.

So much, then, for the connection of d'Arvieux with the Turkish ceremony as an idea. Martino shows how many of the passages in the memoirs of d'Arvieux suggest the words and the actions of the Turkish ceremony, especially the descriptions of the costumes, the music, the dancing, and the ceremonies of the dervishes. Many of these passages are repeated

almost verbally in the Turkish ceremony; in other cases the
similarity of the actions is nearly identical. The " muphty " of
the ceremony is the " dedé," or superior, of the dervishes; the
word *muphty* was substituted for *dedé* because the latter was
unknown in France, whereas the former was known, such a
character having appeared in French tragedy. So similar to
dervish ceremonies is a part of the Turkish interlude that the Tri-
politan envoy who witnessed a performance of " Le Bourgeois
gentilhomme " in 1704 was greatly pleased to see represented
the manners of his country. The other part of the Turkish
ceremony deals with the conferring of the rank of " mamamouchi " upon Jourdain. It is thought by some that this word
represents a parody of the rank of " muta ferraca," with which
the aforesaid Turkish envoy, Suleïman Aga, adorned himself.[1]
No such ceremony of investiture, however, is found in the
memoirs of d'Arvieux as a feature of Oriental countries. According to Mr. Martino we have here a parody on the reception of a knight into the order of Notre Dame of Mount Carmel.
This order had been established by Henry IV in 1607 as the
continuation in France of the order of Saint Lazarus. Now,
at the time of his collaboration with Molière, d'Arvieux was
very desirous of being received into this order, which Louis
XIV was about to revive in great splendor. And he was sub-
sequently admitted. His own description of the ceremony in
his memoirs shows many points of similarity with the " mamamouchi " ceremony, and these similarities are greatly increased
if we consult the full description of the reception and profession of faith of knights of the order of Mount Carmel as
contained in the " Mémoires, règles, statuts, cérémonies et
privilèges des ordres militaires de Notre-Dame du Mont Carmel et de Saint-Lazare de Jérusalem " (Lyons, 1649). It seems
to us that Mr. Martino has well established the similarity, and

[1] See also the note to page 70, line 13.

shown fully the extent of the real collaboration of d'Arvieux
with Molière. This collaboration in no wise affects the reputa-
tion of Molière, for he undoubtedly gave to the material fur-
nished him all the dramatic value that could be put into it.
The Turkish ceremony, dramatically speaking, is still the work
of Molière. He took the suggestions offered by d'Arvieux and
used them in the very best manner possible to produce the
desired effect. That he may have received help also from Lulli,
the musician, seems probable in view of the passage in Loret's
"La Muse historique," under date of December 18, 1660:

> Ensuite on dansa le Balet
> Peu sérieux, mais trés folet,
> Sur tout dans un Récit Turquesque,
> Si singulier et si burlesque,
> Et dont Baptiste étoit Auteur,
> Que sans doute tout spectateur
> En eut la rate épanoüye . . . [1]

This Baptiste cannot well have been any other than Jean-
Baptiste Lulli, the leading court musician. In any event it is of
moment to note the interest in a ballet that was "turquesque"
and "burlesque" as early as 1660, ten years before the production of "Le Bourgeois gentilhomme."

If Martino's theory of the origin of the Turkish ceremony is
correct, the ideas previously held by some that the ceremony
was a travesty on the consecration of bishops must be given
up. Moreover, it is inconceivable that Molière would have ven-
tured such a thing, especially in a comedy designed for the
entertainment of so orthodox a king as Louis XIV. Similarly
the charge of Molière's enemies that the ceremony is a mockery
of the Christian religion must be abandoned, although it must

---

[1] Loret, "La Muse historique," Livet's edition, 1878, Vol. III, page 293,
second column.

be admitted that it contains elements of travesty on the Mohammedan faith, especially in the burlesque use of the word *Hou*, a most solemn and holy word to the Mohammedans, meaning God, whose utterance by profane lips was blasphemy.

Were it necessary to justify the absurdity of the Turkish ceremony, and to seek analogies for such a farce in real life, reference might be made to an actual occurrence in 1687. In that year the abbé of Saint Martin of Caen, a rather simple-minded soul, was tricked into believing that the king of Siam had created him a mandarin of the first class, and he submitted to ridiculous ceremonies of initiation at the hands of the youth of Caen disguised as Siamese mandarins.[1] No doubt similar jests have been perpetrated many times in one form or another. Literary justification already existed for Molière in an episode in Book XI of Charles Sorel's burlesque romance " Francion," which had been printed several decades before. Here the pedant Hortensius is the victim of a hoax, whereby he is made to believe that he has been elected king of Poland.[2]

The Turkish ceremony was not printed *in extenso* in the first edition of the play. There the main features only were given, the rest of the action being merely summarized in stage directions. Perhaps this was done because the public of that time knew the stage business so well. In the edition of 1682 the burlesque was printed in full, and later, with some slight modifications, in 1734. This latter text is the one usually adopted by editors, and it also is undoubtedly based upon the best traditions of Molière's acting. We have, however, preferred the text of 1682, which was edited by La Grange, one

1 See a full account well documented by N. M. Bernardin in the *Revue de Paris* for August 1, 1902.

2 See Livet's edition of " Le Bourgeois gentilhomme," pages lxi–lxiv. See, further, Émile Roy, " La Vie et les œuvres de Charles Sorel," Paris, 1891, where many borrowings of Molière from Sorel's romances are set forth ; see especially page 91 for hoaxes similar to the coronation of Hortensius.

of Molière's own troupe of actors, who played the part of
Cléonte, since we feel that this text in all probability approaches
closest to the original presentation.[1]

Performances of "Le Bourgeois Gentilhomme"

The stage setting of the play is relatively simple, being merely
a room in Jourdain's house. It does not change throughout the
play. At the rear of the somewhat elegant apartment is a sort
of colonnade, through which may be seen another room. It is
through this second room that the more formal entrances are
made, such as the several ballets of the interludes. In Molière's
day it was difficult to have the elaborate stage setting and
scenery of modern times. The stage was small, usually not
over fifteen feet in width. It was encumbered on either side
by benches or seats, where sat the fashionable young men of
the day, who paid a higher price for the privilege of occupying
these conspicuous places. This peculiar custom of allowing part
of the audience on the stage itself lasted until 1759, and was a
cause of much annoyance to authors and actors. Our modern
boxes, at least those nearest the stage, are a direct evolution
from the older stage seats. Lighting effects were unknown, since
the only source of illumination was candles, which gave but feeble
light compared to that used to-day. Owing to the frequent tur-
bulence of that part of the audience which stood in the pit, now
the orchestra and parquet, it was necessary to protect the actors
from possible attack by a sort of low grating along the front of
the stage. There were usually no wings to the stage, the presence
of the audience there preventing their use for entrances and exits.

The first performance of "Le Bourgeois gentilhomme" was
at the palace at Chambord, near Orléans, where the king and

[1] See the Despois-Mesnard edition, Vol. VIII, page 178, note 2, and page
183; also the article by Pierre Martino, already cited, page 40, note 2.

court had gone for a hunting visit. It is generally agreed that
the date was October 14, 1670, although there is some evidence
that it was a day earlier. There were further performances at
Chambord on October 16, 20, and 21. Then the court repaired
to Saint-Germain-en-Laye, where performances took place on
November 9, 11, and 13. All these court performances were
most elegantly staged and costumed. The first public performance was in the Palais Royal theater, Molière's regular play-
house in Paris, Sunday, November 23, 1670. The play had
what was then considered a good run, being repeated seven
times in 1670 and twenty-eight times in 1671. It has not
proved one of the most popular of Molière's productions, however, as a glance at an interesting table prepared by Trollope
will show.[1] Up to 1870 "Le Bourgeois gentilhomme" had
been played in Paris five hundred twenty-six times, whereas
"Le Misanthrope" and "Les Femmes savantes" had had
twice as many performances, and "Le Tartuffe" nearly four
times as many.

There have been many elaborate revivals of the play.[2] On
these occasions the entire play with all the interludes, including
the closing *Ballet des Nations*, is usually given. Lulli's music is
used, and the actors of the Comédie Française unite with the
singers and dancers of the Opéra. The earliest of these great
revivals was on December 30, 1716, with a series of subsequent performances. Other revivals occurred in 1736, 1792,
1852, 1876. The greatest revival of all took place October 28,
1880, at the two hundredth anniversary of the founding of the
Comédie Française, and from all descriptions this was a remarkable occasion.[3] Aside from these more elaborate revivals

---

[1] Henry M. Trollope, "Life of Molière," pages 282–283.

[2] See a list in Livet's edition, page xiv.

[3] Accounts may be found in Livet's edition, page lv, and in Moland's edition,
pages 11–15. Auguste Vitu's interesting comments on this performance are also
found there.

the play is not usually given with all the interludes of singing and dancing, on account of the greater length and the greater cost of such a performance. In foreign lands the play has always been a favorite, especially for the French clubs of American colleges. A long list of translations, adaptations, and imitations of " Le Bourgeois gentilhomme " may be made.[1] The theme has been often handled by French dramatists in varying manner. Among the best imitations may be mentioned Labiche's " La Poudre aux yeux," and especially Augier's " Le Gendre de monsieur Poirier."

THE CHARACTERS

In analyzing the characters of " Le Bourgeois gentilhomme " we must note the cleverness with which they are contrasted, the one with the other. This is known as the principle of foil. By such a process of contrast each character stands out much more sharply. It may be said that Molière is past master in this art of contrast. He never brings two characters together without adding greatly to our understanding of them, and he does this by means so natural that the listener or reader thinks he himself discovers the contrasts which the author desires to emphasize. The fact that Molière was an actor, and an eminent one, accounts for much of his genius in this respect, since his training made him feel, and gave him the skill to make others feel, these most subtle dramatic values. In the judgment of many, no other dramatist in the world's literature is Molière's equal in this respect. It is also of considerable importance to note how the language of each character belongs most naturally to that character; for instance, Covielle uses words and expressions quite different from those of his master Cléonte; similarly

[1] See the Despois-Mesnard edition of Molière, Vol. VIII, page 37; also Livet's edition of this play, pages xvi ff.

Nicole has a manner of speech all her own, which is in perfect harmony with her limited education and modest social station, and yet leaves us a vivid picture of her rugged character. Again, fully alive to the psychological value of first impressions, Molière makes the first entrance of each person an epitome of the character of that person. Our attention is immediately aroused, and it is then an easy matter to retain our interest. With these general principles in mind, it will be easier for us to appreciate the characters as individuals.

Monsieur Jourdain. The mainspring of M. Jourdain's character is vanity. It is the basis of his ambition and accounts for all his actions, even the most absurd. If this quality is duly understood and correctly interpreted, as it must have been by Molière who played the part, the apparent inconsistencies of the later burlesque scenes disappear, and these scenes assume their proper logical connection with the play. It is vanity which forces Jourdain to dress and act like people of quality, and which leads him to think that he is succeeding in this imitation. Vanity makes him aspire to the possibility of a lofty alliance for his daughter, even a marriage with a duke. Vanity urges him to associate only with people of noble rank, and vanity again blinds him to the absurdity of such an association. Dorante and Covielle rely with safety upon this blindness, and play tricks on Jourdain which would have been impossible were their victim not controlled by his fixed idea. Vanity again leads him to show off his lately acquired knowledge, and makes it impossible for him to see how poorly he repeats what has been told him. In this portion of his rôle Jourdain somewhat resembles Strepsiades in Aristophanes' " Clouds." In short, Jourdain is a perfect character for comedy, since he does not, and cannot, see himself as others see him. Yet he is not so completely dominated by this master impulse that he does not reveal other qualities. Note the cropping out of his bourgeois

and common-sense nature in his preference for the simple popular ditty instead of the artificial pastoral poetry that he does
not understand. Note also the shopkeeper's blood reasserting
itself in the accuracy of his knowledge of Dorante's debt to
him. He realizes fully that he must loan Dorante money, but
at the same time he is very careful to note down the amounts
and to carry the memorandum on his person. As with many
of the characters which Molière has created and held up to our
ridicule, we are led to feel a certain sympathy for Jourdain.
Despite his vanity we sympathize with his sincere desire for
knowledge and self-improvement. He appeals to us by his
frankness and naïveté, above all by his good nature, which
enables him to recover so quickly from rebuffs. We even pity
his ignorance. In this connection it is of importance to note that
Jourdain inherited his wealth, a fact of moment in estimating his
character, since, if he had made his money himself, it is scarcely
probable that the process would have left him such a fool. In
this respect he is to be contrasted with Monsieur Poirier in
Augier's play. The character of Jourdain has been compared
with that of Lord Dundreary, as it was played by the English
actor E. A. Sothern in Tom Taylor's " Our American Cousin."

The art of a dramatic writer can be tested in no better way
than by observing his method of using subordinate characters
to enhance the picture of his chief personage. Molière is
nowhere greater in this respect than in his treatment of Jourdain. There is not a single character from the tailor appren-
tices to Madame Jourdain herself who does not contribute
some share, either by way of contrast or by way of incentive
to Jourdain's action, to that perfect picture of his character
which we perceive. The unity of action in this drama has
been much discussed, and it has sometimes been denied; but
no further unity is necessary than that of Jourdain himself.
He is the pivot of the play; indeed, he is the play. Molière

has centered in him the treatment and the characterization which he had in varying measure previously given to Arnolphe in " L'Ecole des femmes," and to George Dandin. Jourdain is thus the composite picture of the vanities of many of Molière's earlier creations.

As has been stated, Molière himself played the rôle of Jourdain. His expressive face, his alertness, his volubility, and his general dramatic skill combined to give an interpretation that won the applause of his contemporaries, and that has been the tradition for this rôle through the centuries. The costume contributed its share to this result. The dressing gown was striped, and lined with green and yellowish-gold taffeta. The feather hat had similar colors. The knee breeches were of red, the jersey and the stockings of green silk. An Indian scarf served as a girdle for the dressing gown. In the Turkish ceremony a Turkish tunic, turban, and sword were worn.

Madame Jourdain. Madame Jourdain is the chief foil or contrast to her husband. She is of the old bourgeoisie and is not ashamed of it, preferring to keep her own station in life and scorning all efforts of her husband to change it. Although lacking in outer refinement and elegance, she possesses the homely virtues of modesty, prudence, domesticity, and common sense. She is keen-witted, and sharp of speech, and even leaves sometimes the impression of severity. Indeed, she must often have made things uncomfortable for her husband. Her use of homely, direct speech contrasts well with her husband's striving to imitate the talk of people of quality. With Nicole she represents Molière's normal, common-sense philosophy of life. The rôle was played by a man, the celebrated Hubert, who excelled in the rôles of elderly women, it being a long-established tradition that such parts should be played by men.

Lucile. The rôle of Lucile is not one of major importance. What little we see of her leads to the impression that she is more cultured than her mother. We see her largely through the eyes of her lover Cléonte and in the famous description of her charms given by him. This picture, in Act III, scene ix, is without doubt that of Armande Béjart, the capricious young wife of Molière, who made his life so unhappy because of their mutual uncongeniality. Inasmuch as Armande played the rôle of Lucile, an accurate description of her was dramatically effective. Moreover, it was well known that despite her faults she exercised the same fascination over Molière as Lucile in the play exercises over Cléonte. The name Lucile is taken from early Italian comedy.

Cléonte. This was a favorite name in classic comedy to give to the rôle of leading lover. Here he is Molière's ideal young man of the middle class, and with Madame Jourdain, Covielle, and Nicole he represents the common-sense standpoint of the author. The rôle of young lover is usually a sympathetic one, and Cléonte's is no exception to the rule. It may, however, be said that his character is not entirely consistent, for, immediately after his frank and manly reply to Jourdain's question " Êtes-vous gentilhomme ? " which always wins applause, he agrees to deceive his future father-in-law with the Turkish ceremony and its attendant nonsense. On the principle, however, that all is fair in love he does not thereby lose our sympathy ; he had to do something desperate to win his sweetheart, who herself joins in the fun the moment she realizes its importance for them both.

Dorimène. This name is indicative of a coquette and even of a courtesan. Molière used it also in " Le Mariage forcé." In " Le Bourgeois gentilhomme " her character is rather undeveloped, and is therefore hard to estimate. Her chief value seems to be as a foil to show off the bourgeois, common-sense, domestic virtues of Madame Jourdain. Dorimène is far from domestic, suggesting rather the social butterfly. She is evidently rich, otherwise Dorante would not pay her court.

Dorante. The name was a favorite one for lovers' rôles, but here we have a parasitic nobleman of somewhat uncertain ancestry. He is clever in a bad way, using Jourdain for his own purposes, and preventing him from divulging the truth. In another man's house he gives orders with complete coolness and self-assurance. That Molière felt free to represent this detestable type of nobleman marks a high tide in his favor with the king, who had supported Molière during the hostilities connected with the production of " Le Tartuffe." The courtiers could scarcely have been pleased with this accurate and vivid representation of many of their own methods and characteristics. Yet, on the other hand, it is not improbable that Dorante's conduct, however reprehensible it appears to-day, formed one of the main elements of humor to the public of Molière's time. It was probably considered amusing, as it had been for centuries in the history of comedy, to see an old or eccentric man fooled and deceived, no matter by what methods. Indeed, J. J. Rousseau's criticism was that Dorante was clearly the " honnête homme " of the play whose successful tricks the public applauded. This type of scheming, unscrupulous nobleman became common in comedy after Molière, especially in the morally decadent eighteenth century.

Nicole. With Madame Jourdain, Nicole represents the common-sense, practical, rough and ready, but morally sound and vigorous, outlook on life. This type of servant is common in Molière, for Nicole is very like Martine in " Les Femmes savantes," Dorine in " Le Tartuffe," and Toinette in " Le Malade imaginaire," all of them zealous, faithful, and sensible servants, who frequently add a touch of democracy to the plays in which they appear. While the threatened beating of Nicole by Jourdain is indicative of a different relative position of servants and masters from that which prevails to-day, due allowance must be made for Molière's desire to make the most of a comic situation.

Molière created this part especially for Mademoiselle Beauval, a new member of his company, whose ability to laugh in the opening scene of the third act won the favor of Louis XIV, despite the fact that he had disliked her laughing in other rôles and had hitherto, on this account, refused his sanction to her admission to the troupe. This laughing episode in the rôle of Nicole is always a severe test of a comédienne's ability.

Covielle. Both the name and the character of this clever, quick-witted servant are taken from old Italian comedy, where such rôles were popular and important. Here, too, Covielle has a leading part. Although in most scenes he is merely the foil of his master, in the planning and execution of the Turkish ceremony he leads the way. Following the example of Terence and other writers of ancient comedy, Molière was ever alive to the dramatic possibilities of the shrewd servant who aids the purposes of his master. The best example is Scapin in " Les Fourberies de Scapin." Morally, Covielle is superior to Scapin, however, since real fidelity to his master's interests is his chief concern.

The various teachers do not have individually very important parts, but jointly they contribute much to the comedy of the play. It should be noted that each has his distinct personality, and that vanity in one direction or another is their dominant characteristic. This is particularly true of the Maître de Philosophie, whose grammar lesson forms one of the most ludicrous scenes of the entire comedy. This scene may well be considered an epitome of the play, and as such it is quoted more often than any other.

LE BOURGEOIS GENTILHOMME

COMÉDIE–BALLET DE MOLIÈRE

Représentée pour la première fois, à Chambord, le 14 octobre 1670

PERSONNAGES ET ACTEURS

MONSIEUR JOURDAIN, *bourgeois* . (*vain*) . . . . . MOLIÈRE

MADAME JOURDAIN, *sa femme* . . . . HUBERT

LUCILE, *fille de M. Jourdain* . . . . Mlle MOLIÈRE

CLÉONTE, *amoureux de Lucile* . . . . LA GRANGE

DORIMÈNE, *marquise* . . . . Mlle DEBRIE

DORANTE, *comte, amant de Dorimène* . . . . . . LA THORILLIÈRE [1]

NICOLE, *servante de M. Jourdain* . . . . Mlle BEAUVAL

COVIELLE, *valet de Cléonte* . . . . * * *

UN MAÎTRE DE MUSIQUE . . . . BEAUVAL

UN ÉLÈVE DU MAÎTRE DE MUSIQUE . . . . GAYE

UN MAÎTRE À DANSER . . . . * * *

UN MAÎTRE D'ARMES . . . . DEBRIE

UN MAÎTRE DE PHILOSOPHIE . . . . DU CROISY

UN MAÎTRE TAILLEUR . . . . * * *

UN GARÇON TAILLEUR . . . . * * *

DEUX LAQUAIS, PLUSIEURS MUSICIENS, MUSICIENNES, JOUEURS D'INS-
TRUMENTS, DANSEURS, CUISINIERS, GARÇONS TAILLEURS ET AUTRES
PERSONNAGES DES INTERMÈDES DU BALLET

La scène est à Paris, dans la maison de M. Jourdain.

[1] The edition of Ch.-L. Livet assigns La Thorillière to Covielle's rôle and says
he played also the part of Dorante and that of the *maître à danser*. Now he
might have doubled as the *maître à danser* and as *either* Dorante *or* Covielle,
but he could not have played both Covielle and Dorante, since they are together
in Act IV in the scene immediately before the Turkish ceremony, and also in
the last two scenes of Act V. La Thorillière's specialty was dignified parts, and
the best evidence assigns him to the rôle of Dorante. Confusion has arisen
because of his son, who also became an actor and played, usually as the *maître
à danser*, in later productions. He was, however, too young to have played in
1670, not having been born until 1659.

2

LE BOURGEOIS GENTILHOMME

COMÉDIE-BALLET

L'ouverture se fait par un grand assemblage d'instruments, et dans le milieu du théâtre on voit un élève du Maître de Musique qui compose sur une table un air que le Bourgeois a demandé pour une sérénade. 5

ACTE PREMIER

SCÈNE PREMIÈRE

Un MAÎTRE DE MUSIQUE, *un* ÉLÈVE DU MAÎTRE DE MUSIQUE, *composant sur une table qui est au milieu du théâtre. Une* MUSICIENNE, *deux* MUSICIENS, *un* MAÎTRE À DANSER, DANSEURS

LE MAÎTRE DE MUSIQUE, *aux musiciens.* Venez, entrez dans cette salle, et vous reposez là, en attendant qu'il vienne. 10

LE MAÎTRE À DANSER, *aux danseurs.* Et vous aussi, de ce côté.

LE MAÎTRE DE MUSIQUE, *à son élève.* Est-ce fait?

L'ÉLÈVE. Oui.

LE MAÎTRE DE MUSIQUE. Voyons . . . Voilà qui est bien. 15

LE MAÎTRE À DANSER. Est-ce quelque chose de nouveau?

LE MAÎTRE DE MUSIQUE. Oui, c'est un air pour une sérénade que je lui ai fait composer ici, en attendant que notre homme fût éveillé.

LE MAÎTRE À DANSER. Peut-on voir ce que c'est? 20

LE MAÎTRE DE MUSIQUE. Vous l'allez entendre, avec le dialogue, quand il viendra. Il ne tardera guère.

3

LE MAÎTRE À DANSER. Nos occupations, à vous et à moi, ne sont pas petites maintenant.

LE MAÎTRE DE MUSIQUE. Il est vrai. Nous avons trouvé ici un homme comme il nous le faut à tous deux. Ce nous est
5 une douce rente que ce monsieur Jourdain, avec les visions de noblesse et de galanterie qu'il est allé se mettre en tête; et votre danse et ma musique auraient à souhaiter que tout le monde lui ressemblât.

LE MAÎTRE À DANSER. Non pas entièrement; et je voudrais,
10 pour lui, qu'il se connût mieux qu'il ne fait aux choses que nous lui donnons.

LE MAÎTRE DE MUSIQUE. Il est vrai qu'il les connaît mal, mais il les paye bien; et c'est de quoi maintenant nos arts ont plus besoin que de toute autre chose.

15 LE MAÎTRE À DANSER. Pour moi, je vous l'avoue, je me repais un peu de gloire. Les applaudissements me touchent; et je tiens que, dans tous les beaux-arts, c'est un supplice assez fâcheux que de se produire à des sots, que d'essuyer sur des compositions la barbarie d'un stupide. Il y a plaisir, ne m'en
20 parlez point, à travailler pour des personnes qui soient capables de sentir les délicatesses d'un art, qui sachent faire un doux accueil aux beautés d'un ouvrage, et par de chatouillantes approbations vous régaler de votre travail. Oui, la récompense la plus agréable qu'on puisse recevoir des choses que l'on fait,
25 c'est de les voir connues, de les voir caressées d'un applaudissement qui vous honore. Il n'y a rien, à mon avis, qui nous paye mieux que cela de toutes nos fatigues; et ce sont des douceurs exquises que des louanges éclairées.

LE MAÎTRE DE MUSIQUE. J'en demeure d'accord, et je les
30 goûte comme vous. Il n'y a rien assurément qui chatouille davantage que les applaudissements que vous dites; mais cet encens ne fait pas vivre. Des louanges toutes pures ne mettent point un homme à son aise: il y faut mêler du solide; et la

meilleure façon de louer, c'est de louer avec les mains. C'est un homme, à la vérité, dont les lumières sont petites, qui parle à tort et à travers de toutes choses et n'applaudit qu'à contre-sens ; mais son argent redresse les jugements de son esprit : il a du discernement dans sa bourse, ses louanges sont mon- 5 nayées ; et ce bourgeois ignorant nous vaut mieux, comme vous voyez, que le grand seigneur éclairé qui nous a introduits ici.

Le Maître à Danser. Il y a quelque chose de vrai dans ce que vous dites ; mais je trouve que vous appuyez un peu trop sur l'argent ; et l'intérêt est quelque chose de si bas, qu'il ne faut 10 jamais qu'un honnête homme montre pour lui de l'attachement.

Le Maître de Musique. Vous recevez fort bien pourtant l'argent que notre homme vous donne.

Le Maître à Danser. Assurément ; mais je n'en fais pas mon bonheur ; et je voudrais qu'avec son bien il eût encore 15 quelque bon goût des choses.

Le Maître de Musique. Je le voudrais aussi, et c'est à quoi nous travaillons tous deux autant que nous pouvons. Mais, en tous cas, il nous donne moyen de nous faire connaître dans le monde, et il payera pour les autres ce que les autres 20 loueront pour lui.

Le Maître à Danser. Le voilà qui vient.

SCÈNE II

M. Jourdain, *en robe de chambre et en bonnet de nuit,* Le Maître de Musique, Le Maître à Danser, L'Élève du Maître de Musique, *une* Musicienne, *deux* Musiciens, Danseurs, *deux* Laquais 25

M. Jourdain. Eh bien, messieurs, qu'est-ce ? Me ferez-vous voir votre petite drôlerie ?

Le Maître à Danser. Comment ? quelle petite drôlerie ?

M. Jourdain. Hé ! la . . . Comment appelez-vous cela ? Votre prologue ou dialogue de chansons et de danse. 30

Le Maître à Danser. Ah, ah!

Le Maître de Musique. Vous nous y voyez préparés.

M. Jourdain. Je vous ai fait un peu attendre, mais c'est que je me fais habiller aujourd'hui comme les gens de qualité, 5 et mon tailleur m'a envoyé des bas de soie que j'ai pensé ne mettre jamais.

Le Maître de Musique. Nous ne sommes ici que pour attendre votre loisir.

M. Jourdain. Je vous prie (tous deux) de ne vous point en 10 aller, qu'on ne m'ait apporté mon habit, afin que vous me puissiez voir.

Le Maître à Danser. Tout ce qu'il vous plaira.

M. Jourdain. Vous me verrez équipé comme il faut, depuis les pieds jusqu'à la tête.

15 Le Maître de Musique. Nous n'en doutons point.

M. Jourdain. Je me suis fait faire cette indienne-ci.

Le Maître à Danser. Elle est fort belle.

M. Jourdain. Mon tailleur m'a dit que les gens de qualité étaient comme cela le matin.

20 Le Maître de Musique. Cela vous sied à merveille.

M. Jourdain. Laquais! holà! mes deux laquais!

Premier Laquais. Que voulez-vous, monsieur?

M. Jourdain. Rien. C'est pour voir si vous m'entendez bien. (*Au Maître de Musique et au Maître à Danser.*) Que 25 dites-vous de mes livrées?

Le Maître à Danser. Elles sont magnifiques.

M. Jourdain, *entr'ouvrant sa robe, et faisant voir son haut-de-chausses étroit de velours rouge, et sa camisole de velours vert.* Voici encore un petit déshabillé pour faire le matin mes 30 exercices.

Le Maître de Musique. Il est galant.

M. Jourdain. Laquais!

Premier Laquais. Monsieur.

M. Jourdain. L'autre laquais !

Second Laquais. Monsieur.

M. Jourdain, *ôtant sa robe de chambre.* Tenez ma robe. (*Au Maître de Musique et au Maître à Danser.*) Me trouvez-vous bien comme cela ?

Le Maître à Danser. Fort bien. On ne peut pas mieux.

M. Jourdain. Voyons un peu votre affaire.

Le Maître de Musique. Je voudrais bien auparavant vous faire entendre un air (*montrant son élève*) qu'il vient de com- poser pour la sérénade que vous m'avez demandée. C'est un de mes écoliers, qui a pour ces sortes de choses un talent admirable.

M. Jourdain. Oui ; mais il ne fallait pas faire faire cela par un écolier ; et vous n'étiez pas trop bon vous-même pour cette besogne-là.

Le Maître de Musique. Il ne faut pas, monsieur, que le nom d'écolier vous abuse. Ces sortes d'écoliers en savent autant que les plus grands maîtres, et l'air est aussi beau qu'il s'en puisse faire. Écoutez seulement.

M. Jourdain, *à ses laquais.* Donnez-moi ma robe pour mieux entendre ... Attendez, je crois que je serai mieux sans robe ... Non, redonnez-la-moi, cela ira mieux.

La Musicienne, *chantant.*

> Je languis nuit et jour, et mon mal est extrême,
> Depuis qu'à vos rigueurs vos beaux yeux m'ont soumis ;
> Si vous traitez ainsi, belle Iris, qui vous aime,
> Hélas ! que pourriez-vous faire à vos ennemis ?

M. Jourdain. Cette chanson me semble un peu lugubre ; elle endort, et je voudrais que vous la pussiez un peu ragaillardir par-ci par-là.

Le Maître de Musique. Il faut, monsieur, que l'air soit accommodé aux paroles.

M. JOURDAIN. On m'en apprit un tout à fait joli, il y a quelque temps. Attendez . . . La . . . Comment est-ce qu'il dit?

LE MAÎTRE À DANSER. Par ma foi, je ne sais.

M. JOURDAIN. Il y a du mouton dedans.

5 LE MAÎTRE À DANSER. Du mouton?

M. JOURDAIN. Oui. Ah! (*Il chante.*)

Je croyais Jeanneton
Aussi douce que belle;
Je croyais Jeanneton
10 Plus douce qu'un mouton.
Hélas! hélas! elle est cent fois
Mille fois plus cruelle
Que n'est le tigre au bois.

N'est-il pas joli?

15 LE MAÎTRE DE MUSIQUE. Le plus joli du monde.

LE MAÎTRE À DANSER. Et vous le chantez bien.

M. JOURDAIN. C'est sans avoir appris la musique.

LE MAÎTRE DE MUSIQUE. Vous devriez l'apprendre, monsieur, comme vous faites la danse. Ce sont deux arts qui ont
20 une étroite liaison ensemble.

LE MAÎTRE À DANSER. Et qui ouvrent l'esprit d'un homme aux belles choses.

M. JOURDAIN. Est-ce que les gens de qualité apprennent aussi la musique?

25 LE MAÎTRE DE MUSIQUE. Oui, monsieur.

M. JOURDAIN. Je l'apprendrai donc. Mais je ne sais quel temps je pourrai prendre; car, outre le maître d'armes qui me montre, j'ai arrêté encore un maître de philosophie, qui doit commencer ce matin.

30 LE MAÎTRE DE MUSIQUE. La philosophie est quelque chose; mais la musique, monsieur, la musique . . .

LE MAÎTRE À DANSER. La musique et la danse . . . La musique et la danse, c'est là tout ce qu'il faut.

LE MAÎTRE DE MUSIQUE. Il n'y a rien qui soit si utile dans un État que la musique.

LE MAÎTRE À DANSER. Il n'y a rien qui soit si nécessaire aux hommes que la danse.

LE MAÎTRE DE MUSIQUE. Sans la musique, un État ne 5 peut subsister.

LE MAÎTRE À DANSER. Sans la danse, un homme ne saurait rien faire.

LE MAÎTRE DE MUSIQUE. Tous les désordres, toutes les guerres qu'on voit dans le monde n'arrivent que pour n'appren- 10 dre pas la musique.

LE MAÎTRE À DANSER. Tous les malheurs des hommes, tous les revers funestes dont les histoires sont remplies, les bévues des politiques, et les manquements des grands capitaines, tout cela n'est venu que faute de savoir danser. 15

M. JOURDAIN. Comment cela ?

LE MAÎTRE DE MUSIQUE. La guerre ne vient-elle pas d'un manque d'union entre les hommes ?

M. JOURDAIN. Cela est vrai.

LE MAÎTRE DE MUSIQUE. Et, si tous les hommes apprenaient 20 la musique, ne serait-ce pas le moyen de s'accorder ensemble et de voir dans le monde la paix universelle ?

M. JOURDAIN. Vous avez raison.

LE MAÎTRE À DANSER. Lorsqu'un homme a commis un manquement dans sa conduite, soit aux affaires de sa famille, 25 ou au gouvernement d'un État, ou au commandement d'une armée, ne dit-on pas toujours : Un tel a fait un mauvais pas dans une telle affaire ?

M. JOURDAIN. Oui, on dit cela.

LE MAÎTRE À DANSER. Et faire un mauvais pas, peut-il 30 procéder d'autre chose que de ne savoir pas danser ?

M. JOURDAIN. Cela est vrai, et vous avez raison tous deux.

LE MAÎTRE À DANSER. C'est pour vous faire voir l'excellence et l'utilité de la danse et de la musique.

M. JOURDAIN. Je comprends cela à cette heure.

LE MAÎTRE DE MUSIQUE. Voulez-vous voir nos deux affaires ?

5   M. JOURDAIN. Oui.

LE MAÎTRE DE MUSIQUE. Je vous l'ai déjà dit, c'est un petit essai que j'ai fait autrefois des diverses passions que peut exprimer la musique.

M. JOURDAIN. Fort bien.

10   LE MAÎTRE DE MUSIQUE, *aux musiciens*. Allons, avancez. (*À M. Jourdain.*) Il faut vous figurer qu'ils sont habillés en bergers.

M. JOURDAIN. Pourquoi toujours des bergers ? On ne voit que cela partout.

LE MAÎTRE À DANSER. Lorsqu'on a des personnes à faire
15 parler en musique, il faut bien que, pour la vraisemblance, on donne dans la bergerie. Le chant a été de tout temps affecté aux bergers ; et il n'est guère naturel, en dialogue, que des princes ou des bourgeois chantent leurs passions.

M. JOURDAIN. Passe, passe. Voyons.

DIALOGUE EN MUSIQUE

UNE MUSICIENNE, DEUX MUSICIENS

LA MUSICIENNE

20   Un cœur, dans l'amoureux empire,
De mille soins est toujours agité :
On dit qu'avec plaisir on languit, on soupire ;
Mais, quoi qu'on puisse dire,
Il n'est rien de si doux que notre liberté.

PREMIER MUSICIEN

25   Il n'est rien de si doux que les tendres ardeurs
Qui font vivre deux cœurs
Dans une même envie.

On ne peut être heureux sans amoureux désirs :
　　　Ôtez l'amour de la vie,
　　　Vous en ôtez les plaisirs.

SECOND MUSICIEN

Il serait doux d'entrer sous l'amoureuse loi,
　　Si l'on trouvait en amour de la foi :   5
　　　Mais, hélas ! ô rigueur cruelle !
　　On ne voit point de bergère fidèle :
Et ce sexe inconstant, trop indigne du jour,
Doit faire pour jamais renoncer à l'amour.

PREMIER MUSICIEN
Aimable ardeur ! . . .   10

LA MUSICIENNE
Franchise heureuse ! . . .

SECOND MUSICIEN
Sexe trompeur ! . . .

PREMIER MUSICIEN
Que tu m'es précieuse !

LA MUSICIENNE
Que tu plais à mon cœur !

SECOND MUSICIEN
Que tu me fais d'horreur !   15

PREMIER MUSICIEN
Ah ! quitte, pour aimer, cette haine mortelle.

LA MUSICIENNE
On peut, on peut te montrer
Une bergère fidèle.

SECOND MUSICIEN
Hélas ! où la rencontrer ?

LA MUSICIENNE

Pour défendre notre gloire,
Je te veux offrir mon cœur.

SECOND MUSICIEN

Mais, bergère, puis-je croire
Qu'il ne sera point trompeur?

LA MUSICIENNE

5   Voyons par expérience
Qui des deux aimera mieux.

SECOND MUSICIEN

Qui manquera de constance,
Le puissent perdre les Dieux!

TOUS TROIS ENSEMBLE

À des ardeurs si belles
10   Laissons-nous enflammer:
Ah! qu'il est doux d'aimer,
Quand deux cœurs sont fidèles!

M. JOURDAIN.   Est-ce tout?
LE MAÎTRE DE MUSIQUE.   Oui.
15 M. JOURDAIN.   Je trouve cela bien troussé, et il y a là-dedans
de petits dictons assez jolis.

LE MAÎTRE À DANSER.   Voici, pour mon affaire, un petit
essai des plus beaux mouvements et des plus belles attitudes
dont une danse puisse être variée.

20 M. JOURDAIN.   Sont-ce encore des bergers?
LE MAÎTRE À DANSER.   C'est ce qu'il vous plaira. (*Aux
danseurs.*) Allons.

ENTRÉE DE BALLET

*Quatre danseurs exécutent tous les mouvements différents et
toutes les sortes de pas que le Maître à Danser leur commande,*
25   *et cette danse fait le premier intermède.*

ACTE II

SCÈNE PREMIÈRE

M. Jourdain, Le Maître de Musique, Le Maître à Danser

M. Jourdain. Voilà qui n'est point sot, et ces gens-là se trémoussent bien.

Le Maître de Musique. Lorsque la danse sera mêlée avec la musique, cela fera plus d'effet encore, et vous verrez quelque chose de galant dans le petit ballet que nous avons ajusté pour vous. 5

M. Jourdain. C'est pour tantôt au moins, et la personne pour qui j'ai fait faire tout cela me doit faire l'honneur de venir dîner céans.

Le Maître à Danser. Tout est prêt.

Le Maître de Musique. Au reste, monsieur, ce n'est pas 10 assez; il faut qu'une personne comme vous, qui êtes magnifique et qui avez de l'inclination pour les belles choses, ait un concert de musique chez soi tous les mercredis ou tous les jeudis.

M. Jourdain. Est-ce que les gens de qualité en ont?

Le Maître de Musique. Oui, monsieur.

M. Jourdain. J'en aurai donc. Cela sera-t-il beau? 15

Le Maître de Musique. Sans doute. Il vous faudra trois voix: un dessus, une haute-contre et une basse, qui seront accompagnées d'une basse de viole, d'un théorbe et d'un clavecin pour les basses continues, avec deux dessus de violon pour 20 jouer les ritournelles.

M. Jourdain. Il y faudra mettre aussi une trompette marine. La trompette marine est un instrument qui me plaît et qui est harmonieux.

Le Maître de Musique. Laissez-nous gouverner les choses. 25

13

M. JOURDAIN. Au moins, n'oubliez pas tantôt de m'envoyer des musiciens pour chanter à table.

LE MAÎTRE DE MUSIQUE. Vous aurez tout ce qu'il vous faut.

M. JOURDAIN. Mais surtout, que le ballet soit beau.

5 LE MAÎTRE À DANSER. Vous en serez content, et, entre autres choses, de certains menuets que vous y verrez.

M. JOURDAIN. Ah! les menuets sont ma danse; et je veux que vous me les voyiez danser. Allons, mon maître.

LE MAÎTRE À DANSER. Un chapeau, monsieur, s'il vous 10 plaît. (*M. Jourdain va prendre le chapeau de son laquais et le met par-dessus son bonnet de nuit. Son maître lui prend les mains et le fait danser sur un air de menuet qu'il chante.*) La, la, la; La, la, la, la, la, la; La, la, la, *bis;* La, la, la; La, la. En cadence, s'il vous plaît. La, la, la, la. La jambe droite. La, la, 15 la. Ne remuez point tant les épaules. La, la, la, la, la; La, la, la, la. Vos deux bras sont estropiés. La, la, la, la, la. Haussez la tête. Tournez la pointe du pied en dehors. La, la, la. Dressez votre corps.

M. JOURDAIN. Euh?

20 LE MAÎTRE DE MUSIQUE. Voilà qui est le mieux du monde.

M. JOURDAIN. À propos. Apprenez-moi comme il faut faire une révérence pour saluer une marquise; j'en aurai besoin tantôt.

LE MAÎTRE À DANSER. Une révérence pour saluer une marquise?

25 M. JOURDAIN. Oui. Une marquise qui s'appelle Dorimène.

LE MAÎTRE À DANSER. Donnez-moi la main.

M. JOURDAIN. Non. Vous n'avez qu'à faire; je le retiendrai bien.

LE MAÎTRE À DANSER. Si vous voulez la saluer avec beaucoup de respect, il faut faire d'abord une révérence en arrière, 30 puis marcher vers elle avec trois révérences en avant, et à la dernière vous baisser jusqu'à ses genoux.

M. JOURDAIN. Faites un peu. (*Après que le Maître à Danser a fait les trois révérences.*) Bon.

SCÈNE II

M. Jourdain, Le Maître de Musique, Le Maître à Danser, *un* Laquais

Le Laquais. Monsieur, voilà votre maître d'armes qui est là.

M. Jourdain. Dis-lui qu'il entre ici pour me donner leçon. (*Au Maître de Musique et au Maître à Danser.*) Je veux que vous me voyiez faire.

SCÈNE III

M. Jourdain, *un* Maître d'Armes, Le Maître de Musique, Le Maître à Danser, *un* Laquais, *tenant deux fleurets*

Le Maître d'Armes, *après avoir pris les deux fleurets de la* 5 *main du laquais et en avoir présenté un à M. Jourdain.* Allons, monsieur, la révérence. Votre corps droit. Un peu penché sur la cuisse gauche. Les jambes point tant écartées. Vos pieds sur une même ligne. Votre poignet à l'opposite de votre hanche. La pointe de votre épée vis-à-vis de votre épaule. Le bras pas 10 tout à fait si étendu. La main gauche à la hauteur de l'œil. L'épaule gauche plus quartée. La tête droite. Le regard assuré. Avancez. Le corps ferme. Touchez-moi l'épée de quarte, et achevez de même. Une, deux. Remettez-vous. Redoublez de pied ferme. Une, deux. Un saut en arrière. Quand vous portez 15 la botte, monsieur, il faut que l'épée parte la première et que le corps soit bien effacé. Une, deux. Allons, touchez-moi l'épée de tierce, et achevez de même. Avancez. Le corps ferme. Avancez. Partez de là. Une, deux. Remettez-vous. Redoublez. Une, deux. Un saut en arrière. En garde, monsieur, en garde! 20 (*Le Maître d'Armes lui pousse deux ou trois bottes, en lui disant: En garde!*)

M. Jourdain. Euh?

Le Maître de Musique. Vous faites des merveilles.

Le Maître d'Armes. Je vous l'ai déjà dit, tout le secret des armes ne consiste qu'en deux choses : à donner et à ne point recevoir ; et, comme je vous fis voir l'autre jour par raison démonstrative, il est impossible que vous receviez, si vous savez
5 détourner l'épée de votre ennemi de la ligne de votre corps : ce qui ne dépend seulement que d'un petit mouvement du poignet, ou en dedans ou en dehors.

M. Jourdain. De cette façon donc, un homme, sans avoir du cœur, est sûr de tuer son homme et de n'être point tué ?

10 Le Maître d'Armes. Sans doute. N'en vîtes-vous pas la démonstration ?

M. Jourdain. Oui.

Le Maître d'Armes. Et c'est en quoi l'on voit de quelle considération nous autres nous devons être dans un État, et
15 combien la science des armes l'emporte hautement sur toutes les autres sciences inutiles, comme la danse, la musique, la . . .

Le Maître à Danser. Tout beau ! monsieur le tireur d'armes. Ne parlez de la danse qu'avec respect.

Le Maître de Musique. Apprenez, je vous prie, à mieux
20 traiter l'excellence de la musique.

Le Maître d'Armes. Vous êtes de plaisantes gens, de vouloir comparer vos sciences à la mienne !

Le Maître de Musique. Voyez un peu l'homme d'importance !

Le Maître à Danser. Voilà un plaisant animal, avec son
25 plastron !

Le Maître d'Armes. Mon petit maître à danser, je vous ferais danser comme il faut. Et vous, mon petit musicien, je vous ferais chanter de la belle manière.

Le Maître à Danser. Monsieur le batteur de fer, je vous
30 apprendrai votre métier.

M. Jourdain, au Maître à Danser. Êtes-vous fou de l'aller quereller, lui qui entend la tierce et la quarte, et qui sait tuer un homme par raison démonstrative ?

LE MAÎTRE À DANSER. Je me moque de sa raison démonstrative, et de sa tierce et de sa quarte.

M. JOURDAIN, *au Maître à Danser.* Tout doux, vous dis-je.

LE MAÎTRE D'ARMES, *au Maître à Danser.* Comment?
petit impertinent! 5

M. JOURDAIN. Hé! mon maître d'armes!

LE MAÎTRE À DANSER, *au Maître d'Armes.* Comment?
grand cheval de carrosse!

M. JOURDAIN. Hé! mon maître à danser!

LE MAÎTRE D'ARMES. Si je me jette sur vous . . . 10

M. JOURDAIN, *au Maître d'Armes.* Doucement!

LE MAÎTRE À DANSER. Si je mets sur vous la main . . .

M. JOURDAIN, *au Maître à Danser.* Tout beau!

LE MAÎTRE D'ARMES. Je vous étrillerai d'un air . . .

M. JOURDAIN, *au Maître d'Armes.* De grâce! 15

LE MAÎTRE À DANSER. Je vous rosserai d'une manière . . .

M. JOURDAIN, *au Maître à Danser.* Je vous prie . . .

LE MAÎTRE DE MUSIQUE. Laissez-nous un peu lui apprendre
à parler.

M. JOURDAIN, *au Maître de Musique.* Mon Dieu! arrêtez-vous. 20

SCÈNE IV

Un MAÎTRE DE PHILOSOPHIE, M. JOURDAIN, LE MAÎTRE DE MUSIQUE,
LE MAÎTRE À DANSER, LE MAÎTRE D'ARMES, *un* LAQUAIS

M. JOURDAIN. Holà! monsieur le Philosophe, vous arrivez
tout à propos avec votre philosophie. Venez un peu mettre la
paix entre ces personnes-ci.

LE MAÎTRE DE PHILOSOPHIE. Qu'est-ce donc? Qu'y a-t-il,
messieurs?
25

M. JOURDAIN. Ils se sont mis en colère pour la préférence
de leurs professions, jusqu'à se dire des injures et vouloir en
venir aux mains.

Le Maître de Philosophie. Eh quoi, messieurs, faut-il s'emporter de la sorte ? Et n'avez-vous point lu le docte traité que Sénèque a composé de la colère ? Y a-t-il rien de plus bas et de plus honteux que cette passion qui fait d'un homme une

5 bête féroce ? Et la raison ne doit-elle pas être maîtresse de tous nos mouvements ?

Le Maître à Danser. Comment, monsieur ! il vient nous dire des injures à tous deux en méprisant la danse, que j'exerce, et la musique, dont il fait profession !

10 Le Maître de Philosophie. Un homme sage est au-dessus de toutes les injures qu'on lui peut dire ; et la grande réponse qu'on doit faire aux outrages, c'est la modération et la patience.

Le Maître d'Armes. Ils ont tous deux l'audace de vouloir

15 comparer leurs professions à la mienne !

Le Maître de Philosophie. Faut-il que cela vous émeuve ? Ce n'est pas de vaine gloire et de condition que les hommes doivent disputer entre eux ; et ce qui nous distingue parfaite-ment les uns des autres, c'est la sagesse et la vertu.

20 Le Maître à Danser. Je lui soutiens que la danse est une science à laquelle on ne peut faire assez d'honneur.

Le Maître de Musique. Et moi, que la musique en est une que tous les siècles ont révérée.

Le Maître d'Armes. Et moi, je leur soutiens à tous deux

25 que la science de tirer des armes est la plus belle et la plus nécessaire de toutes les sciences.

Le Maître de Philosophie. Et que sera donc la philo-sophie ? Je vous trouve tous trois bien impertinents de parler devant moi avec cette arrogance, et de donner impudemment

30 le nom de science à des choses que l'on ne doit pas même honorer du nom d'art, et qui ne peuvent être comprises que sous le nom de métier misérable de gladiateur, de chanteur et de baladin !

LE MAÎTRE D'ARMES. Allez, philosophe de chien !

LE MAÎTRE DE MUSIQUE. Allez, bélître de pédant !

LE MAÎTRE À DANSER. Allez, cuistre fieffé !

LE MAÎTRE DE PHILOSOPHIE. Comment ! marauds que vous
êtes ! . . .   5

(*Le Philosophe se jette sur eux, et tous trois le chargent de coups.*)

M. JOURDAIN. Monsieur le Philosophe !

LE MAÎTRE DE PHILOSOPHIE. Infâmes ! coquins ! insolents !

M. JOURDAIN. Monsieur le Philosophe !

LE MAÎTRE D'ARMES. La peste l'animal !   10

M. JOURDAIN. Messieurs !

LE MAÎTRE DE PHILOSOPHIE. Impudents !

M. JOURDAIN. Monsieur le Philosophe !

LE MAÎTRE À DANSER. Diantre soit de l'âne bâté !

M. JOURDAIN. Messieurs !   15

LE MAÎTRE DE PHILOSOPHIE. Scélérats !

M. JOURDAIN. Monsieur le Philosophe !

LE MAÎTRE DE MUSIQUE. Au diable l'impertinent !

M. JOURDAIN. Messieurs !

LE MAÎTRE DE PHILOSOPHIE. Fripons ! gueux ! traîtres !   20
imposteurs !

M. JOURDAIN. Monsieur le Philosophe ! Messieurs ! Monsieur le Philosophe ! Messieurs ! Monsieur le Philosophe !

(*Ils sortent en se battant.*)

SCÈNE V

M. JOURDAIN, *un* LAQUAIS

M. JOURDAIN. Oh ! battez-vous tant qu'il vous plaira, je n'y   25
saurais que faire, et je n'irai pas gâter ma robe pour vous
séparer. Je serais bien fou de m'aller fourrer parmi eux, pour
recevoir quelque coup qui me ferait mal.

SCÈNE VI

Le Maître de Philosophie, M. Jourdain, un Laquais

Le Maître de Philosophie, *en raccommodant son collet.*
Venons à notre leçon.

M. Jourdain. Ah! monsieur, je suis fâché des coups qu'ils
vous ont donnés.

5   Le Maître de Philosophie. Cela n'est rien. Un philosophe sait recevoir comme il faut les choses, et je vais composer
contre eux une satire du style de Juvénal, qui les déchirera de
la belle façon. Laissons cela. Que voulez-vous apprendre?

M. Jourdain. Tout ce que je pourrai, car j'ai toutes les
10 envies du monde d'être savant; et j'enrage que mon père et
ma mère ne m'aient pas fait bien étudier dans toutes les
sciences quand j'étais jeune.

Le Maître de Philosophie. Ce sentiment est raisonnable,
Nam, sine doctrina, vita est quasi mortis imago. Vous entendez
15 cela, et vous savez le latin, sans doute.

M. Jourdain. Oui, mais faites comme si je ne le savais pas.
Expliquez-moi ce que cela veut dire.

Le Maître de Philosophie. Cela veut dire que *Sans la
science la vie est presque une image de la mort.*

20   M. Jourdain. Ce latin-là a raison.

Le Maître de Philosophie. N'avez-vous point quelques
principes, quelques commencements des sciences?

M. Jourdain. Oh! oui. Je sais lire et écrire.

Le Maître de Philosophie. Par où vous plaît-il que
25 nous commencions? Voulez-vous que je vous apprenne la
logique?

M. Jourdain. Qu'est-ce que c'est que cette logique?

Le Maître de Philosophie. C'est elle qui enseigne les
trois opérations de l'esprit.

30   M. Jourdain. Qui sont-elles, ces trois opérations de l'esprit?

LE MAÎTRE DE PHILOSOPHIE. La première, la seconde et la troisième. La première est de bien concevoir par le moyen des universaux ; la seconde, de bien juger par le moyen des catégories ; et la troisième, de bien tirer une conséquence par le moyen des figures *Barbara*, *Celarent*, *Darii*, *Ferio*, 5 *Baralipton*, etc.

M. JOURDAIN. Voilà des mots qui sont trop rébarbatifs. Cette logique-là ne me revient point. Apprenons autre chose qui soit plus joli.

LE MAÎTRE DE PHILOSOPHIE. Voulez-vous apprendre la 10 morale ?

M. JOURDAIN. La morale ?

LE MAÎTRE DE PHILOSOPHIE. Oui.

M. JOURDAIN. Qu'est-ce qu'elle dit, cette morale ?

LE MAÎTRE DE PHILOSOPHIE. Elle traite de la félicité, en- 15 seigne aux hommes à modérer leurs passions, et . . .

M. JOURDAIN. Non, laissons cela. Je suis bilieux comme tous les diables, et il n'y a morale qui tienne ; je me veux mettre en colère tout mon soûl quand il m'en prend envie.

LE MAÎTRE DE PHILOSOPHIE. Est-ce la physique que vous 20 voulez apprendre ?

M. JOURDAIN. Qu'est-ce qu'elle chante, cette physique ?

LE MAÎTRE DE PHILOSOPHIE. La physique est celle qui explique les principes des choses naturelles et les propriétés du corps ; qui discourt de la nature des éléments, des métaux, des 25 minéraux, des pierres, des plantes et des animaux, et nous enseigne les causes de tous les météores, l'arc-en-ciel, les feux volants, les comètes, les éclairs, le tonnerre, la foudre, la pluie, la neige, la grêle, les vents et les tourbillons.

M. JOURDAIN. Il y a trop de tintamarre là-dedans, trop de 30 brouillamini.

LE MAÎTRE DE PHILOSOPHIE. Que voulez-vous donc que je vous apprenne ?

M. Jourdain.   Apprenez-moi l'orthographe.

Le Maître de Philosophie.   Très volontiers.

M. Jourdain.   Après, vous m'apprendrez l'almanach, pour savoir quand il y a de la lune, et quand il n'y en a point.

5   Le Maître de Philosophie.   Soit.   Pour bien suivre votre pensée, et traiter cette matière en philosophe, il faut commencer, selon l'ordre des choses, par une exacte connaissance de la nature des lettres et de la différente manière de les prononcer toutes.   Et là-dessus j'ai à vous dire que les lettres sont divisées
10 en voyelles, ainsi dites voyelles parce qu'elles expriment les voix ; et en consonnes, ainsi appelées consonnes parce qu'elles sonnent avec les voyelles et ne font que marquer les diverses articulations des voix.   Il y a cinq voyelles ou voix, A, E, I, O, U.

M. Jourdain.   J'entends tout cela.

15   Le Maître de Philosophie.   La voix A se forme en ouvrant fort la bouche : A.

M. Jourdain.   A, A.   Oui.

Le Maître de Philosophie.   La voix E se forme en rapprochant la mâchoire d'en bas de celle d'en haut : A, E.

20   M. Jourdain.   A, E, A, E.   Ma foi ! oui.   Ah ! que cela est beau !

Le Maître de Philosophie.   Et la voix I, en rapprochant encore davantage les mâchoires l'une de l'autre, et écartant les deux coins de la bouche vers les oreilles : A, E, I.

M. Jourdain.   A, E, I, I, I, I.   Cela est vrai.   Vive la science !

25   Le Maître de Philosophie.   La voix O se forme en rouvrant les mâchoires et rapprochant les lèvres par les deux coins, le haut et le bas : O.

M. Jourdain.   O, O.   Il n'y a rien de plus juste.   A, E, I, O, I, O.   Cela est admirable !   I, O, I, O.

30   Le Maître de Philosophie.   L'ouverture de la bouche fait justement comme un petit rond qui représente un O.

M. Jourdain.   O, O, O.   Vous avez raison, O.   Ah ! la belle chose que de savoir quelque chose !

Le Maître de Philosophie. La voix U se forme en rapprochant les dents sans les joindre entièrement, et allongeant les deux lèvres en dehors, les approchant aussi l'une de l'autre, sans les joindre tout à fait : U.

M. Jourdain. U, U. Il n'y a rien de plus véritable, U.   5

Le Maître de Philosophie. Vos deux lèvres s'allongent comme si vous faisiez la moue ; d'où vient que, si vous la voulez faire à quelqu'un et vous moquer de lui, vous ne sauriez lui dire que U.

M. Jourdain. U, U. Cela est vrai. Ah ! que n'ai-je étudié 10 plus tôt pour savoir tout cela !

Le Maître de Philosophie. Demain, nous verrons les autres lettres, qui sont les consonnes.

M. Jourdain. Est-ce qu'il y a des choses aussi curieuses qu'à celles-ci ?   15

Le Maître de Philosophie. Sans doute. La consonne D, par exemple, se prononce en donnant du bout de la langue audessus des dents d'en haut : DA.

M. Jourdain. DA, DA. Oui. Ah ! les belles choses ! les belles choses !   20

Le Maître de Philosophie. L'F, en appuyant les dents d'en haut sur la lèvre de dessous : FA.

M. Jourdain. FA, FA. C'est la vérité. Ah, mon père et ma mère, que je vous veux de mal !

Le Maître de Philosophie. Et l'R, en portant le bout de 25 la langue jusqu'au haut du palais ; de sorte qu'étant frôlée par l'air qui sort avec force, elle lui cède et revient toujours au même endroit, faisant une manière de tremblement : R, RA.

M. Jourdain. R, R, RA ; R, R, R, R, R, RA. Cela est vrai. Ah ! l'habile homme que vous êtes ! et que j'ai perdu de 30 temps ! R, R, R, RA.

Le Maître de Philosophie. Je vous expliquerai à fond toutes ces curiosités.

M. Jourdain. Je vous en prie. Au reste, il faut que je vous fasse une confidence. Je suis amoureux d'une personne de grande qualité ; et je souhaiterais que vous m'aidassiez à lui écrire quelque chose dans un petit billet que je veux laisser 5 tomber à ses pieds.

Le Maître de Philosophie. Fort bien.

M. Jourdain. Cela sera galant ; oui.

Le Maître de Philosophie. Sans doute. Sont-ce des vers que vous lui voulez écrire ?

10   M. Jourdain. Non, non, point de vers.

Le Maître de Philosophie. Vous ne voulez que de la prose ?

M. Jourdain. Non, je ne veux ni prose ni vers.

Le Maître de Philosophie. Il faut bien que ce soit l'un 15 ou l'autre.

M. Jourdain. Pourquoi ?

Le Maître de Philosophie. Par la raison, monsieur, qu'il n'y a pour s'exprimer que la prose ou les vers.

M. Jourdain. Il n'y a que la prose ou les vers ?

20   Le Maître de Philosophie. Non, monsieur. Tout ce qui n'est point prose est vers, et tout ce qui n'est point vers est prose.

M. Jourdain. Et comme l'on parle, qu'est-ce que c'est donc que cela ?

25   Le Maître de Philosophie. De la prose.

M. Jourdain. Quoi ! quand je dis, « Nicole, apportez-moi mes pantoufles et me donnez mon bonnet de nuit », c'est de la prose ?

Le Maître de Philosophie. Oui, monsieur.

30   M. Jourdain. Par ma foi, il y a plus de quarante ans que je dis de la prose sans que j'en susse rien ; et je vous suis le plus obligé du monde de m'avoir appris cela. Je voudrais donc lui mettre dans un billet : *Belle marquise, vos beaux yeux me*

font mourir d'amour ; mais je voudrais que cela fût mis d'une
manière galante, que cela fût tourné gentiment.

LE MAÎTRE DE PHILOSOPHIE. Mettre que les feux de ses
yeux réduisent votre cœur en cendres, que vous souffrez nuit
et jour pour elle les violences d'un . . .

M. JOURDAIN. Non, non, non ; je ne veux point tout cela.
Je ne veux que ce que je vous ai dit : *Belle marquise, vos beaux
yeux me font mourir d'amour.*

LE MAÎTRE DE PHILOSOPHIE. Il faut bien étendre un peu
la chose.

M. JOURDAIN. Non, vous dis-je ; je ne veux que ces seules
paroles-là dans le billet, mais tournées à la mode, bien arran-
gées comme il faut. Je vous prie de me dire un peu, pour voir,
les diverses manières dont on les peut mettre.

LE MAÎTRE DE PHILOSOPHIE. On les peut mettre, premièrement, comme vous avez dit : *Belle marquise, vos beaux yeux me
font mourir d'amour.* Ou bien : *D'amour mourir me font, belle
marquise, vos beaux yeux.* Ou bien : *Vos yeux beaux d'amour
me font, belle marquise, mourir.* Ou bien : *Mourir vos beaux
yeux, belle marquise, d'amour me font.* Ou bien : *Me font vos
yeux beaux mourir, belle marquise, d'amour.*

M. JOURDAIN. Mais, de toutes ces façons-là, laquelle est la
meilleure ?

LE MAÎTRE DE PHILOSOPHIE. Celle que vous avez dite :
Belle marquise, vos beaux yeux me font mourir d'amour.

M. JOURDAIN. Cependant je n'ai point étudié, et j'ai fait cela
tout du premier coup. Je vous remercie de tout mon cœur, et
vous prie de venir demain de bonne heure.

LE MAÎTRE DE PHILOSOPHIE. Je n'y manquerai pas.

SCÈNE VII

M. Jourdain, *un* Laquais

M. Jourdain, *à son laquais.* Comment, mon habit n'est point encore arrivé?

Le Laquais. Non, monsieur.

M. Jourdain. Ce maudit tailleur me fait bien attendre pour
5 un jour où j'ai tant d'affaires. J'enrage. Que la fièvre quartaine puisse serrer bien fort le bourreau de tailleur! Au diable le tailleur! La peste étouffe le tailleur! Si je le tenais maintenant, ce tailleur détestable, ce chien de tailleur-là, ce traître de tailleur, je . . .

SCÈNE VIII

10 M. Jourdain, *un* Maître Tailleur, *un* Garçon Tailleur, *portant l'habit de* M. Jourdain, *un* Laquais

M. Jourdain. Ah! vous voilà! Je m'allais mettre en colère contre vous.

Le Maître Tailleur. Je n'ai pas pu venir plus tôt, et j'ai
15 mis vingt garçons après votre habit.

M. Jourdain. Vous m'avez envoyé des bas de soie si étroits que j'ai eu toutes les peines du monde à les mettre, et il y a déjà deux mailles de rompues.

Le Maître Tailleur. Ils ne s'élargiront que trop.

20 M. Jourdain. Oui, si je romps toujours des mailles. Vous m'avez aussi fait faire des souliers qui me blessent furieusement.

Le Maître Tailleur. Point du tout, monsieur.

M. Jourdain. Comment, point du tout!

Le Maître Tailleur. Non, ils ne vous blessent point.

25 M. Jourdain. Je vous dis qu'ils me blessent, moi.

Le Maître Tailleur. Vous vous imaginez cela.

M. Jourdain. Je me l'imagine parce que je le sens. Voyez la belle raison!

LE MAÎTRE TAILLEUR. Tenez, voilà le plus bel habit de la cour et le mieux assorti. C'est un chef-d'œuvre que d'avoir inventé un habit sérieux qui ne fût pas noir; et je le donne en six coups aux tailleurs les plus éclairés.

M. JOURDAIN. Qu'est-ce que c'est que ceci? vous avez mis 5 les fleurs en enbas.

LE MAÎTRE TAILLEUR. Vous ne m'aviez point dit que vous les vouliez en enhaut.

M. JOURDAIN. Est-ce qu'il faut dire cela?

LE MAÎTRE TAILLEUR. Oui, vraiment. Toutes les personnes 10 de qualité les portent de la sorte.

M. JOURDAIN. Les personnes de qualité portent les fleurs en enbas?

LE MAÎTRE TAILLEUR. Oui, monsieur.

M. JOURDAIN. Oh! voilà qui est donc bien. 15

LE MAÎTRE TAILLEUR. Si vous voulez, je les mettrai en enhaut.

M. JOURDAIN. Non, non.

LE MAÎTRE TAILLEUR. Vous n'avez *only* qu'à dire.

M. JOURDAIN. Non, vous dis-je; vous avez bien fait. Croyez-vous que l'habit m'aille bien? 20

LE MAÎTRE TAILLEUR. Belle demande! Je défie un peintre, avec son pinceau, de vous faire rien de plus juste. J'ai chez moi un garçon qui, pour monter une rhingrave, est le plus grand génie du monde; et un autre qui, pour assembler un pourpoint, est le héros de notre temps. —————— 25

M. JOURDAIN. La perruque et les plumes sont-elles comme il faut?

LE MAÎTRE TAILLEUR. Tout est bien.

M. JOURDAIN, *en regardant l'habit du tailleur.* Ah! ah! monsieur le tailleur, voilà de mon étoffe du dernier habit que vous 30 m'avez fait. Je la reconnais bien.

LE MAÎTRE TAILLEUR. C'est que l'étoffe me sembla si belle que j'en ai voulu lever un habit pour moi.

M. Jourdain. Oui, mais il ne fallait pas le lever avec le mien.

Le Maître Tailleur. Voulez-vous mettre votre habit ?

M. Jourdain. Oui, donnez-le moi.

Le Maître Tailleur. Attendez. Cela ne va pas comme
5 cela. J'ai amené des gens pour vous habiller en cadence, et
ces sortes d'habits se mettent avec cérémonie. Holà ! entrez,
vous autres.

SCÈNE IX

M. Jourdain, Le Maître Tailleur, Le Garçon Tailleur, Garçons
Tailleurs *dansants*, un Laquais

10   Le Maître Tailleur, *à ses garçons*. Mettez cet habit à
monsieur, de la manière que vous faites aux personnes de
qualité.

Première entrée de ballet

Les quatre garçons tailleurs dansants s'approchent de M. Jour-
dain. Deux lui arrachent le haut-de-chausses de ses exercices ;
15   *les deux autres lui ôtent la camisole ; après quoi, toujours en*
cadence, ils lui mettent son habit neuf. M. Jourdain se promène
au milieu d'eux, et leur montre son habit, pour voir s'il est bien.

Garçon Tailleur. Mon gentilhomme, donnez, s'il vous
plaît, aux garçons quelque chose pour boire.

20   M. Jourdain. Comment m'appelez-vous ?

Garçon Tailleur. Mon gentilhomme.

M. Jourdain. Mon gentilhomme ! Voilà ce que c'est de se
mettre en personne de qualité. Allez-vous-en demeurer toujours
habillé en bourgeois, on ne vous dira point : mon gentilhomme.
25 Tenez, voilà pour mon gentilhomme.

Garçon Tailleur. Monseigneur, nous vous sommes bien
obligés.

M. Jourdain. Monseigneur ! Oh ! oh ! Monseigneur !
Attendez, mon ami : Monseigneur mérite quelque chose, et ce

n'est pas une petite parole que Monseigneur. Tenez, voilà ce que Monseigneur vous donne.

GARÇON TAILLEUR. Monseigneur, nous allons boire tous à la santé de Votre Grandeur.

M. JOURDAIN. Votre Grandeur ! Oh ! oh ! oh ! Attendez ; 5 ne vous en allez pas. À moi, Votre Grandeur ! (*Bas, à part.*) Ma foi ! s'il va jusqu'à l'Altesse, il aura toute la bourse. (*Haut.*) Tenez, voilà pour Ma Grandeur.

GARÇON TAILLEUR. Monseigneur, nous la remercions très humblement de ses libéralités.   10

M. JOURDAIN. Il a bien fait, je lui allais tout donner.

SCÈNE X

DEUXIÈME ENTRÉE DE BALLET

Les quatre garçons tailleurs se réjouissent, en dansant, de la libéralité de M. Jourdain.

ACTE III

SCÈNE PREMIÈRE

M. Jourdain, *deux* Laquais

M. Jourdain. Suivez-moi, que j'aille un peu montrer mon habit par la ville ; et surtout ayez soin tous deux de marcher immédiatement sur mes pas, afin qu'on voie bien que vous êtes à moi.

Laquais. Oui, monsieur.

5   M. Jourdain. Appelez-moi Nicole, que je lui donne quelques ordres. Ne bougez, la voilà.

SCÈNE II

M. Jourdain, Nicole, *deux* Laquais

M. Jourdain. Nicole !

Nicole. Plaît-il ?

M. Jourdain. Écoutez.

10   Nicole, *riant*. Hi, hi, hi, hi, hi.

M. Jourdain. Qu'as-tu à rire ?

Nicole. Hi, hi, hi, hi, hi, hi.

M. Jourdain. Que veut dire cette coquine-là ?

Nicole. Hi, hi, hi. Comme vous voilà bâti ! Hi, hi, hi.

15   M. Jourdain. Comment donc ?

Nicole. Ah ! ah ! Mon Dieu ! Hi, hi, hi, hi, hi.

M. Jourdain. Quelle friponne est-ce là ! Te moques-tu de moi ?

Nicole. Nenni, monsieur, j'en serais bien fâchée. Hi, hi, 20 hi, hi, hi, hi.

M. Jourdain. Je te baillerai sur le nez si tu ris davantage.

NICOLE. Monsieur, je ne puis pas m'en empêcher. Hi, hi, hi, hi, hi, hi.

M. JOURDAIN. Tu ne t'arrêteras pas?

NICOLE. Monsieur, je vous demande pardon; mais vous êtes si plaisant que je ne saurais me tenir de rire. Hi, hi, hi. 5

M. JOURDAIN. Mais voyez quelle insolence!

NICOLE. Vous êtes tout à fait drôle comme cela. Hi, hi.

M. JOURDAIN. Je te . . .

NICOLE. Je vous prie de m'excuser. Hi, hi, hi, hi.

M. JOURDAIN. Tiens, si tu ris encore le moins du monde, je 10 te jure que je t'appliquerai sur la joue le plus grand soufflet qui se soit jamais donné.

NICOLE. Eh bien, monsieur, voilà qui est fait, je ne rirai plus.

M. JOURDAIN. Prends-y bien garde. Il faut que, pour tantôt, tu nettoies . . . 15

NICOLE. Hi, hi.

M. JOURDAIN. Que tu nettoies comme il faut . . .

NICOLE. Hi, hi.

M. JOURDAIN. Il faut, dis-je, que tu nettoies la salle, et . . .

NICOLE. Hi, hi. 20

M. JOURDAIN. Encore?

NICOLE, *tombant à force de rire.* Tenez, monsieur, battez-moi plutôt, et me laissez rire tout mon soûl; cela me fera plus de bien. Hi, hi, hi, hi, hi.

M. JOURDAIN. J'enrage. 25

NICOLE. De grâce, monsieur, je vous prie de me laisser rire. Hi, hi, hi.

M. JOURDAIN. Si je te prends . . .

NICOLE. Monsieur . . . -eur, je crèverai . . . -ai, si je ne ris. Hi, hi, hi. 30

M. JOURDAIN. Mais a-t-on jamais vu une pendarde comme celle-là, qui me vient rire insolemment au nez, au lieu de recevoir mes ordres?

NICOLE. Que voulez-vous que je fasse, monsieur?

M. JOURDAIN. Que tu songes, coquine, à préparer ma maison pour la compagnie qui doit venir tantôt.

NICOLE, *se relevant.*   Ah! par ma foi, je n'ai plus envie de
5 rire; et toutes vos compagnies font tant de désordre céans, que ce mot est assez pour me mettre en mauvaise humeur.

M. JOURDAIN. Ne dois-je point pour toi fermer ma porte à tout le monde?

NICOLE. Vous devriez au moins la fermer à certaines gens.

SCÈNE III

MADAME JOURDAIN, M. JOURDAIN, NICOLE, *deux* LAQUAIS

10   Mme JOURDAIN. Ah! ah! voici une nouvelle histoire. Qu'est-ce que c'est donc, mon mari, que cet équipage-là? Vous moquez-vous du monde, de vous être fait enharnacher de la sorte, et avez-vous envie qu'on se raille partout de vous?

M. JOURDAIN. Il n'y a que des sots et des sottes, ma femme,
15 qui se railleront de moi.

Mme JOURDAIN. Vraiment, on n'a pas attendu jusqu'à cette heure; et il y a longtemps que vos façons de faire donnent à rire à tout le monde.

M. JOURDAIN. Qui est donc tout ce monde-là, s'il vous
20 plaît?

Mme JOURDAIN. Tout ce monde-là est un monde qui a raison, et qui est plus sage que vous. Pour moi, je suis scandalisée de la vie que vous menez. Je ne sais plus ce que c'est que notre maison. On dirait qu'il est céans carême-prenant tous
25 les jours, et dès le matin, de peur d'y manquer, on y entend des vacarmes de violons et de chanteurs dont tout le voisinage se trouve incommodé.

NICOLE. Madame parle bien. Je ne saurais plus voir mon ménage propre avec cet attirail de gens que vous faites venir chez vous. Ils ont des pieds qui vont chercher de la boue dans tous les quartiers de la ville pour l'apporter ici ; et la pauvre Françoise est presque sur les dents à frotter les planchers que vos biaux maîtres viennent crotter régulièrement tous les jours.

M. JOURDAIN. Ouais ! notre servante Nicole, vous avez le caquet bien affilé pour une paysanne.

Mme JOURDAIN. Nicole a raison, et son sens est meilleur que le vôtre. Je voudrais bien savoir ce que vous pensez faire d'un maître à danser à l'âge que vous avez.

NICOLE. Et d'un grand maître tireur d'armes qui vient, avec ses battements de pied, ébranler toute la maison et nous déraciner tous les carriaux de notre salle.

M. JOURDAIN. Taisez-vous, ma servante et ma femme.

Mme JOURDAIN. Est-ce que vous voulez apprendre à danser, pour quand vous n'aurez plus de jambes ?

NICOLE. Est-ce que vous avez envie de tuer quelqu'un ?

M. JOURDAIN. Taisez-vous, vous dis-je, vous êtes des ignorantes l'une et l'autre, et vous ne savez pas les prérogatives de tout cela.

Mme JOURDAIN. Vous devriez bien plutôt songer à marier votre fille, qui est en âge d'être pourvue.

M. JOURDAIN. Je songerai à marier ma fille, quand il se présentera un parti pour elle ; mais je veux songer aussi à apprendre les belles choses.

NICOLE. J'ai encore ouï dire, madame, qu'il a pris aujourd'hui, pour renfort de potage, un maître de philosophie.

M. JOURDAIN. Fort bien. Je veux avoir de l'esprit et savoir raisonner des choses parmi les honnêtes gens.

Mme JOURDAIN. N'irez-vous point l'un de ces jours au collège vous faire donner le fouet, à votre âge ?

M. JOURDAIN. Pourquoi non ? Plût à Dieu l'avoir tout à l'heure, le fouet, devant tout le monde, et savoir ce qu'on apprend au collège !

NICOLE. Oui, ma foi, cela vous rendrait la jambe bien mieux faite.

M. JOURDAIN. Sans doute.

Mme JOURDAIN. Tout cela est fort nécessaire pour conduire 5 votre maison.

M. JOURDAIN. Assurément. Vous parlez toutes deux comme des bêtes, et j'ai honte de votre ignorance. (À Mme Jourdain.) Par exemple, savez-vous, vous, ce que c'est que vous dites à cette heure?

10 Mme JOURDAIN. Oui, je sais que ce que je dis est fort bien dit, et que vous devriez songer à vivre d'autre sorte.

M. JOURDAIN. Je ne parle pas de cela. Je vous demande ce que c'est que les paroles que vous dites ici?

Mme JOURDAIN. Ce sont des paroles bien sensées, et votre 15 conduite ne l'est guère.

M. JOURDAIN. Je ne parle pas de cela, vous dis-je. Je vous demande, ce que je parle avec vous, ce que je vous dis à cette heure, qu'est-ce que c'est?

Mme JOURDAIN. Des chansons.

20 M. JOURDAIN. Hé non! ce n'est pas cela. Ce que nous disons tous deux, le langage que nous parlons à cette heure?

Mme JOURDAIN. Eh bien?

M. JOURDAIN. Comment est-ce que cela s'appelle?

Mme JOURDAIN. Cela s'appelle comme on veut l'appeler.

25 M. JOURDAIN. C'est de la prose, ignorante.

Mme JOURDAIN. De la prose!

M. JOURDAIN. Oui, de la prose. Tout ce qui est prose n'est point vers, et tout ce qui n'est point vers n'est point prose. Hé, voilà ce que c'est d'étudier. (À Nicole.) Et toi, sais-tu bien 30 comme il faut faire pour dire un U?

NICOLE. Comment?

M. JOURDAIN. Oui, qu'est-ce que tu fais quand tu dis un U?

NICOLE. Quoi?

M. Jourdain. Dis un peu U, pour voir.

Nicole. Eh bien, U.

M. Jourdain. Qu'est-ce que tu fais?

Nicole. Je dis U.

M. Jourdain. Oui; mais quand tu dis U, qu'est-ce que tu fais? 5

Nicole. Je fais ce que vous me dites.

M. Jourdain. Oh! l'étrange chose que d'avoir à faire à des bêtes! Tu allonges les lèvres en dehors et approches la mâchoire d'en haut de celle d'en bas. U, vois-tu? U. Je fais la moue, U.   10

Nicole. Oui, cela est biau!

Mme Jourdain. Voilà qui est admirable.

M. Jourdain. C'est bien autre chose, si vous aviez vu O, et DA, DA, et FA, FA.

Mme Jourdain. Qu'est-ce que c'est donc que tout ce 15 galimatias-là!

Nicole. De quoi est-ce que tout cela guérit?

M. Jourdain. J'enrage quand je vois des femmes ignorantes.

Mme Jourdain. Allez. Vous devriez envoyer promener tous ces gens-là avec leurs fariboles.   20

Nicole. Et surtout ce grand escogriffe de maître d'armes, qui remplit de poudre tout mon ménage.

M. Jourdain. Ouais! ce maître d'armes vous tient fort au cœur! Je te veux faire voir ton impertinence tout à l'heure. (*Il fait apporter les fleurets et en donne un à Nicole.*) Tiens; 25 raison démonstrative. La ligne du corps. Quand on pousse en quarte, on n'a qu'à faire cela; et quand on pousse en tierce, on n'a qu'à faire cela. Voilà le moyen de n'être jamais tué; et cela n'est-il pas beau d'être assuré de son fait, quand on se bat contre quelqu'un? Là, pousse-moi un peu pour voir.   30

Nicole. Eh bien, quoi? (*Nicole lui pousse plusieurs coups.*)

M. Jourdain. Tout beau! Holà! Oh! doucement. Diantre soit la coquine!

NICOLE. Vous me dites de pousser.

M. JOURDAIN. Oui ; mais tu me pousses en tierce avant que
de pousser en quarte, et tu n'as pas la patience que je pare.

Mme JOURDAIN. Vous êtes fou, mon mari, avec toutes vos
fantaisies ; et cela vous est venu depuis que vous vous mêlez
de hanter la noblesse.

M. JOURDAIN. Lorsque je hante la noblesse, je fais paraître
mon jugement ; et cela est plus beau que de hanter votre
bourgeoisie.

Mme JOURDAIN. Çamon, vraiment ! Il y a fort à gagner à
fréquenter vos nobles, et vous avez bien opéré avec ce beau
monsieur le comte, dont vous vous êtes embéguiné.

M. JOURDAIN. Paix ! Songez à ce que vous dites. Savez-
vous bien, ma femme, que vous ne savez pas de qui vous parlez,
quand vous parlez de lui ? C'est une personne d'importance
plus que vous ne pensez, un seigneur que l'on considère à la
cour, et qui parle au roi tout comme je vous parle. N'est-ce
pas une chose qui m'est tout à fait honorable, que l'on voie
venir chez moi si souvent une personne de cette qualité, qui
m'appelle son cher ami et me traite comme si j'étais son égal ?
Il a pour moi des bontés qu'on ne devinerait jamais ; et devant
tout le monde il me fait des caresses dont je suis moi-même
confus.

Mme JOURDAIN. Oui, il a des bontés pour vous, et vous fait
des caresses ; mais il vous emprunte votre argent.

M. JOURDAIN. Eh bien ! ne m'est-ce pas de l'honneur de
prêter de l'argent à un homme de cette condition-là ? Et puis-je
faire moins pour un seigneur qui m'appelle son cher ami ?

Mme JOURDAIN. Et ce seigneur, que fait-il pour vous ?

M. JOURDAIN. Des choses dont on serait étonné, si on les
savait.

Mme JOURDAIN. Et quoi ?

M. JOURDAIN. Baste ! je ne puis pas m'expliquer. Il suffit

que si je lui ai prêté de l'argent, il me le rendra bien, et avant
qu'il soit peu.

Mme JOURDAIN.   Oui, attendez-vous à cela.

M. JOURDAIN.   Assurément.   Ne me l'a-t-il pas dit ?

Mme JOURDAIN.   Oui, oui ; il ne manquera pas d'y faillir.   5

M. JOURDAIN.   Il m'a juré sa foi de gentilhomme.

Mme JOURDAIN.   Chansons !

M. JOURDAIN.   Ouais ! vous êtes bien obstinée, ma femme.
Je vous dis qu'il me tiendra parole, j'en suis sûr.

Mme JOURDAIN.   Et moi je suis sûre que non, et que toutes 10
les caresses qu'il vous fait ne sont que pour vous enjôler.

M. JOURDAIN.   Taisez-vous.   Le voici.

Mme JOURDAIN.   Il ne nous faut plus que cela.   Il vient
peut-être encore vous faire quelque emprunt ; et il me semble
que j'ai dîné quand je le vois.   15

M. JOURDAIN.   Taisez-vous, vous dis-je.

SCÈNE IV

DORANTE, M. JOURDAIN, Mme JOURDAIN, NICOLE

DORANTE.   Mon cher ami, monsieur Jourdain, comment vous
portez-vous ?

M. JOURDAIN.   Fort bien, monsieur, pour vous rendre mes
petits services.   20

DORANTE.   Et madame Jourdain, que voilà, comment se
porte-t-elle ?

Mme JOURDAIN.   Madame Jourdain se porte comme elle peut.

DORANTE.   Comment ! monsieur Jourdain, vous voilà le plus
propre du monde !   25

M. JOURDAIN.   Vous voyez.

DORANTE.   Vous avez tout à fait bon air avec cet habit, et
nous n'avons point de jeunes gens à la cour qui soient mieux
faits que vous.

M. JOURDAIN. Hai, hai ! *He flatters his weaknesses*

Mme JOURDAIN, *à part.* Il le gratte par où il se démange.

DORANTE. Tournez-vous. Cela est tout à fait galant.

Mme JOURDAIN, *à part.* Oui, aussi *foolish* sot par derrière que par
5 devant.

DORANTE. Ma foi, monsieur Jourdain, j'avais une impatience
étrange de vous voir. Vous êtes l'homme du monde que
j'estime le plus, et je parlais de vous encore ce matin dans la
chambre du roi.

10 M. JOURDAIN. Vous me faites beaucoup d'honneur, monsieur. (*À Mme Jourdain.*) Dans la chambre du roi !

DORANTE. Allons, mettez.

M. JOURDAIN. Monsieur, je sais le respect que je vous dois.

DORANTE. Mon Dieu ! mettez. Point de cérémonie entre
15 nous, je vous prie.

M. JOURDAIN. Monsieur . . .

DORANTE. Mettez, vous dis-je, monsieur Jourdain ; vous êtes
mon ami.

M. JOURDAIN. Monsieur, je suis votre serviteur.

20 DORANTE. Je ne me couvrirai point si vous ne vous couvrez.

M. JOURDAIN, *se couvrant.* J'aime mieux être incivil qu'importun. *boresome*

DORANTE. Je suis votre débiteur, comme vous le savez.

Mme JOURDAIN, *à part.* Oui, nous ne le savons que trop.

25 DORANTE. Vous m'avez généreusement prêté de l'argent en
plusieurs occasions ; et vous m'avez obligé de la meilleure grâce
du monde, assurément.

M. JOURDAIN. Monsieur, vous vous moquez.

DORANTE. Mais je sais rendre ce qu'on me prête, et recon-
30 naître les plaisirs qu'on me fait.

M. JOURDAIN. Je n'en doute point, monsieur.

DORANTE. Je veux sortir d'affaire avec vous ; et je viens ici
pour faire nos comptes ensemble.

M. Jourdain, *bas à Mme Jourdain.* Eh bien! vous voyez votre impertinence, ma femme.

Dorante. Je suis homme qui aime à m'acquitter le plus tôt que je puis.

M. Jourdain, *bas à Mme Jourdain.* Je vous le disais bien.   5

Dorante. Voyons un peu ce que je vous dois.

M. Jourdain, *bas à Mme Jourdain.* Vous voilà, avec vos soupçons ridicules!

Dorante. Vous souvenez-vous bien de tout l'argent que vous m'avez prêté?   10

M. Jourdain. Je crois que oui. J'en ai fait un petit mémoire. Le voici. Donné à vous, une fois, deux cents louis.

Dorante. Cela est vrai.

M. Jourdain. Une autre fois, six-vingts.

Dorante. Oui.   15

M. Jourdain. Et une autre fois, cent quarante.

Dorante. Vous avez raison.

M. Jourdain. Ces trois articles font quatre cent soixante louis, qui valent cinq mille soixante livres.

Dorante. Le compte est fort bon. Cinq mille soixante   20 livres.

M. Jourdain. Mille huit cent trente-deux livres à votre plumassier.

Dorante. Justement.

M. Jourdain. Deux mille sept cent quatre-vingts livres à   25 votre tailleur.

Dorante. Il est vrai.

M. Jourdain. Quatre mille trois cent septante-neuf livres, douze sols huit deniers à votre marchand.

Dorante. Fort bien. Douze sols huit deniers. Le compte   30 est juste.

M. Jourdain. Et mille sept cent quarante-huit livres sept sols quatre deniers à votre sellier.

DORANTE. Tout cela est véritable. Qu'est-ce que cela fait?

M. JOURDAIN. Somme totale, quinze mille huit cents livres.

DORANTE. Somme totale est juste: quinze mille huit cents
livres. Mettez encore deux cents pistoles que vous m'allez
5 donner; cela fera justement dix-huit mille francs que je vous
payerai au premier jour.

Mme JOURDAIN, bas à M. Jourdain. Eh bien, ne l'avais-je
pas bien deviné?

M. JOURDAIN, bas à Mme Jourdain. Paix!

10   DORANTE. Cela vous incommodera-t-il de me donner ce que
je vous dis?

M. JOURDAIN. Eh non!

Mme JOURDAIN, bas à M. Jourdain. Cet homme-là fait de
vous une vache à lait.

15   M. JOURDAIN, bas à Mme Jourdain. Taisez-vous.

DORANTE. Si cela vous incommode, j'en irai chercher ailleurs.

M. JOURDAIN. Non, monsieur.

Mme JOURDAIN, bas à M. Jourdain. Il ne sera pas content
qu'il ne vous ait ruiné.

20   M. JOURDAIN, bas à Mme Jourdain. Taisez-vous, vous
dis-je!

DORANTE. Vous n'avez qu'à me dire si cela vous embarrasse.

M. JOURDAIN. Point, monsieur.

Mme JOURDAIN, bas à M. Jourdain. C'est un vrai enjôleux.

25   M. JOURDAIN, bas à Mme Jourdain. Taisez-vous donc.

Mme JOURDAIN, bas à M. Jourdain. Il vous sucera jusqu'au
dernier sou.

M. JOURDAIN, bas à Mme Jourdain. Vous tairez-vous?

DORANTE. J'ai force gens qui m'en prêteraient avec joie;
30 mais comme vous êtes mon meilleur ami, j'ai cru que je vous
ferais tort si j'en demandais à quelque autre.

M. JOURDAIN. C'est trop d'honneur, monsieur, que vous me
faites. Je vais quérir votre affaire.

Mme Jourdain, *bas à M. Jourdain.* Quoi! vous allez encore lui donner cela?

M. Jourdain, *bas à Mme Jourdain.* Que faire? Voulez-vous que je refuse un homme de cette condition-là, qui a parlé de moi ce matin dans la chambre du roi? 5

Mme Jourdain, *bas à M. Jourdain.* Allez, vous êtes une vraie dupe.

SCÈNE V

DORANTE, Mme JOURDAIN, NICOLE

Dorante. Vous me semblez toute mélancolique. Qu'avez-vous, madame Jourdain?

Mme Jourdain. J'ai la tête plus grosse que le poing, et si 10 elle n'est pas enflée.

Dorante. Mademoiselle votre fille, où est-elle, que je ne la vois point?

Mme Jourdain. Mademoiselle ma fille est bien où elle est.

Dorante. Comment se porte-t-elle? 15

Mme Jourdain. Elle se porte sur ses deux jambes.

Dorante. Ne voulez-vous point, un de ces jours, venir voir avec elle le ballet et la comédie que l'on fait chez le roi?

Mme Jourdain. Oui, vraiment, nous avons fort envie de rire; fort envie de rire nous avons! 20

Dorante. Je pense, madame Jourdain, que vous avez eu bien des amants dans votre jeune âge, belle et d'agréable humeur comme vous étiez.

Mme Jourdain. Tredame, monsieur! est-ce que madame Jourdain est décrépite, et la tête lui grouille-t-elle déjà? 25

Dorante. Ah! ma foi, madame Jourdain, je vous demande pardon; je ne songeais pas que vous êtes jeune, et je rêve le plus souvent. Je vous prie d'excuser mon impertinence.

SCÈNE VI

M. Jourdain, Mme Jourdain, Dorante, Nicole

M. Jourdain, *à Dorante*. Voilà deux cents louis bien comptés.

Dorante. Je vous assure, monsieur Jourdain, que je suis tout à vous, et que je brûle de vous rendre un service à la cour.

M. Jourdain. Je vous suis trop obligé.

5 Dorante. Si madame Jourdain veut voir le divertissement royal, je lui ferai donner les meilleures places de la salle.

Mme Jourdain. Madame Jourdain vous baise les mains.

Dorante, *bas à M. Jourdain*. Notre belle marquise, comme je vous ai mandé par mon billet, viendra tantôt ici pour le 10 ballet et le repas; et je l'ai fait consentir enfin au cadeau que vous lui voulez donner.

M. Jourdain. Tirons-nous un peu plus loin, pour cause.

Dorante. Il y a huit jours que je ne vous ai vu, et je ne vous ai point mandé de nouvelles du diamant que vous me 15 mîtes entre les mains pour lui en faire présent de votre part; mais c'est que j'ai eu toutes les peines du monde à vaincre son scrupule, et ce n'est que d'aujourd'hui qu'elle s'est résolue à l'accepter.

M. Jourdain. Comment l'a-t-elle trouvé ?

20 Dorante. Merveilleux! et je me trompe fort, ou la beauté de ce diamant fera pour vous sur son esprit un effet admirable.

M. Jourdain. Plût au ciel !

Mme Jourdain, *à Nicole*. Quand il est une fois avec lui, il ne peut le quitter.

25 Dorante. Je lui ai fait valoir comme il faut la richesse de ce présent et la grandeur de votre amour.

M. Jourdain. Ce sont, monsieur, des bontés qui m'accablent; et je suis dans une confusion la plus grande du monde, de voir une personne de votre qualité s'abaisser pour moi à ce que 30 vous faites.

DORANTE. Vous moquez-vous? Est-ce qu'entre amis on s'arrête à ces sortes de scrupules, et ne feriez-vous pas pour moi la même chose, si l'occasion s'en offrait?

M. JOURDAIN. Oh! assurément, et de très grand cœur.

Mme JOURDAIN, *bas à Nicole*. Que sa présence me pèse sur 5 les épaules!

DORANTE. Pour moi, je ne regarde rien quand il faut servir un ami; et lorsque vous me fîtes confidence de l'ardeur que vous aviez prise pour cette marquise agréable chez qui j'avais commerce, vous vîtes que d'abord je m'offris de moi-même à 10 servir votre amour.

M. JOURDAIN. Il est vrai. Ce sont des bontés qui me confondent.

Mme JOURDAIN, *à Nicole*. Est-ce qu'il ne s'en ira point?

NICOLE. Ils se trouvent bien ensemble. 15

DORANTE. Vous avez pris le bon biais pour toucher son cœur. Les femmes aiment surtout les dépenses qu'on fait pour elles; et vos fréquentes sérénades et vos bouquets continuels, ce superbe feu d'artifice qu'elle trouva sur l'eau, le diamant qu'elle a reçu de votre part, et le cadeau que vous lui préparez, 20 tout cela lui parle bien mieux en faveur de votre amour que toutes les paroles que vous auriez pu lui dire vous-même.

M. JOURDAIN. Il n'y a point de dépenses que je ne fisse si par là je pouvais trouver le chemin de son cœur. Une femme de qualité a pour moi des charmes ravissants; et c'est un hon- 25 neur que j'achèterais au prix de toute chose.

Mme JOURDAIN, *bas à Nicole*. Que peuvent-ils tant dire ensemble? Va-t'en un peu tout doucement prêter l'oreille.

DORANTE. Ce sera tantôt que vous jouirez à votre aise du plaisir de sa vue; et vos yeux auront tout le temps de se satisfaire. 30

M. JOURDAIN. Pour être en pleine liberté, j'ai fait en sorte que ma femme ira dîner chez ma sœur, où elle passera toute l'après-dînée.

DORANTE. Vous avez fait prudemment, et votre femme aurait pu nous embarrasser. J'ai donné pour vous l'ordre qu'il faut au cuisinier, et à toutes les choses qui sont nécessaires pour le ballet. Il est de mon invention ; et pourvu que l'exécution 5 puisse répondre à l'idée, je suis sûr qu'il sera trouvé . . .

M. JOURDAIN, *s'aperçoit que Nicole écoute, et lui donne un soufflet.* Ouais. Vous êtes bien impertinente ! (*À Dorante.*) Sortons, s'il vous plaît.

SCÈNE VII

Mme JOURDAIN, NICOLE

NICOLE. Ma foi, madame, la curiosité m'a coûté quelque 10 chose ; mais je crois qu'il y a quelque anguille sous roche, et ils parlent de quelque affaire où ils ne veulent pas que vous soyez.

Mme JOURDAIN. Ce n'est pas d'aujourd'hui, Nicole, que j'ai conçu des soupçons de mon mari. Je suis la plus trompée du 15 monde, ou il y a quelque amour en campagne, et je travaille à découvrir ce que ce peut être. Mais songeons à ma fille. Tu sais l'amour que Cléonte a pour elle. C'est un homme qui me revient, et je veux aider sa recherche, et lui donner Lucile, si je puis.

20 NICOLE. En vérité, madame, je suis la plus ravie du monde de vous voir dans ces sentiments ; car si le maître vous revient, le valet ne me revient pas moins, et je souhaiterais que notre mariage se pût faire à l'ombre du leur.

Mme JOURDAIN. Va-t'en lui parler de ma part, et lui dire 25 que tout à l'heure il me vienne trouver, pour faire ensemble à mon mari la demande de ma fille.

NICOLE. J'y cours, madame, avec joie, et je ne pouvais recevoir une commission plus agréable. (*Seule.*) Je vais, je pense, bien réjouir les gens.

SCÈNE VIII

CLÉONTE, COVIELLE, NICOLE

NICOLE, *à Cléonte*. Ah ! vous voilà tout à propos. Je suis une ambassadrice de joie, et je viens . . .

CLÉONTE. Retire-toi, perfide ! et ne me viens point amuser avec tes traîtresses paroles.

NICOLE. Est-ce ainsi que vous recevez . . .   5

CLÉONTE. Retire-toi, te dis-je, et va-t'en dire de ce pas à ton infidèle maîtresse qu'elle n'abusera de sa vie le trop simple Cléonte.

NICOLE. Quel vertigo est-ce donc là ? Mon pauvre Covielle, dis-moi un peu ce que cela veut dire.   10

COVIELLE. Ton pauvre Covielle, petite scélérate ! Allons vite, ôte-toi de mes yeux, vilaine, et me laisse en repos.

NICOLE. Quoi ! tu me viens aussi . . .

COVIELLE. Ôte-toi de mes yeux, te dis-je, et ne me parle de ta vie.   15

NICOLE, *à part*. Ouais ! quelle mouche les a piqués tous deux ? Allons de cette belle histoire informer ma maîtresse.

SCÈNE IX

CLÉONTE, COVIELLE

CLÉONTE. Quoi ! traiter un amant de la sorte, et un amant le plus fidèle et le plus passionné de tous les amants !

COVIELLE. C'est une chose épouvantable que ce qu'on nous 20 fait à tous deux.

CLÉONTE. Je fais voir pour une personne toute l'ardeur et toute la tendresse qu'on peut imaginer ; je n'aime rien au monde qu'elle, et je n'ai qu'elle dans l'esprit ; elle fait tous mes soins, tous mes désirs, toute ma joie ; je ne parle que d'elle, je ne 25

pense qu'à elle, je ne fais des songes que d'elle, je ne respire
que par elle, mon cœur vit tout en elle, et voilà de tant d'amitié
la digne récompense ! Je suis deux jours sans la voir, qui sont
pour moi deux siècles effroyables ; je la rencontre par hasard ;
5 mon cœur à cette vue se sent tout transporté, ma joie éclate
sur mon visage, je vole avec ravissement vers elle ; et l'infidèle
détourne de moi ses regards et passe brusquement, comme si
de sa vie elle ne m'avait vu !

COVIELLE. Je dis les mêmes choses que vous.

10 CLÉONTE. Peut-on rien voir d'égal, Covielle, à cette perfidie
de l'ingrate Lucile ?

COVIELLE. Et à celle, monsieur, de la pendarde de Nicole ?

CLÉONTE. Après tant de sacrifices ardents, de soupirs et de
vœux que j'ai faits à ses charmes.

15 COVIELLE. Après tant d'assidus hommages, de soins et de
services que je lui ai rendus dans sa cuisine !

CLÉONTE. Tant de larmes que j'ai versées à ses genoux.

COVIELLE. Tant de seaux d'eau que j'ai tirés au puits pour
elle !

20 CLÉONTE. Tant d'ardeur que j'ai fait paraître à la chérir
plus que moi-même !

COVIELLE. Tant de chaleur que j'ai soufferte à tourner la
broche à sa place !

CLÉONTE. Elle me fuit avec mépris !

25 COVIELLE. Elle me tourne le dos avec effronterie !

CLÉONTE. C'est une perfidie digne des plus grands châtiments.

COVIELLE. C'est une trahison à mériter mille soufflets.

CLÉONTE. Ne t'avise point, je te prie, de me jamais parler
30 pour elle.

COVIELLE. Moi, monsieur ! Dieu m'en garde !

CLÉONTE. Ne viens point m'excuser l'action de cette infidèle.

COVIELLE. N'ayez pas peur.

CLÉONTE. Non, vois-tu, tous tes discours pour la défendre ne serviront de rien.

COVIELLE. Qui songe à cela ?

CLÉONTE. Je veux contre elle conserver mon ressentiment, et rompre ensemble tout commerce. 5

COVIELLE. J'y consens.

CLÉONTE. Ce monsieur le comte qui va chez elle lui donne peut-être dans la vue ; et son esprit, je le vois bien, se laisse éblouir à la qualité. Mais il me faut, pour mon honneur, prévenir l'éclat de son inconstance. Je veux faire autant de pas 10 qu'elle au changement où je la vois courir, et ne lui laisser pas toute la gloire de me quitter.

COVIELLE. C'est fort bien dit, et j'entre pour mon compte dans tous vos sentiments.

CLÉONTE. Donne la main à mon dépit, et soutiens ma réso- 15 lution contre tous les restes d'amour qui me pourraient parler pour elle. Dis-m'en, je t'en conjure, tout le mal que tu pourras ; fais-moi de sa personne une peinture qui me la rende méprisable ; et marque-moi bien, pour m'en dégoûter, tous les défauts que tu peux voir en elle. 20

COVIELLE. Elle, monsieur ! voilà une belle mijaurée, une pimpesouée bien bâtie pour vous donner tant d'amour ! Je ne lui vois rien que de très médiocre, et vous trouverez cent personnes qui seront plus dignes de vous. Premièrement, elle a les yeux petits.

CLÉONTE. Cela est vrai, elle a les yeux petits ; mais elle les 25 a pleins de feu, les plus brillants, les plus perçants du monde, les plus touchants qu'on puisse voir.

COVIELLE. Elle a la bouche grande.

CLÉONTE. Oui ; mais on y voit des grâces qu'on ne voit point aux autres bouches ; et cette bouche, en la voyant, inspire 30 des désirs, est la plus attrayante, la plus amoureuse du monde.

COVIELLE. Pour sa taille, elle n'est pas grande.

CLÉONTE. Non ; mais elle est aisée et bien prise.

COVIELLE. Elle affecte une nonchalance dans son parler et dans ses actions.

CLÉONTE. Il est vrai ; mais elle a grâce à tout cela ; et ses manières sont engageantes, ont je ne sais quel charme à
5 s'insinuer dans les cœurs.

COVIELLE. Pour de l'esprit . . .

CLÉONTE. Ah ! elle en a, Covielle, du plus fin, du plus délicat.

COVIELLE. Sa conversation . . .

CLÉONTE. Sa conversation est charmante.

10 COVIELLE. Elle est toujours sérieuse.

CLÉONTE. Veux-tu de ces enjouements épanouis, de ces joies toujours ouvertes ? Et vois-tu rien de plus impertinent que des femmes qui rient à tout propos ?

COVIELLE. Mais enfin elle est capricieuse autant que per-
15 sonne du monde.

CLÉONTE. Oui, elle est capricieuse, j'en demeure d'accord ; mais tout sied bien aux belles ; on souffre tout des belles.

COVIELLE. Puisque cela va comme cela, je vois bien que vous avez envie de l'aimer toujours.

20 CLÉONTE. Moi ! j'aimerais mieux mourir, et je vais la haïr autant que je l'ai aimée.

COVIELLE. Le moyen, si vous la trouvez si parfaite ?

CLÉONTE. C'est en quoi ma vengeance sera plus éclatante, en quoi je veux faire mieux voir la force de mon cœur à la haïr, à la
25 quitter, toute belle, toute pleine d'attraits, toute aimable que je la trouve. La voici.

SCÈNE X

LUCILE, CLÉONTE, COVIELLE, NICOLE

NICOLE, *à Lucile*. Pour moi, j'en ai été toute scandalisée.

LUCILE. Ce ne peut être, Nicole, que ce que je te dis. Mais le voilà.

30 CLÉONTE, *à Covielle*. Je ne veux pas seulement lui parler.

COVIELLE. Je veux vous imiter.

LUCILE. Qu'est-ce donc, Cléonte ? Qu'avez-vous ?

NICOLE. Qu'as-tu donc, Covielle ?

LUCILE. Quel chagrin vous possède ?

NICOLE. Quelle mauvaise humeur te tient ?   5

LUCILE. Êtes-vous muet, Cléonte ?

NICOLE. As-tu perdu la parole, Covielle ?

CLÉONTE. Que voilà qui est scélérat !

COVIELLE. Que cela est Judas !

LUCILE. Je vois bien que la rencontre de tantôt a troublé 10
votre esprit.

CLÉONTE, *à Covielle.* Ah, ah ! on voit ce qu'on a fait.

NICOLE. Notre accueil de ce matin t'a fait prendre la chèvre.

COVIELLE, *à Cléonte.* On a deviné l'enclouure.

LUCILE. N'est-il pas vrai, Cléonte, que c'est là le sujet de 15
votre dépit ?

CLÉONTE. Oui, perfide, ce l'est, puisqu'il faut parler ; et j'ai
à vous dire que vous ne triompherez pas, comme vous pensez,
de votre infidélité ; que je veux être le premier à rompre avec
vous, et que vous n'aurez pas l'avantage de me chasser. J'aurai 20
de la peine, sans doute, à vaincre l'amour que j'ai pour vous ;
cela me causera des chagrins ; je souffrirai un temps : mais j'en
viendrai à bout, et je me percerai plutôt le cœur que d'avoir la
faiblesse de retourner à vous.

COVIELLE, *à Nicole.* Queussi, queumi.   25

LUCILE. Voilà bien du bruit pour un rien. Je veux vous
dire, Cléonte, le sujet qui m'a fait, ce matin, éviter votre abord.

CLÉONTE, *voulant s'en aller pour éviter Lucile.* Non ; je ne
veux rien écouter.

NICOLE, *à Covielle.* Je te veux apprendre la cause qui nous 30
a fait passer si vite.

CLÉONTE, *voulant aussi s'en aller pour éviter Nicole.* Je ne
veux rien entendre.

LUCILE, *suivant Cléonte*. Sachez que ce matin . . .

CLÉONTE, *marchant toujours sans regarder Lucile*. Non, vous dis-je.

NICOLE, *suivant Covielle*. Apprends que . . .

5   COVIELLE, *marchant aussi sans regarder Nicole*. Non, traî-tresse.

LUCILE. Écoutez.

CLÉONTE. Point d'affaire.

NICOLE. Laisse-moi dire.

10   COVIELLE. Je suis sourd.

LUCILE. Cléonte !

CLÉONTE. Non.

NICOLE. Covielle !

COVIELLE. Point !

15   LUCILE. Arrêtez !

CLÉONTE. Chansons !

NICOLE. Entends-moi.

COVIELLE. Bagatelles !

LUCILE. Un moment.

20   CLÉONTE. Point du tout.

NICOLE. Un peu de patience.

COVIELLE. Tarare !

LUCILE. Deux paroles.

CLÉONTE. Non ; c'en est fait.

25   NICOLE. Un mot.

COVIELLE. Plus de commerce.

LUCILE, *s'arrêtant*. Eh bien, puisque vous ne voulez pas m'écouter, demeurez dans votre pensée, et faites ce qu'il vous plaira.

30   NICOLE, *s'arrêtant aussi*. Puisque tu fais comme cela, prends-le tout comme tu voudras.

CLÉONTE, *se retournant vers Lucile*. Sachons donc le sujet d'un si bel accueil.

LUCILE, *s'en allant à son tour pour éviter Cléonte.* Il ne me plaît plus de le dire.

COVIELLE, *se retournant vers Nicole.* Apprends-nous un peu cette histoire.

NICOLE, *s'en allant aussi à son tour pour éviter Covielle.* Je 5 ne veux plus, moi, te l'apprendre.

CLÉONTE, *suivant Lucile.* Dites-moi . . .

LUCILE, *marchant toujours sans regarder Cléonte.* Non ; je ne veux rien dire.

COVIELLE, *suivant Nicole.* Conte-moi . . .   10

NICOLE, *marchant aussi sans regarder Covielle.* Non ; je ne conte rien.

CLÉONTE. De grâce !

LUCILE. Non, vous dis-je.

COVIELLE. Par charité !   15

NICOLE. Point d'affaire.

CLÉONTE. Je vous en prie.

LUCILE. Laissez-moi.

COVIELLE. Je t'en conjure.

NICOLE. Ôte-toi de là.   20

CLÉONTE. Lucile !

LUCILE. Non !

COVIELLE. Nicole !

NICOLE. Point.

CLÉONTE. Au nom des dieux !   25

LUCILE. Je ne veux pas.

COVIELLE. Parle-moi.

NICOLE. Point du tout.

CLÉONTE. Éclaircissez mes doutes.

LUCILE. Non ; je n'en ferai rien.   30

COVIELLE. Guéris-moi l'esprit.

NICOLE. Non ; il ne me plaît pas.

CLÉONTE. Eh bien, puisque vous vous souciez si peu de me

tirer de peine, et de vous justifier du traitement indigne que
vous avez fait à ma flamme, vous me voyez, ingrate, pour la
dernière fois ; et je vais loin de vous, mourir de douleur et
d'amour.

5   COVIELLE, *à Nicole*. Et moi, je vais suivre ses pas.

LUCILE, *à Cléonte, qui veut sortir*. Cléonte !

NICOLE, *à Covielle, qui suit son maître*. Covielle !

CLÉONTE, *s'arrêtant*. Hé ?

COVIELLE, *s'arrêtant aussi*. Plaît-il ?

10   LUCILE. Où allez-vous ?

CLÉONTE. Où je vous ai dit.

COVIELLE. Nous allons mourir.

LUCILE. Vous allez mourir, Cléonte ?

CLÉONTE. Oui, cruelle, puisque vous le voulez.

15   LUCILE. Moi, je veux que vous mouriez ?

CLÉONTE. Oui, vous le voulez.

LUCILE. Qui vous le dit ?

CLÉONTE, *s'approchant de Lucile*. N'est-ce pas le vouloir que
de ne vouloir pas éclaircir mes soupçons ?

20   LUCILE. Est-ce ma faute ? Et si vous aviez voulu m'écouter,
ne vous aurais-je pas dit que l'aventure dont vous vous plaignez
a été causée ce matin par la présence d'une vieille tante qui
veut à toute force que la seule approche d'un homme désho-
nore une fille, qui perpétuellement nous sermonne sur ce
25 chapitre, et nous figure tous les hommes comme des diables
qu'il faut fuir ?

NICOLE, *à Covielle*. Voilà le secret de l'affaire.

CLÉONTE. Ne me trompez-vous point, Lucile ?

COVIELLE, *à Nicole*. Ne m'en donnes-tu point à garder ?

30   LUCILE, *à Cléonte*. Il n'est rien de plus vrai.

NICOLE, *à Covielle*. C'est la chose comme elle est.

COVIELLE, *à Cléonte*. Nous rendrons-nous à cela ?

CLÉONTE. Ah ! Lucile, qu'avec un mot de votre bouche vous

savez apaiser de choses dans mon cœur ! et que facilement on
se laisse persuader aux personnes qu'on aime !

COVIELLE. Qu'on est aisément amadoué par ces diantres
d'animaux-là !

SCÈNE XI

Mᵐᵉ JOURDAIN, CLÉONTE, LUCILE, COVIELLE, NICOLE

Mᵐᵉ JOURDAIN. Je suis bien aise de vous voir, Cléonte, et
vous voilà tout à propos. Mon mari vient ; prenez vite votre
temps pour lui demander Lucile en mariage.

CLÉONTE. Ah ! madame, que cette parole m'est douce, et
qu'elle flatte mes désirs ! Pouvais-je recevoir un ordre plus
charmant, une faveur plus précieuse ?

SCÈNE XII

CLÉONTE, M. JOURDAIN, Mᵐᵉ JOURDAIN, LUCILE, COVIELLE, NICOLE

CLÉONTE. Monsieur, je n'ai voulu prendre personne, pour
vous faire une demande que je médite il y a longtemps. Elle
me touche assez pour m'en charger moi-même ; et, sans autre
détour, je vous dirai que l'honneur d'être votre gendre est une
faveur glorieuse que je vous prie de m'accorder.

M. JOURDAIN. Avant que de vous rendre réponse, monsieur,
je vous prie de me dire si vous êtes gentilhomme.

CLÉONTE. Monsieur, la plupart des gens sur cette question
n'hésitent pas beaucoup. On tranche le mot aisément. Ce
nom ne fait aucun scrupule à prendre, et l'usage aujourd'hui
semble en autoriser le vol. Pour moi, je vous l'avoue, j'ai les
sentiments sur cette matière un peu plus délicats. Je trouve
que toute imposture est indigne d'un honnête homme, et qu'il
y a de la lâcheté à déguiser ce que le ciel nous a fait naître, à

se parer aux yeux du monde d'un titre dérobé, à se vouloir
donner pour ce qu'on n'est pas. Je suis né de parents, sans
doute, qui ont tenu des charges honorables. Je me suis acquis
dans les armes l'honneur de six ans de services, et je me trouve
5 assez de bien pour tenir dans le monde un rang assez passable ;
mais, avec tout cela, je ne veux point me donner un nom où
d'autres, en ma place, croiraient pouvoir prétendre ; et je vous
dirai franchement que je ne suis point gentilhomme.

M. Jourdain. Touchez là, monsieur. Ma fille n'est pas
10 pour vous.

Cléonte. Comment ?

M. Jourdain. Vous n'êtes point gentilhomme, vous n'aurez
pas ma fille.

Mme Jourdain. Que voulez-vous donc dire avec votre gen-
15 tilhomme ? Est-ce que nous sommes, nous autres, de la côte
de Saint-Louis ?

M. Jourdain. Taisez-vous, ma femme ; je vous vois venir.

Mme Jourdain. Descendons-nous tous deux que de bonne
bourgeoisie ?

20 M. Jourdain. Voilà pas le coup de langue ?

Mme Jourdain. Et votre père n'était-il pas marchand, aussi
bien que le mien ?

M. Jourdain. Peste soit de la femme ! Elle n'y a jamais
manqué. Si votre père a été marchand, tant pis pour lui ; mais
25 pour le mien, ce sont des malavisés qui disent cela. Tout ce
que j'ai à vous dire, moi, c'est que je veux avoir un gendre
gentilhomme.

Mme Jourdain. Il faut à votre fille un mari qui lui soit
propre, et il vaut mieux pour elle un honnête homme riche et
30 bien fait qu'un gentilhomme gueux et mal bâti.

Nicole. Cela est vrai. Nous avons le fils du gentilhomme
de notre village, qui est le plus grand malitorne et le plus sot
dadais que j'aie jamais vu.

M. Jourdain, à *Nicole*. Taisez-vous, impertinente. Vous vous fourrez toujours dans la conversation. J'ai du bien assez pour ma fille, je n'ai besoin que d'honneurs, et je la veux faire marquise.

Mme Jourdain. Marquise ?   5

M. Jourdain. Oui, marquise.

Mme Jourdain. Hélas ! Dieu m'en garde !

M. Jourdain. C'est une chose que j'ai résolue.

Mme Jourdain. C'est une chose, moi, où je ne consentirai point. Les alliances avec plus grand que soi sont sujettes 10 toujours à de fâcheux inconvénients. Je ne veux point qu'un gendre puisse à ma fille reprocher ses parents, et qu'elle ait des enfants qui aient honte de m'appeler leur grand'maman. S'il fallait qu'elle me vînt visiter en équipage de grand'dame, et qu'elle manquât par mégarde à saluer quelqu'un du quartier, 15 on ne manquerait pas aussitôt de dire cent sottises. « Voyez-vous, dirait-on, cette madame la marquise qui fait tant la glo-rieuse ? C'est la fille de monsieur Jourdain, qui était trop heureuse, étant petite, de jouer à la madame avec nous. Elle n'a pas toujours été si relevée que la voilà, et ses deux grands- 20 pères vendaient du drap auprès de la porte Saint-Innocent. Ils ont amassé du bien à leurs enfants, qu'ils payent maintenant peut-être bien cher en l'autre monde, et l'on ne devient guère si riches à être honnêtes gens.» Je ne veux point tous ces caquets, et je veux un homme, en un mot, qui m'ait obligation 25 de ma fille et à qui je puisse dire : « Mettez-vous là, mon gendre, et dînez avec moi.»

M. Jourdain. Voilà bien les sentiments d'un petit esprit, de vouloir demeurer toujours dans la bassesse. Ne me répliquez pas davantage : ma fille sera marquise en dépit de tout le monde ; 30 et si vous me mettez en colère, je la ferai duchesse.

SCÈNE XIII

Mᵐᵉ JOURDAIN, LUCILE, CLÉONTE, NICOLE, COVIELLE

Mᵐᵉ JOURDAIN. Cléonte, ne perdez point courage encore. (*À Lucile.*) Suivez-moi, ma fille, et venez dire résolument à votre père que, si vous ne l'avez, vous ne voulez épouser personne.

SCÈNE XIV

CLÉONTE, COVIELLE

5   COVIELLE. Vous avez fait de belles affaires avec vos beaux sentiments.

CLÉONTE. Que veux-tu? j'ai un scrupule là-dessus que l'exemple ne saurait vaincre.

COVIELLE. Vous moquez-vous, de le prendre sérieusement
10 avec un homme comme cela? Ne voyez-vous pas qu'il est fou? Et vous coûtait-il quelque chose de vous accommoder à ses chimères?

CLÉONTE. Tu as raison; mais je ne croyais pas qu'il fallût faire ses preuves de noblesse pour être gendre de monsieur
15 Jourdain.

COVIELLE, *riant.* Ah, ah, ah.

CLÉONTE. De quoi ris-tu?

COVIELLE. D'une pensée qui me vient pour jouer notre homme et vous faire obtenir ce que vous souhaitez.

20   CLÉONTE. Comment?

COVIELLE. L'idée est tout à fait plaisante.

CLÉONTE. Quoi donc?

COVIELLE. Il s'est fait depuis peu une certaine mascarade qui vient le mieux du monde ici, et que je prétends faire entrer
25 dans une bourle que je veux faire à notre ridicule. Tout cela sent un peu sa comédie; mais avec lui on peut hasarder toute

chose, il n'y faut point chercher tant de façons, et il est homme
à y jouer son rôle à merveille, à donner aisément dans toutes
les faribobes qu'on s'avisera de lui dire. J'ai les acteurs, j'ai les
habits tout prêts ; laissez-moi faire seulement.

CLÉONTE. Mais apprends-moi . . .   5

COVIELLE. Je vais vous instruire de tout. Retirons-nous, le
voilà qui revient.

SCÈNE XV

M. JOURDAIN, *seul*

Que diable est-ce là ! Ils n'ont rien que les grands seigneurs
à me reprocher, et moi, je ne vois rien de si beau que de hanter
les grands seigneurs ; il n'y a qu'honneur et que civilité avec 10
eux, et je voudrais qu'il m'eût coûté deux doigts de la main et
être né comte ou marquis.

SCÈNE XVI

M. JOURDAIN, *un* LAQUAIS

LE LAQUAIS. Monsieur, voici monsieur le comte et une dame
qu'il mène par la main.

M. JOURDAIN. Hé mon Dieu ! j'ai quelques ordres à donner. 15
Dis-leur que je vais venir ici tout à l'heure.

SCÈNE XVII

DORIMÈNE, DORANTE, LE LAQUAIS

LE LAQUAIS. Monsieur dit comme cela qu'il va venir ici tout
à l'heure.

DORANTE. Voilà qui est bien.

SCÈNE XVIII

DORIMÈNE, DORANTE

DORIMÈNE. Je ne sais pas, Dorante ; je fais encore ici une
étrange démarche, de me laisser amener par vous dans une
maison où je ne connais personne.

DORANTE. Quel lieu voulez-vous donc, madame, que mon
5 amour choisisse pour vous régaler, puisque, pour fuir l'éclat,
vous ne voulez ni votre maison, ni la mienne ?

DORIMÈNE. Mais vous ne dites pas que je m'engage insensiblement chaque jour à recevoir de trop grands témoignages
de votre passion. J'ai beau me défendre des choses, vous
10 fatiguez ma résistance, et vous avez une civile opiniâtreté qui
me fait venir doucement à tout ce qu'il vous plaît. Les visites
fréquentes ont commencé ; les déclarations sont venues ensuite,
qui après elles ont traîné les sérénades et les cadeaux, que les
présents ont suivis. Je me suis opposée à tout cela, mais vous
15 ne vous rebutez point, et pied à pied vous gagnez mes résolu-
tions. Pour moi, je ne puis plus répondre de rien, et je crois
qu'à la fin vous me ferez venir au mariage dont je me suis
tant éloignée.

DORANTE. Ma foi, madame, vous y devriez déjà être. Vous
20 êtes veuve et ne dépendez que de vous. Je suis maître de
moi, et vous aime plus que ma vie. A quoi tient-il que dès
aujourd'hui vous ne fassiez tout mon bonheur ?

DORIMÈNE. Mon Dieu ! Dorante, il faut des deux parts
bien des qualités pour vivre heureusement ensemble ; et les
25 deux plus raisonnables personnes du monde ont souvent peine
à composer une union dont ils soient satisfaits.

DORANTE. Vous vous moquez, madame, de vous y figurer
tant de difficultés ; et l'expérience que vous avez faite ne conclut rien pour tous les autres.

30 DORIMÈNE. Enfin, j'en reviens toujours là. Les dépenses

que je vous vois faire pour moi m'inquiètent par deux raisons :
l'une, qu'elles m'engagent plus que je ne voudrais ; et l'autre,
que je suis sûre, sans vous déplaire, que vous ne les faites point
que vous ne vous incommodiez ; et je ne veux point cela.

DORANTE. Ah, madame ! ce sont des bagatelles, et ce n'est 5
pas par là . . .

DORIMÈNE. Je sais ce que je dis ; et entre autres le diamant
que vous m'avez forcée à prendre est d'un prix . . .

DORANTE. Hé, madame, de grâce, ne faites point tant valoir
une chose que mon amour trouve indigne de vous, et souffrez . . . 10
Voici le maître du logis.

SCÈNE XIX

M. JOURDAIN, DORIMÈNE, DORANTE

M. JOURDAIN, *après avoir fait deux révérences, se trouvant
trop près de Dorimène.* Un peu plus loin, madame.

DORIMÈNE. Comment ?

M. JOURDAIN. Un pas, s'il vous plaît.   15

DORIMÈNE. Quoi donc ?

M. JOURDAIN. Reculez un peu pour la troisième.

DORANTE. Madame, monsieur Jourdain sait son monde.

M. JOURDAIN. Madame, ce m'est une gloire bien grande de
me voir assez fortuné pour être si heureux que d'avoir le bon- 20
heur que vous ayez eu la bonté de m'accorder la grâce de me
faire l'honneur de m'honorer de la faveur de votre présence ; et
si j'avais aussi le mérite pour mériter un mérite comme le vôtre,
et que le ciel . . . envieux de mon bien . . . m'eût accordé . . .
l'avantage de me voir digne . . . des . . .   25

DORANTE. Monsieur Jourdain, en voilà assez ; madame n'aime
pas les grands compliments, et elle sait que vous êtes homme
d'esprit. (*Bas à Dorimène.*) C'est un bon bourgeois assez
ridicule, comme vous voyez, dans toutes ses manières.

Dorimène, *bas à Dorante.* Il n'est pas malaisé de s'en apercevoir.

Dorante. Madame, voilà le meilleur de mes amis.

M. Jourdain. C'est trop d'honneur que vous me faites.

5 Dorante. Galant homme tout à fait.

Dorimène. J'ai beaucoup d'estime pour lui.

M. Jourdain. Je n'ai rien fait encore, madame, pour mériter cette grâce.

Dorante, *bas à M. Jourdain.* Prenez bien garde au moins à
10 ne lui point parler du diamant que vous lui avez donné.

M. Jourdain, *bas à Dorante.* Ne pourrais-je pas seulement lui demander comment elle le trouve ?

Dorante, *bas à M. Jourdain.* Comment ? gardez-vous-en bien. Cela serait vilain à vous ; et pour agir en galant homme,
15 il faut que vous fassiez comme si ce n'était pas vous qui lui eussiez fait ce présent. (*Haut.*) Monsieur Jourdain, madame, dit qu'il est ravi de vous voir chez lui.

Dorimène. Il m'honore beaucoup.

M. Jourdain, *bas à Dorante.* Que je vous suis obligé, mon-
20 sieur, de lui parler ainsi pour moi.

Dorante, *bas à M. Jourdain.* J'ai eu une peine effroyable à la faire venir ici.

M. Jourdain, *bas à Dorante.* Je ne sais quelles grâces vous en rendre.

25 Dorante. Il dit, madame, qu'il vous trouve la plus belle personne du monde.

Dorimène. C'est bien de la grâce qu'il me fait.

M. Jourdain. Madame, c'est vous qui faites les grâces, et . . .

30 Dorante. Songeons à manger.

SCÈNE XX

M. Jourdain, Dorimène, Dorante, *un* Laquais

Le Laquais, *à M. Jourdain.* Tout est prêt, monsieur.

Dorante. Allons donc nous mettre à table, et qu'on fasse venir les musiciens.

SCÈNE XXI

Entrée de ballet

Six cuisiniers, qui ont préparé le festin, dansent ensemble et font le troisième intermède ; après quoi ils apportent une table cou- 5 *verte de plusieurs mets.*

ACTE IV

SCÈNE PREMIÈRE

DORIMÈNE, M. JOURDAIN, DORANTE, *une* MUSICIENNE, *deux* MUSICIENS, LAQUAIS

DORIMÈNE. Comment ! Dorante, voilà un repas tout à fait magnifique !

M. JOURDAIN. Vous vous moquez, madame, et je voudrais qu'il fût plus digne de vous être offert.

5 (*Dorimène, M. Jourdain, Dorante et les trois musiciens se mettent à table.*)

DORANTE. Monsieur Jourdain a raison, madame, de parler de la sorte, et il m'oblige de vous faire si bien les honneurs de chez lui. Je demeure d'accord avec lui que le repas n'est pas
10 digne de vous. Comme c'est moi qui l'ai ordonné, et que je n'ai pas sur cette matière les lumières de nos amis, vous n'avez pas ici un repas fort savant, et vous y trouverez des incongruités de bonne chère, et des barbarismes de bon goût. Si Damis s'en était mêlé, tout serait dans les règles ; il y aurait
15 partout de l'élégance et de l'érudition, et il ne manquerait pas de vous exagérer lui-même toutes les pièces du repas qu'il vous donnerait, et de vous faire tomber d'accord de sa haute capacité dans la science des bons morceaux ; de vous parler d'un pain de rive à biseau doré, relevé de croûte partout, croquant tendre-
20 ment sous la dent ; d'un vin à sève veloutée, armé d'un vert qui n'est point trop commandant ; d'un carré de mouton gourmandé de persil ; d'une longe de veau de rivière, longue comme

cela, blanche, délicate, et qui sous les dents est une vraie pâte
d'amande; de perdrix relevées d'un fumet surprenant; et pour
son opéra, d'une soupe à bouillon perlé, soutenue d'un jeune
gros dindon, cantonné de pigeonneaux, et couronnée d'oignons
blancs mariés avec la chicorée. Mais, pour moi, je vous avoue 5
mon ignorance; et, comme monsieur Jourdain a fort bien dit,
je voudrais que le repas fût plus digne de vous être offert.

DORIMÈNE. Je ne réponds à ce compliment qu'en mangeant
comme je fais.

M. JOURDAIN. Ah! que voilà de belles mains! 10

DORIMÈNE. Les mains sont médiocres, monsieur Jourdain;
mais vous voulez parler du diamant, qui est fort beau.

M. JOURDAIN. Moi, madame? Dieu me garde d'en vouloir
parler! Ce ne serait pas agir en galant homme, et le diamant
est fort peu de chose. 15

DORIMÈNE. Vous êtes bien dégoûté.

M. JOURDAIN. Vous avez trop de bonté . . .

DORANTE, après avoir fait signe à M. Jourdain. Allons, qu'on
donne du vin à monsieur Jourdain, et à ces messieurs qui nous
feront la grâce de nous chanter un air à boire. 20

DORIMÈNE. C'est merveilleusement assaisonner la bonne
chère que d'y mêler la musique, et je me vois ici admirablement
régalée.

M. JOURDAIN. Madame, ce n'est pas . . .

DORANTE. Monsieur Jourdain, prêtons silence à ces mes- 25
sieurs; ce qu'ils nous diront vaudra mieux que tout ce que
nous pourrions dire.

LES MUSICIENS ET LA MUSICIENNE prennent des verres,
chantent deux chansons à boire, et sont soutenus de toute la
symphonie. 30

PREMIÈRE CHANSON À BOIRE

PREMIER ET DEUXIÈME MUSICIENS ENSEMBLE, *un verre à la main*

Un petit doigt, Philis, pour commencer le tour.
Ah! qu'un verre en vos mains a d'agréables charmes!
    Vous et le vin, vous vous prêtez des armes, *you become allies*
Et je sens pour tous deux redoubler mon amour;
5   Entre lui, vous et moi, jurons, jurons, ma belle,
        Une ardeur éternelle.

Qu'en mouillant votre bouche il en reçoit d'attraits,
Et que l'on voit par lui votre bouche embellie!
    Ah! l'un de l'autre ils me donnent envie,
10   Et de vous et de lui je m'enivre à longs traits;
Entre lui, vous et moi, jurons, jurons, ma belle,
        Une ardeur éternelle.

SECONDE CHANSON À BOIRE

DEUXIÈME ET TROISIÈME MUSICIENS ENSEMBLE

    Buvons, chers amis, buvons:
    Le temps qui fuit nous y convie;
15   Profitons de la vie
        Autant que nous pouvons.
    Quand on a passé l'onde noire,
    Adieu le bon vin, nos amours;
        Dépêchons-nous de boire,
20   On ne boit pas toujours.

    Laissons raisonner les sots
    Sur le vrai bonheur de la vie;
        Notre philosophie
        Le met parmi les pots.
25   Les biens, le savoir et la gloire
    N'ôtent point les soucis fâcheux;
        Et ce n'est qu'à bien boire
        Que l'on peut être heureux.

TOUS TROIS ENSEMBLE

Sus, sus, du vin partout ; versez, garçons, versez ;
Versez, versez toujours, tant qu'on vous dise assez.

DORIMÈNE. Je ne crois pas qu'on puisse mieux chanter, et
cela est tout à fait beau.

M. JOURDAIN. Je vois encore ici, madame, quelque chose 5
de plus beau.

DORIMÈNE. Ouais ! Monsieur Jourdain est galant plus que
je ne pensais.

DORANTE. Comment, madame ? pour qui prenez-vous monsieur Jourdain ?   10

M. JOURDAIN. Je voudrais bien qu'elle me prît pour ce que
je dirais.

DORIMÈNE. Encore !

DORANTE, à Dorimène. Vous ne le connaissez pas.

M. JOURDAIN. Elle me connaîtra quand il lui plaira.   15

DORIMÈNE. Oh ! je le quitte.

DORANTE. Il est homme qui a toujours la riposte en main.
Mais vous ne voyez pas que monsieur Jourdain, madame, mange
tous les morceaux que vous touchez.

DORIMÈNE. Monsieur Jourdain est un homme qui me ravit.   20

M. JOURDAIN. Si je pouvais ravir votre cœur, je serais . . .

SCÈNE II

Mᵐᵉ JOURDAIN, M. JOURDAIN, DORIMÈNE, DORANTE, MUSICIENS,
MUSICIENNE, LAQUAIS

Mᵐᵉ JOURDAIN. Ah, ah ! je trouve ici bonne compagnie, et
je vois bien qu'on ne m'y attendait pas. C'est donc pour cette
belle affaire-ci, monsieur mon mari, que vous avez eu tant
d'empressement à m'envoyer dîner chez ma sœur ? Je viens de 25
voir un théâtre là-bas, et je vois ici un banquet à faire noces.

Voilà comme vous dépensez votre bien, et c'est ainsi que vous
festinez les dames en mon absence, et que vous leur donnez la
musique et la comédie, tandis que vous m'envoyez promener!

DORANTE. Que voulez-vous dire, madame Jourdain, et quelles
5 fantaisies sont les vôtres de vous aller mettre en tête que votre
mari dépense son bien, et que c'est lui qui donne ce régale à
madame? Apprenez que c'est moi, je vous prie; qu'il ne fait
seulement que me prêter sa maison, et que vous devriez un peu
mieux regarder aux choses que vous dites.

10 M. JOURDAIN. Oui, impertinente, c'est monsieur le comte
qui donne tout ceci à madame, qui est une personne de qualité.
Il me fait l'honneur de prendre ma maison et de vouloir que je
sois avec lui.

Mme JOURDAIN. Ce sont des chansons que cela; je sais ce
15 que je sais.

DORANTE. Prenez, madame Jourdain, prenez de meilleures
lunettes.

Mme JOURDAIN. Je n'ai que faire de lunettes, monsieur, et
je vois assez clair; il y a longtemps que je sens les choses, et
20 je ne suis pas une bête. Cela est fort vilain à vous, pour un
grand seigneur, de prêter la main, comme vous faites, aux sottises de mon mari. Et vous, madame, pour une grand'dame,
cela n'est ni beau ni honnête à vous de mettre la dissension
dans un ménage, et de souffrir que mon mari soit amoureux
25 de vous.

DORIMÈNE. Que veut donc dire tout ceci? Allez, Dorante,
vous vous moquez de m'exposer aux sottes visions de cette
extravagante.

DORANTE, *suivant Dorimène qui sort*. Madame, holà! ma-
30 dame, où courez-vous?

M. JOURDAIN. Madame . . . Monsieur le comte, faites-lui
excuses, et tâchez de la ramener.

SCÈNE III

Mme Jourdain, M. Jourdain, Laquais

M. Jourdain. Ah! impertinente que vous êtes, voilà de vos
beaux faits! Vous me venez faire des affronts devant tout le
monde, et vous chassez de chez moi des personnes de qualité!

Mme Jourdain. Je me moque de leur qualité.

M. Jourdain. Je ne sais qui me tient, maudite, que je ne 5
vous fende la tête avec les pièces du repas que vous êtes venue
troubler.

(*Les laquais emportent la table.*)

Mme Jourdain, *sortant*. Je me moque de cela. Ce sont mes
droits que je défends et j'aurai pour moi toutes les femmes.   10

M. Jourdain. Vous faites bien d'éviter ma colère.

SCÈNE IV

M. Jourdain, *seul*

Elle est arrivée là bien malheureusement. J'étais en humeur
de dire de jolies choses, et jamais je ne m'étais senti tant
d'esprit . . . Qu'est-ce que c'est que cela?

SCÈNE V

M. Jourdain, Covielle *déguisé*   15

Covielle. Monsieur, je ne sais pas si j'ai l'honneur d'être
connu de vous.

M. Jourdain. Non, monsieur.

Covielle, *étendant la main à un pied de terre.* Je vous ai vu
que vous n'étiez pas plus grand que cela.   20

M. Jourdain. Moi?

Covielle. Oui, vous étiez le plus bel enfant du monde, et toutes les dames vous prenaient dans leurs bras pour vous baiser.

M. Jourdain. Pour me baiser ?

Covielle. Oui, j'étais grand ami de feu monsieur votre père.

5 M. Jourdain. De feu monsieur mon père ?

Covielle. Oui. C'était un fort honnête gentilhomme.

M. Jourdain. Comment dites-vous ?

Covielle. Je dis que c'était un fort honnête gentilhomme.

M. Jourdain. Mon père ?

10 Covielle. Oui.

M. Jourdain. Vous l'avez fort connu ?

Covielle. Assurément.

M. Jourdain. Et vous l'avez connu pour gentilhomme ?

Covielle. Sans doute.

15 M. Jourdain. Je ne sais donc pas comment le monde est fait.

Covielle. Comment ?

M. Jourdain. Il y a de sottes gens qui me veulent dire qu'il a été marchand.

Covielle. Lui, marchand ? C'est pure médisance, il ne l'a 20 jamais été. Tout ce qu'il faisait, c'est qu'il était fort obligeant, fort officieux, et comme il se connaissait fort bien en étoffes, il en allait choisir de tous les côtés, les faisait apporter chez lui, et en donnait à ses amis pour de l'argent.

M. Jourdain. Je suis ravi de vous connaître, afin que vous 25 rendiez ce témoignage-là, que mon père était gentilhomme.

Covielle. Je le soutiendrai devant tout le monde.

M. Jourdain. Vous m'obligerez. Quel sujet vous amène ?

Covielle. Depuis avoir connu feu monsieur votre père, honnête gentilhomme, comme je vous ai dit, j'ai voyagé par 30 tout le monde.

M. Jourdain. Par tout le monde ?

Covielle. Oui.

M. Jourdain. Je pense qu'il y a bien loin en ce pays-là.

Covielle. Assurément. Je ne suis revenu de tous mes longs voyages que depuis quatre jours ; et par l'intérêt que je prends à tout ce qui vous touche, je viens vous annoncer la meilleure nouvelle du monde.

M. Jourdain. Quelle ? 5

Covielle. Vous savez que le fils du Grand Turc est ici ?

M. Jourdain. Moi ? non.

Covielle. Comment ! il a un train tout à fait magnifique, tout le monde le va voir, et il a été reçu en ce pays comme un seigneur d'importance. 10

M. Jourdain. Par ma foi, je ne savais pas cela.

Covielle. Ce qu'il y a d'avantageux pour vous, c'est qu'il est amoureux de votre fille.

M. Jourdain. Le fils du Grand Turc ?

Covielle. Oui, et il veut être votre gendre. 15

M. Jourdain. Mon gendre, le fils du Grand Turc !

Covielle. Le fils du Grand Turc, votre gendre. Comme je le fus voir, et que j'entends parfaitement sa langue, il s'entretint avec moi, et après quelques autres discours, il me dit : *Acciam croc soler ouch alla moustaph gidelum amanahem vara-* 20 *hini oussere carbulath ?* C'est-à-dire : N'as-tu point vu une jeune belle personne qui est la fille de monsieur Jourdain, gentil-homme parisien ?

M. Jourdain. Le fils du Grand Turc dit cela de moi ?

Covielle. Oui. Comme je lui eus répondu que je vous 25 connaissais particulièrement, et que j'avais vu votre fille : Ah ! me dit-il, *marababa sahem !* C'est-à-dire : Ah ! que je suis amoureux d'elle !

M. Jourdain. *Marababa sahem* veut dire : Ah ! que je suis amoureux d'elle ? 30

Covielle. Oui.

M. Jourdain. Par ma foi, vous faites bien de me le dire ; car, pour moi, je n'aurais jamais cru que *marababa sahem* eût

voulu dire : Ah ! que je suis amoureux d'elle ! Voilà une langue
admirable que ce turc !

COVIELLE. Plus admirable qu'on ne peut croire. Savez-vous
bien ce que veut dire *cacaracamouchen* ?

5   M. JOURDAIN. *Cacaracamouchen* ? Non.

COVIELLE. C'est-à-dire : (Ma chère âme.)

M. JOURDAIN. *Cacaracamouchen* veut dire : Ma chère âme ?

COVIELLE. Oui.

M. JOURDAIN. Voilà qui est merveilleux ! *Cacaracamouchen*,
10 ma chère âme ! Dirait-on jamais cela ? Voilà qui me confond.

COVIELLE. Enfin, pour achever mon ambassade, il vient vous
demander votre fille en mariage ; et pour avoir un beau-père
qui soit digne de lui, il veut vous faire *mamamouchi*, qui est une
certaine grande dignité de son pays.

15 M. JOURDAIN. *Mamamouchi* ?

COVIELLE. Oui, *mamamouchi*, c'est-à-dire, en notre langue,
paladin. Paladin, ce sont de ces anciens . . . Paladin enfin.
Il n'y a rien de plus noble que cela dans le monde, et vous irez
de pair avec les plus grands seigneurs de la terre.

20 M. JOURDAIN. Le fils du Grand Turc m'honore beaucoup,
et je vous prie de me mener chez lui pour lui en faire mes
remerciements.

COVIELLE. Comment ! le voilà qui va venir ici.

M. JOURDAIN. Il va venir ici ?

25 COVIELLE. Oui ; et il amène toutes choses pour la cérémonie
de votre dignité.

M. JOURDAIN. Voilà qui est bien prompt.

COVIELLE. Son amour ne peut souffrir aucun retardement.

M. JOURDAIN. Tout ce qui m'embarrasse ici, c'est que ma
30 fille est une opiniâtre qui s'est allé mettre dans la tête un certain Cléonte ; et elle jure de n'épouser personne que celui-là.

COVIELLE. Elle changera de sentiment quand elle verra le
fils du Grand Turc ; et puis il se rencontre ici une aventure

merveilleuse : c'est que le fils du Grand Turc ressemble à ce Cléonte, à peu de chose près. Je viens de le voir, on me l'a montré ; et l'amour qu'elle a pour l'un pourra passer aisément à l'autre, et . . . Je l'entends venir ; le voilà.

SCÈNE VI

CLÉONTE, *en Turc, trois* PAGES, *portant la veste de Cléonte,* M. JOURDAIN, COVIELLE

CLÉONTE. *Ambousahim oqui boraf, Jordina salamalequi !* 5

COVIELLE, *à M. Jourdain.* C'est-à-dire : Monsieur Jourdain, votre cœur soit toute l'année comme un rosier fleuri ! Ce sont façons de parler obligeantes de ces pays-là.

M. JOURDAIN. Je suis très humble serviteur de Son Altesse turque. 10

COVIELLE. *Carigar camboto oustin moraf.*

CLÉONTE. *Oustin yoc catamalequi basum base alla moran !*

COVIELLE. Il dit, que le ciel vous donne la force des lions et la prudence des serpents !

M. JOURDAIN. Son Altesse turque m'honore trop, et je lui 15 souhaite toutes sortes de prospérités.

COVIELLE. *Ossa binamen sadoc babally oracaf ouram.*

CLÉONTE. *Bel-men.*

COVIELLE. Il dit que vous alliez vite avec lui vous préparer pour la cérémonie, afin de voir ensuite votre fille et de conclure 20 le mariage.

M. JOURDAIN. Tant de choses en deux mots ?

COVIELLE. Oui, la langue turque est comme cela ; elle dit beaucoup en peu de paroles. Allez vite où il souhaite.

SCÈNE VII

COVIELLE, *seul*

Ha! ha! ha! Ma foi, cela est tout à fait drôle. Quelle dupe!
Quand il aurait appris son rôle par cœur, il ne pourrait pas le
mieux jouer. Ah, ah!

SCÈNE VIII

DORANTE, COVIELLE

COVIELLE. Je vous prie, monsieur, de nous vouloir aider
5 céans dans une affaire qui s'y passe.

DORANTE. Ah! ah! Covielle, qui t'aurait reconnu? Comme
te voilà ajusté!

COVIELLE. Vous voyez. Ah! ah!

DORANTE. De quoi ris-tu?

10   COVIELLE. D'une chose, monsieur, qui le mérite bien.

DORANTE. Comment?

COVIELLE. Je vous le donnerais en bien des fois, monsieur,
à deviner le stratagème dont nous nous servons auprès de
monsieur Jourdain, pour porter son esprit à donner sa fille à
15 mon maître.

DORANTE. Je ne devine pas le stratagème, mais je devine
qu'il ne manquera pas de faire son effet, puisque tu l'entreprends.

COVIELLE. Je sais, monsieur, que la bête vous est connue.

DORANTE. Apprends-moi ce que c'est.

20   COVIELLE. Prenez la peine de vous tirer un peu plus loin,
pour faire place à ce que j'aperçois venir. Vous pourrez voir
une partie de l'histoire, tandis que je vous conterai le reste.

La Cérémonie turque pour anoblir le Bourgeois se fait en danse et
en musique, et compose le quatrième intermède.

25   *Six Turcs dansants entrent gravement deux à deux, au son de tous les*
instruments. Ils portent trois tapis fort longs, dont ils font plusieurs figures,

et, à la fin de cette première cérémonie, ils les lèvent fort haut ; les Turcs
musiciens, et autres joueurs d'instruments, passent par-dessous ; quatre
Derviches, qui accompagnent le Muphty, ferment cette marche.

    Alors les Turcs étendent les tapis par terre, et se mettent dessus à
genoux ; le Muphty est debout au milieu, qui fait une invocation avec des 5
contorsions et des grimaces, levant le menton, et remuant les mains contre
sa tête, comme si c'était des ailes. Les Turcs se prosternent jusqu'à terre,
chantants **Alli,** *puis se relèvent, chantants* **Alla,** *et continuant alternative-*
ment jusqu'à la fin de l'invocation ; puis ils se lèvent tous, chantants
Alla ekber.   10

    Alors les Derviches amènent devant le Muphty le Bourgeois vêtu à la
turque, rasé, sans turban, sans sabre, auquel il chante gravement ces
paroles.

LE MUPHTY

Se ti sabir,
Ti respondir ;   15
Se non sabir,
Tazir, tazir.

Mi star Muphty,
Ti qui star ti ?
Non intendir ;   20
Tazir, tazir.

    Deux Derviches font retirer le Bourgeois. Le Muphty demande aux
Turcs de quelle religion est le Bourgeois, et chante :

Dice, Turque, qui star quista.
Anabatista ? Anabatista ?   25

LES TURCS *répondent*

Ioc.

LE MUPHTY

Zuinglista ?

LES TURCS

Ioc.

LE MUPHTY

Coffita ?

LES TURCS

Ioc.

LE MUPHTY

Ussita? Morista? Fronista?

LES TURCS

Ioc. Ioc. Ioc.

LE MUPHTY *répète*

Ioc. Ioc. Ioc.
Star pagana?

LES TURCS

Ioc.

LE MUPHTY

Luterana?

LES TURCS

Ioc.

LE MUPHTY

Puritana?

LES TURCS

Ioc.

LE MUPHTY

Bramina? Moffina? Zurina?

LES TURCS

Ioc. Ioc. Ioc.

LE MUPHTY *répète*

Ioc. Ioc. Ioc.
Mahametana? Mahametana?

LES TURCS

Hey valla. Hey valla.

LE MUPHTY

Como chamara? Como chamara?

LES TURCS

Giourdina, Giourdina.

LE MUPHTY

Giourdina.

LE MUPHTY, *sautant, et regardant de côté et d'autre*

Giourdina ? Giourdina ? Giourdina ?

LES TURCS *répètent*

Giourdina ! Giourdina ! Giourdina !

LE MUPHTY

Mahameta per Giourdina   5
Mi pregar sera e matina ;
Voler far un Paladina
De Giourdina, de Giourdina.
Dar turbanta e dar scarcina
Con galera e brigantina   10
Per deffender Palestina.
Mahameta per Giourdina
Mi pregar sera e matina.

Après quoi, le Muphty demande aux Turcs si le Bourgeois est ferme
dans la religion mahométane, et leur chante ces paroles :   15

Star bon Turca Giourdina ? *Bis*

LES TURCS

Hey valla. Hey valla. *Bis*

LE MUPHTY *chante et danse*

Hu la ba ba la chou ba la ba ba la da.

Après que le Muphty s'est retiré, les Turcs dansent, et répètent ces
mêmes paroles :   20

Hu la ba ba la chou ba la ba ba la da.

Le Muphty revient, avec son turban de cérémonie, qui est d'une grosseur démesurée, garni de bougies allumées, à quatre ou cinq rangs.

Deux Derviches l'accompagnent, avec des bonnets pointus, garnis aussi de bougies allumées, portant l'Alcoran ; les deux autres Derviches amènent
5 *le Bourgeois, qui est tout épouvanté de cette cérémonie, et le font mettre à genoux le dos tourné au Muphty, puis, le faisant incliner jusques à mettre ses mains par terre, ils lui mettent l'Alcoran sur le dos, et le font servir de pupitre au Muphty, qui fait une invocation burlesque, fronçant le sourcil, et ouvrant la bouche, sans dire mot ; puis parlant avec véhémence,*
10 *tantôt radoucissant sa voix, tantôt la poussant d'un enthousiasme à faire trembler, en se poussant les côtes avec les mains, comme pour faire sortir ses paroles, frappant quelquefois les mains sur l'Alcoran, et tournant les feuillets avec précipitation, et finit enfin en levant les bras, et criant à haute voix : Hou.*

15 *Pendant cette invocation, les Turcs assistants chantent* Hou, hou, hou, *inclinants à trois reprises, puis se relèvent de même à trois reprises, en chantant* Hou, hou, hou, *et continuant alternativement pendant toute l'invocation du Muphty.*

Après que l'invocation est finie, les Derviches ôtent l'Alcoran de dessus
20 *le dos du Bourgeois, qui crie,* Ouf, *parce qu'il est las d'avoir été longtemps en cette posture, puis ils le relèvent.*

LE MUPHTY, *s'adressant au Bourgeois*

Ti non star furba ?

LES TURCS

No, no, no.

LE MUPHTY

Non star forfanta ?

LES TURCS

25   No, no, no.

LE MUPHTY, *aux Turcs*

Donar turbanta.   Donar turbanta.

Et s'en va.

Les Turcs répètent tout ce que dit le Muphty, et donnent, en dansant et en chantant, le turban au Bourgeois.

LE MUPHTY *revient et donne le sabre au Bourgeois*

Ti star nobile, non star fabola.

Pigliar schiabola.

Puis il se retire.
Les Turcs répètent les mêmes mots, mettants tous le sabre à la main ;
et six d'entre eux dansent autour du Bourgeois, auquel ils feignent de 5
donner plusieurs coups de sabre.

LE MUPHTY *revient, et commande aux Turcs de bâtonner le Bourgeois, et chante*
ces paroles :

Dara, dara, bastonara, bastonara, bastonara.

Puis il se retire.
Les Turcs répètent les mêmes paroles, et donnent au Bourgeois plusieurs
coups de bâton en cadence.
10

LE MUPHTY *revient et chante*

Non tener honta :

Questa star l'ultima affronta.

Les Turcs répètent les mêmes vers.

LE MUPHTY

Au son de tous les instruments, recommence une invocation, appuyé
sur ses Derviches ; après toutes les fatigues de cette cérémonie, les Der- 15
viches le soutiennent par-dessous les bras avec respect, et tous les Turcs,
sautants, dansants et chantants autour du Muphty, se retirent au son de
plusieurs instruments à la turque.

ACTE V

SCÈNE PREMIÈRE

Mme JOURDAIN, M. JOURDAIN

Mme JOURDAIN. Ah, mon Dieu! miséricorde! Qu'est-ce que c'est donc que cela? Quelle figure! Est-ce un *momon* que vous allez porter, et est-il temps d'aller en masque? Parlez donc, qu'est-ce que c'est que ceci? Qui vous a fagoté comme cela?

M. JOURDAIN. Voyez l'impertinente, de parler de la sorte à un *mamamouchi!*

Mme JOURDAIN. Comment donc?

M. JOURDAIN. Oui, il me faut porter du respect maintenant, et l'on vient de me faire *mamamouchi.*

Mme JOURDAIN. Que voulez-vous dire avec votre *mamamouchi?*

M. JOURDAIN. *Mamamouchi,* vous dis-je. Je suis *mamamouchi.*

Mme JOURDAIN. Quelle bête est-ce là?

M. JOURDAIN. *Mamamouchi,* c'est-à-dire, en notre langue, paladin.

Mme JOURDAIN. Baladin? Êtes-vous en âge de danser des ballets?

M. JOURDAIN. Quelle ignorante! Je dis paladin; c'est une dignité dont on vient de me faire la cérémonie.

Mme JOURDAIN. Quelle cérémonie donc?

M. JOURDAIN. *Mahameta per Giourdina.*

Mme JOURDAIN. Qu'est-ce que cela veut dire?

M. JOURDAIN. *Giourdina,* c'est-à-dire Jourdain.

78

Mᵐᵉ Jourdain. Eh bien, quoi, Jourdain?

M. Jourdain. *Voler far un paladina de Giourdina.*

Mᵐᵉ Jourdain. Comment?

M. Jourdain. *Dar turbanta con galera.*

Mᵐᵉ Jourdain. Qu'est-ce à dire cela?   5

M. Jourdain. *Per deffender Palestina.*

Mᵐᵉ Jourdain. Que voulez-vous donc dire?

M. Jourdain. *Dara dara bastonara.*

Mᵐᵉ Jourdain. Qu'est-ce donc que ce jargon-là?

M. Jourdain. *Non tener honta, questa star l'ultima affronta.* 10

Mᵐᵉ Jourdain. Qu'est-ce que c'est donc que tout cela?

M. Jourdain (*chantant et dansant*). *Hou la ba ba la chou ba la ba ba la da.* (*Il tombe par terre.*)

Mᵐᵉ Jourdain. Hélas, mon Dieu! mon mari est devenu fou!   15

M. Jourdain, *se relevant et s'en allant.* Paix, insolente! Portez respect à monsieur le *mamamouchi.*

Mᵐᵉ Jourdain, *seule.* Où est-ce qu'il a donc perdu l'esprit? Courons l'empêcher de sortir. (*Apercevant Dorimène et Dorante.*) Ah, ah! voici justement le reste de notre écu. Je ne vois que 20 chagrin de tous les côtés.

SCÈNE II

Dorimène, Dorante

Dorante. Oui, madame, vous verrez la plus plaisante chose qu'on puisse voir, et je ne crois pas que dans tout le monde il soit possible de trouver encore un homme aussi fou que celui-là. Et puis, madame, il faut tâcher de servir l'amour de Cléonte, et 25 d'appuyer toute sa mascarade. C'est un fort galant homme, et qui mérite que l'on s'intéresse pour lui.

Dorimène. J'en fais beaucoup de cas, et il est digne d'une bonne fortune.

DORANTE. Outre cela, nous avons ici, madame, un ballet qui nous revient, que nous ne devons pas laisser perdre ; et il faut bien voir si mon idée pourra réussir.

• DORIMÈNE. J'ai vu là des apprêts magnifiques, et ce sont
5 des choses, Dorante, que je ne puis plus souffrir. Oui, je veux enfin vous empêcher vos profusions ; et, pour rompre le cours à toutes les dépenses que je vous vois faire pour moi, j'ai résolu de me marier promptement avec vous. C'en est le vrai secret, et toutes ces choses finissent avec le mariage.

10 DORANTE. Ah, madame ! est-il possible que vous ayez pu prendre pour moi une si douce résolution ?

DORIMÈNE. Ce n'est que pour vous empêcher de vous ruiner ; et, sans cela, je vois bien qu'avant qu'il fût peu vous n'auriez pas un sou.

15 DORANTE. Que j'ai d'obligation, madame, aux soins que vous avez de conserver mon bien ! Il est entièrement à vous, aussi bien que mon cœur, et vous en userez de la façon qu'il vous plaira.

DORIMÈNE. J'userai bien de tous les deux. Mais voici votre
20 homme ; la figure en est admirable.

SCÈNE III

M. JOURDAIN, DORIMÈNE, DORANTE

DORANTE. Monsieur, nous venons rendre hommage, madame et moi, à votre nouvelle dignité, et nous réjouir avec vous du mariage que vous faites de votre fille avec le fils du Grand Turc.

M. JOURDAIN, *après avoir fait les révérences à la turque.*
25 Monsieur, je vous souhaite la force des serpents et la prudence des lions.

DORIMÈNE. J'ai été bien aise d'être des premières, monsieur, à venir vous féliciter du haut degré de gloire où vous êtes monté.

M. Jourdain. Madame, je vous souhaite toute l'année votre
rosier fleuri. Je vous suis infiniment obligé de prendre part aux
honneurs qui m'arrivent, et j'ai beaucoup de joie de vous voir
revenue ici, pour vous faire les très humbles excuses de l'extravagance de ma femme.   5

Dorimène. Cela n'est rien ; j'excuse en elle un pareil mouvement. Votre cœur lui doit être précieux ; et il n'est pas étrange
que la possession d'un homme comme vous puisse inspirer
quelques alarmes.

M. Jourdain. La possession de mon cœur est une chose   10
qui vous est toute acquise.

Dorante. Vous voyez, madame, que monsieur Jourdain
n'est pas de ces gens que les prospérités aveuglent, et qu'il sait,
dans sa gloire, connaître encore ses amis.

Dorimène. C'est la marque d'une âme tout à fait généreuse. 15

Dorante. Où est donc Son Altesse turque ? Nous voudrions
bien, comme vos amis, lui rendre nos devoirs.

M. Jourdain. Le voilà qui vient, et j'ai envoyé quérir ma
fille pour lui donner la main.

SCÈNE IV

M. Jourdain, Dorimène, Dorante, Cléonte, *habillé en Turc*

Dorante, *à Cléonte*. Monsieur, nous venons faire la révé- 20
rence à Votre Altesse comme amis de monsieur votre beau-père,
et l'assurer avec respect de nos très humbles services.

M. Jourdain. Où est le truchement, pour lui dire qui vous
êtes, et lui faire entendre ce que vous dites ? Vous verrez qu'il
vous répondra ; et il parle turc à merveille. Holà ! Où diantre 25
est-il allé ? (*À Cléonte.*) *Strouf, strif, strof, straf.* Monsieur est
un *grande segnore, grande segnore, grande segnore ;* et madame
une *granda dama, granda dama.* (*Voyant qu'il ne se fait point*

entendre.) Ah! (*À Cléonte.*) Monsieur, lui *mamamouchi* français, et madame *mamamouchie* française. Je ne puis pas parler
plus clairement. Bon, voici l'interprète.

SCÈNE V

M. Jourdain, Dorimène, Dorante, Cléonte, *habillé en Turc*,
Covielle, *déguisé*

M. Jourdain. Où allez-vous donc? Nous ne saurions rien
5 dire sans vous. (*Montrant Cléonte.*) Dites-lui un peu que monsieur et madame sont des personnes de grande qualité, qui lui
viennent faire la révérence, comme mes amis, et l'assurer de
leurs services. (*À Dorimène et à Dorante.*) Vous allez voir
comme il va répondre.

10 Covielle. *Alabala crociam acci boram alabamen.*

Cléonte. *Catalequi tubal ourin soter amalouchan.*

M. Jourdain, *à Dorimène et à Dorante.* Voyez-vous?

Covielle. Il dit: «Que la pluie des prospérités arrouse en
tout temps le jardin de votre famille.»

15 M. Jourdain. Je vous l'avais bien dit, qu'il parle turc.

Dorante. Cela est admirable!

SCÈNE VI

Cléonte, M. Jourdain, Lucile, Dorimène, Dorante, Covielle

M. Jourdain. Venez, ma fille, approchez-vous, et venez
donner votre main à monsieur, qui vous fait l'honneur de vous
demander en mariage.

20 Lucile. Comment, mon père! comme vous voilà fait! Est-
ce une comédie que vous jouez?

M. Jourdain. Non, non; ce n'est pas une comédie, c'est
une affaire fort sérieuse, et la plus pleine d'honneur pour vous

qui se peut souhaiter. (*Montrant Cléonte.*) Voilà le mari que
je vous donne.

LUCILE.   À moi, mon père ?

M. JOURDAIN.   Oui, à vous. Allons, touchez-lui dans la main,
et rendez grâce au ciel de votre bonheur.   5

LUCILE.   Je ne veux point me marier.

M. JOURDAIN.   Je le veux, moi qui suis votre père.

LUCILE.   Je n'en ferai rien.

M. JOURDAIN.   Ah ! que de bruit ! Allons, vous dis-je. Çà,
votre main.   10

LUCILE.   Non, mon père ; je vous l'ai dit, il n'est point de
pouvoir qui me puisse obliger à prendre un autre mari que
Cléonte ; et je me résoudrai plutôt à toutes les extrémités, que
de . . . (*Reconnaissant Cléonte.*)   Il est vrai que vous êtes mon
père, je vous dois entière obéissance, et c'est à vous à disposer 15
de moi selon vos volontés.

M. JOURDAIN.   Ah ! je suis ravi de vous voir si promptement
revenue dans votre devoir, et voilà qui me plaît, d'avoir une
fille obéissante.

SCÈNE DERNIÈRE

CLÉONTE, Mme JOURDAIN, M. JOURDAIN, LUCILE, DORIMÈNE,
DORANTE, COVIELLE

Mme JOURDAIN.   Comment donc ? qu'est-ce que c'est que ceci ? 20
On dit que vous voulez donner votre fille en mariage à un
carême-prenant.

M. JOURDAIN.   Voulez-vous vous taire, impertinente ? Vous
venez toujours mêler vos extravagances à toutes choses, et il
n'y a pas moyen de vous apprendre à être raisonnable.   25

Mme JOURDAIN.   C'est vous qu'il n'y a pas moyen de rendre
sage, et vous allez de folie en folie. Quel est votre dessein, et
que voulez-vous faire avec cet assemblage ?

M. Jourdain. Je veux marier notre fille avec le fils du Grand Turc.

Mme Jourdain. Avec le fils du Grand Turc?

M. Jourdain. Oui. (*Montrant Covielle.*) Faites-lui faire
5 vos compliments par le truchement que voilà.

Mme Jourdain. Je n'ai que faire du truchement, et je lui dirai bien moi-même, à son nez, qu'il n'aura point ma fille.

M. Jourdain. Voulez-vous vous taire, encore une fois?

Dorante. Comment! madame Jourdain, vous vous opposez
10 à un bonheur comme celui-là? Vous refusez Son Altesse turque pour gendre?

Mme Jourdain. Mon Dieu, monsieur, mêlez-vous de vos affaires.

Dorimène. C'est une grande gloire qui n'est pas à rejeter.

15 Mme Jourdain. Madame, je vous prie aussi de ne vous point embarrasser de ce qui ne vous touche pas.

Dorante. C'est l'amitié que nous avons pour vous qui nous fait intéresser dans vos avantages.

Mme Jourdain. Je me passerai bien de votre amitié.

20 Dorante. Voilà votre fille qui consent aux volontés de son père.

Mme Jourdain. Ma fille consent à épouser un Turc?

Dorante. Sans doute.

Mme Jourdain. Elle peut oublier Cléonte?

25 Dorante. Que ne fait-on pas pour être grand'dame?

Mme Jourdain. Je l'étranglerais de mes mains, si elle avait fait un coup comme celui-là.

M. Jourdain. Voilà bien du caquet. Je vous dis que ce mariage-là se fera.

30 Mme Jourdain. Je vous dis, moi, qu'il ne se fera point.

M. Jourdain. Ah! que de bruit!

Lucile. Ma mère!

Mme Jourdain. Allez, vous êtes une coquine.

M. Jourdain, *à Mme Jourdain.* Quoi! vous la querellez de
ce qu'elle m'obéit?

Mme Jourdain. Oui; elle est à moi aussi bien qu'à vous.

Covielle, *à Mme Jourdain.* Madame!

Mme Jourdain. Que me voulez-vous conter, vous?   5

Covielle. Un mot.

Mme Jourdain. Je n'ai que faire de votre mot.

Covielle, *à M. Jourdain.* Monsieur, si elle veut écouter
une parole en particulier, je vous promets de la faire consentir
à ce que vous voulez.   10

Mme Jourdain. Je n'y consentirai point.

Covielle. Écoutez-moi seulement.

Mme Jourdain. Non.

M. Jourdain, *à Mme Jourdain.* Écoutez-le.

Mme Jourdain. Non; je ne veux pas écouter.   15

M. Jourdain. Il vous dira . . .

Mme Jourdain. Je ne veux point qu'il me dise rien.

M. Jourdain. Voilà une grande obstination de femme!
Cela vous fera-t-il mal de l'entendre?

Covielle. Ne faites que m'écouter; vous ferez après ce   20
qu'il vous plaira.

Mme Jourdain. Eh bien! quoi?

Covielle, *bas à Mme Jourdain.* Il y a une heure, madame,
que nous vous faisons signe. Ne voyez-vous pas bien que tout
ceci n'est fait que pour nous ajuster aux visions de votre mari,   25
que nous l'abusons sous ce déguisement, et que c'est Cléonte
lui-même qui est le fils du Grand Turc?

Mme Jourdain, *bas à Covielle.* Ah, ah!

Covielle, *bas à Mme Jourdain.* Et moi, Covielle, qui suis le
truchement?   30

Mme Jourdain, *bas à Covielle.* Ah! comme cela, je me
rends.

Covielle, *bas à Mme Jourdain.* Ne faites pas semblant de rien.

Mme Jourdain, *haut.* Oui, voilà qui est fait, je consens au mariage.

M. Jourdain. Ah! voilà tout le monde raisonnable. (*À Mme Jourdain.*) Vous ne vouliez pas l'écouter. Je savais bien
5 qu'il vous expliquerait ce que c'est que le fils du Grand Turc.

Mme Jourdain. Il me l'a expliqué comme il faut, et j'en suis satisfaite. Envoyons quérir un notaire.

Dorante. C'est fort bien dit. Et afin, madame Jourdain, que vous puissiez avoir l'esprit tout à fait content, et que vous
10 perdiez aujourd'hui toute la jalousie que vous pourriez avoir conçue de monsieur votre mari, c'est que nous nous servirons du même notaire pour nous marier, madame et moi.

Mme Jourdain. Je consens aussi à cela.

M. Jourdain, *bas à Dorante.* C'est pour lui faire accroire.

15 Dorante, *bas à M. Jourdain.* Il faut bien l'amuser avec cette feinte.

M. Jourdain, *bas.* Bon, bon. (*Haut.*) Qu'on aille vite quérir le notaire.

Dorante. Tandis qu'il viendra et qu'il dressera les contrats,
20 voyons notre ballet, et donnons-en le divertissement à Son Altesse turque.

M. Jourdain. C'est fort bien avisé. Allons prendre nos places.

Mme Jourdain. Et Nicole?

25 M. Jourdain. Je la donne au truchement; et ma femme, à qui la voudra.

Covielle. Monsieur, je vous remercie. (*À part.*) Si l'on en peut voir un plus fou, je l'irai dire à Rome.

La Comédie finit par un petit ballet qui avait été préparé.

BALLET DES NATIONS

PREMIÈRE ENTRÉE

*Un homme vient donner les livres du ballet, qui d'abord est fatigué par
une multitude de gens de provinces différentes, qui crient en musique pour
en avoir, et par trois Importuns, qu'il trouve toujours sur ses pas.*

DIALOGUE DES GENS
qui en musique demandent des livres

TOUS

À moi, Monsieur, à moi de grâce, à moi, Monsieur
Un livre, s'il vous plaît, à votre serviteur.   5

HOMME DU BEL AIR

Monsieur, distinguez-nous parmi des gens qui crient.
Quelques livres ici, les dames vous en prient.

AUTRE HOMME DU BEL AIR

Holà! Monsieur! Monsieur, ayez la charité
    D'en jeter de notre côté.

FEMME DU BEL AIR

Mon Dieu! qu'aux personnes bien faites   10
On sait peu rendre honneur céans!

AUTRE FEMME DU BEL AIR

Ils n'ont des livres et des bancs
Que pour mesdames les grisettes.

GASCON

Aho! l'homme aux libres, qu'on m'en vaille!
J'ai déjà lé poumon usé: 15
Bous boyez qué chacun mé raille;

87

Et jé suis escandalisé
De boir és mains dé la canaille
Cé qui m'est par bous refusé.

AUTRE GASCON

Eh cadédis ! Monseu, boyez qui l'on pût estre :
Un libret, je bous prie, au varon d'Asbarat.
Jé pense, mordy ! qué lé fat
N'a pas l'honnur dé mé connoistre.

LE SUISSE

Mon'-sieur le donneur de papieir,
Que veul dir sty façon de fifre ?
Moi l'écorchair tout mon gosieir
        À crieir,
Sans que je pouvre afoir ein lifre ;
Pardi, mon foi ! Mon'-sieur, je pense fous l'estre ifre.

VIEUX BOURGEOIS BABILLARD

De tout ceci, franc et net,
    Je suis mal satisfait ;
Et cela sans doute est laid
    Que notre fille,
Si bien faite et si gentille,
De tant d'amoureux l'objet,
    N'ait pas à son souhait
    Un livre de ballet,
    Pour lire le sujet
Du divertissement qu'on fait,
Et que toute notre famille
    Si proprement s'habille
Pour être placée au sommet
    De la salle, où l'on met
    Les gens de Lantriguet ;
De tout ceci, franc et net,
    Je suis mal satisfait,
Et cela sans doute est laid.

5

10

15

20

25

30

VIEILLE BOURGEOISE BABILLARDE

Il est vrai que c'est une honte.
Le sang au visage me monte,
Et ce jeteur de vers qui manque au capital,
L'entend fort mal ;
C'est un brutal,   5
Un vrai cheval,
Franc animal,
De faire si peu de compte
D'une fille qui fait l'ornement principal
Du quartier du Palais-Royal,   10
Et que ces jours passés un comte
Fut prendre la première au bal.
Il l'entend mal ;
C'est un brutal,
Un vrai cheval,   15
Franc animal.

HOMMES ET FEMMES DU BEL AIR

Ah ! quel bruit !
　　　Quel fracas !
　　　　　　Quel chaos !
　　　　　　　　　Quel mélange !   20
Quelle confusion !
　　　Quelle cohue étrange !
　　Quel désordre !
　　　　Quel embarras !
On y sèche.   25
　　　L'on n'y tient pas.

GASCON

Bentré ! jé suis à vout.

AUTRE GASCON

J'enrage, Diou mé damne !

LE SUISSE

Ah que ly faire saif dans sty sal de cians !

GASCON

Jé murs.

AUTRE GASCON

Jé perds la tramontane.

LE SUISSE

Mon foi! moy le foudrois estre hors de dedans.

VIEUX BOURGEOIS BABILLARD

Allons, ma mie,
Suivez mes pas,
Je vous en prie,
Et ne me quittez pas;
On fait de nous trop peu de cas,
Et je suis las
De ce tracas;
Tout ce fratras,
Cet embarras
Me pèse par trop sur les bras.
S'il me prend jamais envie
De retourner de ma vie
À ballet ni comédie,
Je veux bien qu'on m'estropie.
Allons, ma mie,
Suivez mes pas,
Je vous en prie,
Et ne me quittez pas;
On fait de nous trop peu de cas.

VIEILLE BOURGEOISE BABILLARDE

Allons, mon mignon, mon fils,
Regagnons notre logis,
Et sortons de ce taudis,
Où l'on ne peut être assis;
Ils seront bien ébaubis
Quand ils nous verront partis.

Trop de confusion règne dans cette salle,
Et j'aimerais mieux être au milieu de la Halle:
Si jamais je reviens à semblable régale,
Je veux bien recevoir des soufflets plus de six.

    Allons, mon mignon, mon fils,   5
    Regagnons notre logis,
    Et sortons de ce taudis,
    Où l'on ne peut être assis.

TOUS

À moi, Monsieur, à moi de grâce, à moi, Monsieur:
Un livre, s'il vous plaît, à votre serviteur.   10

SECONDE ENTRÉE

Les trois Importuns dansent.

TROISIÈME ENTRÉE

TROIS ESPAGNOLS *chantent*

Sé que me muero de amor,
Y solicito el dolor.

Aun muriendo de querer,
De tan buen ayre adolezco,   15
Que es mas de lo que padezco
Lo que quiero padecer,
Y no pudiendo exceder
A mi deseo el rigor.

Sé que me muero de amor,   20
Y solicito el dolor.

Lisonxeame la suerte
Con piedad tan advertida,
Que me assegura la vida
En el riesgo de la muerte.   25

Vivir de su golpe fuerte
Es de mi salud primor.

Sé que, *etc.*

(*Six Espagnols dansent.*)

TROIS MUSICIENS ESPAGNOLS

5   Ay! que locura, con tanto rigor
Quexarse de Amor,
Del niño bonito
Que todo es dulçura!
Ay! que locura!
10   Ay! que locura!

ESPAGNOL, *chantant*

El dolor solicita
El que al dolor se da;
Y nadie de amor muere,
Sino quien no save amar.

DEUX ESPAGNOLS

15   Dulce muerte es el amor
Con correspondencia ygual;
Y si esta gozamos oy
Porque la quieres turbar?

UN ESPAGNOL

Alegrese enamorado,
20   Y tome mi parecer;
Que en esto de querer,
Todo es hallar el vado.

TOUS TROIS, *ensemble*

Vaya, vaya de fiestas!
Vaya de vayle!
25   Alegria, alegria, alegria!
Que esto de dolor es fantasia.

QUATRIÈME ENTRÉE

ITALIENS

Une MUSICIENNE ITALIENNE *fait le premier récit, dont voici les paroles :*

> Di rigori armata il seno,
> Contro amor mi ribellai ;
> Ma fui vinta in un baleno
> In mirar duo vaghi rai ;   5
> Ahi ! che resiste puoco
> Cor di gelo a stral di fuoco !
>
> Ma sì caro è 'l mio tormento,
> Dolce è sì la piaga mia,
> Ch'il penare è 'l mio contento,   10
> E 'l sanarmi è tirannia.
> Ahi ! che più giova e piace,
> Quanto amor è più vivace !

Après l'air que la Musicienne a chanté, deux Scaramouches, deux Trive-
lins, et un Arlequin représentent une nuit à la manière des comédiens 15
italiens, en cadence.

Un Musicien italien se joint à la Musicienne italienne et chante avec elle
les paroles qui suivent :

LE MUSICIEN ITALIEN

> Bel tempo che vola
> Rapisce il contento ;   20
> D'Amor nella scola
> Si coglie il momento.

LA MUSICIENNE

> Insin che florida
>   Ride l'età,
> Che pur tropp' orrida   25
>   Da noi sen và,

TOUS DEUX

Sù cantiamo,
Sù godiamo
Ne' bei dì di gioventù ;
Perduto ben non si racquista più.

MUSICIEN

Pupilla che vaga
Mill' alme incatena
Fà dolce la piaga,
Felice la pena.

MUSICIENNE

Ma poiche frigida
Langue l'età,
Più l'alma rigida
Fiamme non ha.

TOUS DEUX

Sù cantiamo, *etc.*

Après le dialogue italien, les Scaramouches et Trivelins dansent une
réjouissance.

CINQUIÈME ENTRÉE

FRANÇAIS

PREMIER MENUET

DEUX MUSICIENS POITEVINS *dansent, et chantent les paroles qui suivent:*

Ah ! qu'il fait beau dans ces bocages !
Ah ! que le Ciel donne un beau jour !

AUTRE MUSICIEN

Le rossignol, sous ces tendres feuillages,
Chante aux échos son doux retour ;

5

10

15

20

Ce beau séjour,
Ces doux ramages,
Ce beau séjour
Nous invite à l'amour.

SECOND MENUET

TOUS DEUX, *ensemble*

Vois, ma Climène,   5
Vois sous ce chêne
S'entre-baiser ces oiseaux amoureux ;
Ils n'ont rien dans leurs vœux
Qui les gêne ;
De leurs doux feux   10
Leur âme est pleine.
Qu'ils sont heureux !
Nous pouvons tous deux,
Si tu le veux,
Être comme eux.   15

*Six autres Français viennent après, vêtus galamment à la poitevine, trois
en hommes et trois en femmes, accompagnés de huit flûtes et de hautbois,
et dansent les menuets.*

SIXIÈME ENTRÉE

*Tout cela finit par le mélange des trois nations, et les applaudissements
en danse et en musique de toute l'assistance, qui chante les deux vers qui*   20
suivent :

Quels spectacles charmants, quels plaisirs goûtons-nous !
Les Dieux mêmes, les Dieux n'en ont point de plus doux.

Fin du Bourgeois Gentilhomme

NOTES

The heavy figures refer to pages, the light figures to lines

PAGE 1 **Chambord**: a town in the Loire valley on the Cosson, a tributary of the Loire, between Orléans and Blois and slightly east of Blois. Seat of a royal castle and residence under the Bourbons. Here took place the first performance of "Monsieur de Pourceaugnac" (1669) and of "Le Bourgeois gentilhomme" (1670).

2 PERSONNAGES ET ACTEURS. **Maître à Danser**: in modern French *maître de danse* is used. On account of the importance of this rôle, it is always given to one of the most competent actors. — **Deux Laquais . . . du Ballet**: the names of all the singers and dancers of the *intermèdes* who appeared in the first performance are found in the libretto of 1670. They are reprinted in the editions by Despois-Mesnard, Livet, and Moland.

For the music of the songs, the minuet, the Turkish march, etc., see appendix VI of Livet's edition, pp. lxv ff., or Weckerlin's edition of Lulli.

3 3 **se fait**: 'is played.' French has many more reflexive verbs than English. Many of them can be translated only by the English passive voice.

3 5 **le Bourgeois**: this is Monsieur Jourdain, the leading character, who first appears in scene ii.

ACTE PREMIER

3 10 **et vous reposez là**: since *reposez* is a positive imperative, the modern construction would be *reposez-vous*. In the seventeenth century, however, the pronoun object of the last of a series of positive imperatives in the same sentence preceded its verb.

3 15 **Voilà qui est bien** = *voilà ce qui est bien* or *voilà quelque chose qui est bien*, 'that is satisfactory.' *Qui* has a wider and freer use in dialogue than elsewhere. Especially frequent is the concise expression *voilà qui*.

3 18 lui : refers to the pupil. — **notre homme :** refers rather disrespect-fully to Monsieur Jourdain. Molière uses liberally the possessive adjectives to give a touch of contempt or ridicule.

3 19 fût éveillé : in modern construction we should rather expect *soit éveillé*. *awake*

3 21 Vous l'allez entendre : the modern order would be *vous allez l'entendre*. In the seventeenth century certain verbs plus their dependent infinitives were often considered as compound verbs, or at least as compound verb-ideas. Hence *allez entendre*, *doit faire*, *veux offrir*, etc., passed as a sort of future, and pronoun objects of the infinitive were placed before the whole verb-idea, instead of, as now, before the infinitive only. The verbs that were open to such a construction were primarily the modal auxiliaries (*vouloir*, *devoir*, *pouvoir*, *savoir*, *falloir*, *oser*), and also a few others whose function seemed somewhat auxiliary, such as *aller*, *être* (in the sense of *aller*), *venir*, *courir*, *voir*, *faire*, *penser*, *croire*, *daigner*, and even *aimer mieux* and *venir de*. (See A. Haase, " La Syntaxe française du XVIIᵉ siècle," pp. 437–440.)

4 2 petites : here ' unremunerative.'

4 3 Il est vrai : since no clause follows, modern usage prefers here *c'est vrai*.

4 4 un homme comme il nous le faut à tous deux : ' just the man we both need,' '.a man after our own hearts.' — **Ce nous est =** *c'est pour nous*. Molière frequently uses the conjunctive pronoun where we should now expect a disjunctive pronoun with a preposition. — **Ce . . . que ce monsieur Jourdain :** the *que* in such phrases merely serves to introduce and emphasize the logical subject which immediately follows. The best translation of this common construction is to ignore both the *ce* and the *que* and to begin with the logical subject : ' this monsieur Jourdain is an easy source of income for us.'

4 10 qu'il ne fait : ' than he does.' This use of *faire* to avoid repeating a previous verb was more common in Molière's time than it is now.

4 17 c'est . . . que de se produire : ' to exhibit one's talents to fools is quite a cruel punishment.' Compare **4** 4–5. This construction is so common that no further reference to it will be made in these notes.

4 19 un stupide : Molière uses adjectives as substantives very freely.

4 20 qui soient capables . . . qui sachent : there is a touch of affectation in the use of the subjunctive here. The indicative would seem more natural ; see Livet's edition, p. 372. It should be noted, however, that the subjunctive conveys an idea of the uncertainty of there being such persons and also the wish that there were such.

4 22 de chatouillantes approbations : the normal position of adjectives derived from participles is after the noun. Molière is, however, very free in this respect, placing his adjectives wherever he wishes the emphasis.

4 25 connues : 'appreciated,' 'understood.'

4 31 davantage que : now *plus que*. *Davantage* may no longer introduce the second member of a comparison. It is used only to complete the idea of comparison in such phrases as *Marie a beaucoup de livres, mais Jean en a davantage*.

4 32 louanges toutes pures : 'praise only,' *toutes pures* having the sense of 'mere,' 'alone.'

4 33 du solide : see note to **4 19**; *solide* seems to suggest here 'hard cash.'

5 1 louer avec les mains : 'to praise, purse in hand,' 'to pay.' No play on words, with 'applaud' as the other meaning, is here intended, according to the best editors. A gesture of paying money is used by the actor at this phrase.

5 7 le grand seigneur : Dorante, who first appears in Act III, scene iv.

5 9 appuyez . . . sur : 'emphasize.'

5 11 pour lui : in Molière's time the disjunctive *lui* and *elle* referred to things as well as to persons; to-day they refer only to persons or to personified things; *lui* here refers to *intérêt*, or perhaps better to *argent*. There may be a slight idea of personification due to the use of the expression *montrer de l'attachement*; in this case *lui* might well be used even now.

5 22 Le voilà qui vient : 'here he comes.' What is called the exposition of a play is that portion of the opening scenes which exposes to the audience or to the reader a sufficient basis for the complete understanding of the scenes that follow. In other words the exposition is an introduction to the theme or subject of the play. In " Le Bourgeois gentilhomme " this theme is Jourdain and his vanity, and Molière has been greatly praised for the brevity and completeness of this exposition, which has been sufficiently given in the short dialogue between the music teacher and the dancing master. They have revealed enough of Jourdain's character to enable us to proceed in scene ii to a more complete revelation of the Bourgeois by himself. From now on Jourdain becomes the central pivot of the play; in fact he is the play itself.

5 23 **robe de chambre :** Monsieur Jourdain's dressing gown is a most gorgeous one of striped material, lined with green and with reddish yellow. It betrays his lack of taste and his innate vulgarity.

5 30 **prologue ou dialogue :** like Mrs. Malaprop in Sheridan's comedy "The Rivals," Monsieur Jourdain is not very accurate in his use of somewhat unusual words. To him these words seem alike, and neither conveys a very definite meaning. Compare his loose use of *prérogatives* **33** 18.

6 4 **gens de qualité :** 'people of distinguished rank,' 'the higher nobility.' Note how M. Jourdain harps on this phrase, especially in this scene. It is the keynote to his rôle, the fixed idea in his mind.

6 5 **ne mettre jamais :** usually in modern French both negatives precede the infinitive, but Molière here and elsewhere arranges the negatives to suit himself. The *jamais* here has greater emphasis because of its rather unusual position.

6 9 **de ne vous point en aller :** the modern order would bring *ne point* together and *vous en* together, thus : *de ne point vous en aller* ; more emphatically we could also say *de ne vous en aller point*. This is another instance of Molière's freedom in the order of words. Compare note to **6** 5.

6 10 **qu'on ne m'ait apporté mon habit :** the *que* is here equivalent to *avant que*. In the seventeenth century *que* was used very freely where we should now expect *avant que, sans que, jusqu'à ce que, puisque, car, sinon, pour que*, etc. — **me puissiez voir :** see note to **3** 21.

6 16 **indienne :** a dressing gown with very large sleeves. In Molière's day the material was a kind of chintz or painted cloth, and was called *indienne* presumably because it was imported from the Indies. The present cheapness of this material, which was then a luxury, has forced modern actors to substitute here a richer material and to use a different word at this place. According to Livet's edition (p. 207) *indienne* means the garment, but not the material.

6 27 Note again here the gaudiness of Jourdain's costume. This ostentation is quite in harmony with his absurd, pompous manner of ordering his servants about.

7 6 **On ne peut pas mieux :** ' one could n't be better dressed.'

7 17 **écolier :** the definition given shows that *écolier* does not have here the modern meaning of ' schoolboy,' ' beginner.'

7 18 **aussi beau qu'il s'en puisse faire :** ' as beautiful as can be made '; the *il* is impersonal. The subjunctive is used here because of the idea of a superlative contained in *aussi beau que*. It is practically equivalent to *le plus beau que*.

7 23 The music of this serenade was written by Gaye; it may be found on page lxvii of the Livet edition. The *musicienne*, who was disguised as a youth, was Mademoiselle Hilaire du Puy, a relative of Lulli who wrote most of the other music in the play. The serenade is quite in the affected, *précieux* style so fashionable at that time; with its courtly artificiality it is in marked contrast to the simple, popular ballad which follows. Here, then, as in the opening scenes of "Le Misanthrope," Molière criticizes the unnatural, the artificial, and shows his preference for the natural and popular lyric, even if, as here, it be ridiculous.

7 25 Iris (pronounce the *s*) : in Greek mythology the goddess of the rainbow and the messenger of the gods; here it is merely a conventional name in the fashionable poetry of Molière's time. — qui : used by poetic license for *celui qui*.

7 28 vous la pussiez . . . ragaillardir : for the position of the pronoun *la*, see note to 3 21.

8 2 Comment est-ce qu'il dit : 'how *does* the thing go?'

8 4 mouton : Jourdain of course means that the word *mouton* occurs in the song, but he actually says that there is 'some mutton' in it; this is another instance of his slipshod method of talking.

8 7 Jeanneton : feminine (from *Jeanne*), 'Jenny,' a common name in popular poetry. Note the similarity of Jourdain's preference for popular ditties and that of Alceste in "Le Misanthrope." Paulin Paris published (in his edition of the "Historiettes" of Tallemant des Réaux, Vol. III, p. 458) three other couplets of this old song. He said that he had found them in an old collection, but unfortunately he did not give his source. Despois-Mesnard suggest that these verses may be a later parody on the original. They are as follows :

Ah! ne consultez pas | Son visage infidèle; | Ah! ne consultez pas | Ses beaux yeux pleins d'appas. | Hélas! *etc.*

Elle dit chaque jour | Qu'elle n'est point rebelle; | Elle dit chaque jour | Qu'elle est tendre à l'amour. | Hélas! *etc.*

Quand je veux seulement | Lui parler de tendresse, | Quand je veux seulement | Lui dire mon tourment, | Hélas! *etc.*

The music for this song may be found in Livet's edition, p. lxx; Jacquinet's, p. 143.

8 16 Et vous le chantez bien : note that it is the dancing master, not the music master, who compliments Jourdain on his absurd singing. Compare note to 14 20.

8 17 sans avoir appris : here Molière ridicules, as in the case of the false nobleman Mascarille of " Les Précieuses ridicules " (scene ix), the claim made often by the nobility to know everything instinctively.

8 28 montre : ' teach,' or ' give instruction '; this verb now requires a direct object of the subject taught. — **arrêté :** equivalent here to ' hired,' as if he were a servant. The use of this word again emphasizes the vulgarity of Jourdain.

9 1 si utile . . . que la musique : an Academy of Music had been founded by Charles IX in 1570, but it lived only a short time; its charter speaks of the importance of music very much as does the music teacher in this play. Even Plato in his " Republic " acknowledges the importance of music in a state. The Académie Royale de Musique was founded in 1669. Music, as an entertainment at court banquets and at the castles of the nobility, had grown greatly in favor at this time.

9 3 si nécessaire . . . que la danse : dancing was considered a leading accomplishment of all courtiers, and well-bred people studied it seriously. Louis XIV was a graceful dancer and was exceedingly fond of the dance. In 1661 there was established an Académie Royale de Danse of thirteen members. In its charter the importance of dancing was emphasized in terms not unlike the extravagant words of the dancing master in " Le Bourgeois gentilhomme." By 1669, however, the king no longer favored dancing so much, and refrained from appearing in the court productions of ballets and plays, in which he had taken part frequently since 1651. In 1670, therefore, Molière feels no hesitation in presenting to us a ridiculous dancing master full of affectation and conceit. The importance of the profession of dancing master is seen in the fact that Louis XIV paid his writing master 300 livres a year, but his dancing master 2000 livres. The dancing lesson in this play is now usually made longer, in obedience to a tradition established in 1808 by an actor named Faure, who had been an opera dancer and assumed with great success the rôle of the dancing master in " Le Bourgeois gentilhomme " (see note to **14** 8).

9 10 pour n'apprendre pas la musique : we should now say *parce qu'on n'apprend pas la musique.* In Molière's day *pour* not only preceded an infinitive of purpose, which is still a modern construction, but it could also introduce an infinitive causal clause, a construction no longer admitted. Hence the reader of seventeenth-century French must be on his guard to avoid confusing the two possibilities. Note here also that the infinitive is between the negatives. Molière is not bound by any definite rule ; sometimes he places both negatives before the infinitive, and again he puts the infinitive between its negatives. Compare note to **6** 5.

9 21 s'accorder : note the play on this word in its double reference to musical harmony and to harmony in the figurative sense of 'peace,' 'concord.'

9 27 un mauvais pas : 'a misstep,' 'a false step,' in the sense of the modern *faux pas*. Note again the play on words.

9 31 de ne savoir pas : note the position of the negatives, and compare note to **6 5**.

10 16 donne dans la bergerie : 'affect (adopt, ape) the pastoral style.' — **affecté aux bergers :** 'set apart for,' 'used by,' 'affected by shepherds.'

The pastoral style in romance, poetry, and drama, treating in an idealistic manner of the life and the loves of shepherds and shepherdesses, had been very popular in France since its introduction through Italian and Spanish influences early in the seventeenth century. Sannazaro's "Arcadia," 1504; Montemayor's "Diana," 1542; Tasso's "Aminta," 1573; Guarini's "Pastor Fido," 1590, were the chief sources of influence. In France the type received great vogue through the success of d'Urfé's romance "Astrée," which appeared 1607–1627. In French drama the chief pastoral works were Racan's "Les Bergeries," Gombauld's "Amaranthe," and de Viau's "Pyrame et Thisbé." The introduction of Italian opera in France in 1645 still further emphasized this pastoral style. In 1628 Sorel had written his "Berger extravagant" to satirize the absurdities and artificialities of pastoral literature. Molière yielded to the taste of the court and wrote several plays or interludes in plays in which the pastoral style was present, such as "Myrtil et Mélicerte," "Pastorale comique," "Le Sicilien," "Les Amants magnifiques," and "Le Malade imaginaire."

10 19 Passe, passe : "let that pass." Molière made a large use of the so-called independent subjunctive, which has no introductory *que*. The subjunctive is required because of the idea of a wish, which idea is, however, not expressed. Since there is no verb of wishing expressed, the connective *que* becomes unnecessary.

10 20 For the method of singing this trio, see the Despois-Mesnard edition, Vol. VIII, pp. 62–64, with notes, and p. 231. — **l'amoureux empire :** 'the sway of love.' Similarly *l'amoureuse loi* in the third stanza, **11 4.**

12 2 Je te veux offrir : for *je veux t'offrir*. See note to **3 21.**

12 6 mieux : for *le mieux*, 'the better.'

12 7 Qui : *celui qui*, another instance of poetic license.

12 19 dont : *par lesquels.* The seventeenth-century writers often used *qui, où,* and *dont*, where modern usage generally prefers the declinable relative *lequel*; especially is *lequel* now necessary whenever the antecedent is somewhat removed from the relative, since *lequel* in its various forms prevents all ambiguity.

12 23 According to the music written by Lulli, these dancing movements were " (1) un mouvement d'abord grave, puis plus vite ; (2) une Sarabande ; (3) une Bourrée ; (4) une Gaillarde ; (5) une Canarie " (Mangold's edition, p. 80). The *sarabande* was a grave Spanish dance in slow triple time ; the *bourrée* was a lively Auvergne dance ; the *gaillarde* was an obsolete sprightly French dance to lively music ; the *canarie* was an old dance where the partners separated and danced in turn opposite each other, with strange and fantastic poses and gestures intended to imitate the dancing of savages.

12 25 **fait le premier intermède :** ' forms the first interlude.' There is in theory no curtain between the acts. The actors are supposed to remain to watch or to take part in the interludes, and the next act begins where the interlude ends. Hence there is perfect unity of time. There is also complete unity of place, inasmuch as the entire action is in Monsieur Jourdain's house.

For the king and court these interludes of music and dancing seemed more important than the dialogue itself. Certain it is that Lulli, who composed the music of the interludes, received far more applause and far greater rewards than did Molière. For the music of the interludes, see Weckerlin's edition of Lulli ; for a list of the persons taking part in the first performance, see the Moland edition of the play, p. 30 ; the Livet edition, pp. xlvi ff. ; or the Despois-Mesnard edition, pp. 230 ff.

ACTE II

13 1 **Voilà qui n'est point sot :** about the equivalent of ' that is not so bad.' See note to **3** 15.

13 7 **me doit faire :** *doit me faire.* See note to **3** 21.

13 12 **concert de musique :** now *concert* is sufficient. Wednesdays and Thursdays were the customary days for concerts in high society, because there was usually no play or opera on those days. Occasionally in the winter there was opera on Thursdays.

13 13 **chez soi :** modern use requires agreement with *personne*, hence *chez elle.*

13 19 **basse de viole :** an old form of bass viol with from five to seven strings, and having about the range of the modern violoncello, although much larger. It was still in use at the end of the eighteenth century.

— **théorbe** : 'theorbo,' an obsolete instrument, called also an archlute. It was like the lute but designed for low notes also, and might have from nineteen to twenty-eight strings. It had two finger boards, one above the other; one of these was for the bass notes. — **clavecin** : 'harpsichord,' an old type of piano with only three or four octaves.

13 20 basses continues : the sustained bass of an accompaniment.

13 22 Il y faudra mettre : *il faudra y mettre*. The pronominal adverb *y* was treated then, as it is now, like the personal pronoun object. See note to 3 21. — **trompette marine** : this is not a wind instrument as its name might suggest, and as even French audiences and actors sometimes suppose, but an obsolete string instrument of peculiar design. There are several to be seen in the very complete museum of the Paris Conservatoire de Musique. They are about six and a half feet long, and throughout their length are hexagonal in shape, tapering toward the handle, which is somewhat bent. The widest of the six sides is about nine inches at the base, and, since it tapers to the handle, forms an elongated triangle. On this side is stretched the single coarse string. In some instruments there are other resonant strings within the hollow case, but most instruments have but the one string. This string, beginning at the tuning screw, passes near the lower end over a bridge. This bridge is fastened by only one foot, and vibrates on a small square of glass, ivory, or metal. The combination of the coarse string, played by a horsehair bow, and of the loose bridge and vibrating glass, produces a rumbling, trumpet-like sound of no harmony whatsoever. Hence the absurdity of M. Jourdain's remark that it is harmonious. The resemblance to the sound of a trumpet accounts for part of its name; the word *marine* may have been added because seafaring people used the instrument, or because the sound was like that supposed to be made by sea gods with conches. Another suggestion is that *marine* may be a corruption of *mariane*, this name having arisen from the fact that the instrument was much used in the nunneries in medieval times to accompany the singing of the nuns.

The instrument can stand alone on its hexagonal base. It is easy to play, the thumb being used to change the tone. The exact origin is not known, but from medieval times it spread all over Europe, being used often by itinerant musicians and street beggars. As late as 1775 there were three players of this crude instrument, the predecessor of the bass viol, in the orchestra of the French king. The description in the Century Dictionary under "sea-trumpet" is accurate; see further "Le Musée du Conservatoire National de Musique. Catalogue raisonné des instruments," by Gustave Chouquet, Paris (Didot), 1875, Nos. 204, 205; also the two supplements by Léon Pillaut, Paris (Fischbacher), 1894 and 1899.

14 6 menuets : the elegant, aristocratic, and graceful minuet is quite impossible for the awkward, corpulent Jourdain despite his saying *ma danse*; hence the humor of this scene. In dancing the minuet, gentlemen wore their hats, removing them to make bows and salutations at the beginning and end of the figures. The traditional business of Jourdain's taking his lackey's hat and putting it over his own nightcap is amusing. The music of this minuet was composed by Lulli for the festival of Molière's "Amants magnifiques," 1670; for the melody sung by the dancing master, see the Despois-Mesnard edition, pp. 243–244; Livet's edition, p. lxxi; Scheffler's, p. 17.

14 8 Allons, mon maître : this dancing lesson was added to by an actor named Faure, who joined the Comédie Française in 1808; he had previous to the Revolution been a *danseur* at the Opéra. See the L. Moland edition, p. 33, for these additions, which are now usually included in a performance.

14 19 Euh : an exclamation of fatigue and probably also here an appeal for approval. Since the early editions all place an interrogation point after it, the idea of an appeal for approval seems the more probable, especially in view of the music master's commendation.

14 20 Note that it is the music teacher who now compliments Jourdain on his awkward dancing. Compare **8 16**, with the previous flattery by the dancing master when Jourdain sang. Molière always realizes the dramatic value of just such apparently small matters.

14 21 comme : the modern *comment.*

14 25 Dorimène : Jourdain naïvely supposes that a different name might require a different sort of bow.

14 27 Vous n'avez qu'à faire : ' just show me yourself ' (literally, ' you have only to do it ').

14 29 révérence en arrière : a bow made while moving the left foot slowly back of the right.

14 30 révérences en avant : bows made while placing one foot slightly forward. These definitions are taken from the edition of Livet, who quotes descriptions of these *révérences* from the "Dictionnaire des danses," 1787. Compare Jourdain's absurdly literal interpretation of these instructions in Act III, scene xix (**59 12–17**).

15 2 qu'il entre : this subjunctive form is far more categorical than would be the construction *dis-lui d'entrer.*

15 7 la révérence : the peculiar movements of the foil made as a formal salute to one's opponent.

15 12 quartée : a position in fencing, the left shoulder being drawn or bent back so as to expose less the left breast and the heart. — **Le regard assuré :** 'the eyes aimed sharply and steadily at your opponent.'

15 13 moi : the ethical dative, and about equivalent here to English "my" before 'sword.' — **de quarte :** 'in quart,' the fourth position in fencing : wrist on level of belt, forearm straight, elbow resting against body, and blade (or foil) resting at the *right* of the adversary's blade and pointing at his eye ; wrist to be turned *outward* when delivering the blow.

15 14 achevez de même : 'finish the thrust in the position indicated, without disengaging.' — **Remettez-vous :** 'recover your former position.' — **Redoublez de pied ferme :** 'renew the attack without moving the foot.'

15 16 il faut que l'épée parte la première : 'the sword must move forward before the foot is moved.'

15 18 de tierce : 'in tierce,' the third position in fencing : wrist level with the belt, forearm straight, elbow against body, blade resting at *left* of adversary's blade and pointing at his eye ; in thrusting, the wrist is turned *inward*. Compare *de quarte* above.

15 19 Partez de là : 'lunge from there.'

15 24 merveilles : note that, as before (**8 16, 14 20**), Jourdain is flattered by another than the actual teacher.

16 4 il est impossible : governs here the subjunctive, *receviez*.

16 6 seulement : here pleonastic, the *ne . . . que* being sufficient.

16 15 l'emporte hautement sur : 'greatly surpasses.' This conceit of the fencing master sounds more unwarranted and absurd to-day than it did in the time of Molière. Although Richelieu discouraged the resort to arms and forbade dueling under penalty of death, Louis XIV went to another extreme by showing great honor to the masters of this art of defense. In 1656 he even gave hereditary nobility to six of the best fencing masters who had served twenty years ; he also gave the cordon of the order of Saint Michael to several. The fencing masters formed a sort of close corporation of twenty, called an academy, and these alone had the right to give instruction. An apprenticeship of ten years was necessary to join this guild.

16 17 tireur d'armes : this was formerly the correct name for the more modern *maître d'armes*, 'fencing master.' In this play the use of *tireur d'armes* is apparently contemptuous, although one could still say *tirer des armes*, 'to fence,' without disrespect.

16 23 importance : of course ironical here.

16 25 plastron : 'pad,' a padded breast protector made of leather and used by fencers; a similar contrivance was used by cobblers, which may account in part for the tone of contempt here.

16 26 Mon petit : this use of *mon* has in it a touch of contempt, satire, or irony ; so also *sa* in **17** 1–2.

16 29 batteur de fer : 'iron beater,' 'bully,' 'sword eater,' 'swash-buckler,' 'fire eater.'

16 31 de l'aller quereller : *d'aller le quereller.* See note to **3** 21.

17 8 cheval de carrosse : literally 'cart horse,' figuratively 'stupid, coarse, rude fellow.' The *grand* is here added with reference, un-doubtedly, to the great size of the actor de Brie, who played the part of the fencing master.

17 18 lui apprendre à parler : 'teach him how to behave.'

17 27 vouloir en venir aux mains : 'to wish to come to blows about it (*en*).' Some editions have the older order, *en vouloir venir.*

18 3 Sénèque : Lucius Annæus Seneca, Roman philosopher (about 3 B.C.–65 A.D.). His treatise "De Ira," in three books, was written in the reign of Caligula (37–41 A.D.), and addressed to his brother Gallio.

18 9 dont il fait profession : 'which he professes.'

19 1 philosophe de chien : more usually *chien de philosophe,* 'dog of a philosopher'; the phrasing with *chien* as the final word seems more vigorous.

19 3 cuistre fieffé : 'thorough, out-and-out pedant,' 'arrant bottle washer.'

19 7–23 Monsieur le Philosophe : note how often Molière repeats the same phrase to create or sustain comic effect. This has been called *dialogue en écho.* Here the repetition of *Philosophe* is particularly ludi-crous in view of the very unphilosophical conduct of "Monsieur le Philosophe."

19 10 La peste l'animal : an abbreviated form of *la peste soit de l'animal,* 'plague take the fool.'

19 14 Diantre soit de l'âne bâté : 'the devil take the arrant ass'; *bâté* means, 'equipped with a packsaddle (*bât*),' and a donkey so equipped was completely ready for service; hence 'an out-and-out ass,' 'com-plete ass.' The ass being naturally a stupid animal, *bâté* emphasizes this quality strongly. For the use of the subjunctive, see note to **10** 19.

19 25 je n'y saurais que faire : 'I can't help matters,' 'it's no con-cern of mine.' This expression is still current despite two syntactical

peculiarities: *y* is really the indirect object of *faire* (see note to **3** 21);
for *que* we should expect *quoi*.

20 7 Juvénal: Juvenal (about 60–140 A.D.) was a Roman satiric poet,
noted for his bitter style.

20 14 Nam, sine doctrina . . . imago: this quotation was already in
Larivey's "Le Fidelle" (Act II, scene xiv), 1611, where M. Josse uses
it. Originally it came from Dionysius Cato.

20 20 Ce latin-là: note this comic touch; M. Jourdain evidently thinks
of *latin* as a person.

20 29 trois opérations de l'esprit: according to the logic of Aristotle,
these were perception, judgment, reasoning.

20 30 Qui: here, as above with *ce latin*, M. Jourdain thinks of the
trois opérations as persons.

21 3 universaux: a universal in logic is a general abstract conception
or "predicable." In the Aristotelian, or scholastic, logic there were five
universals: genus, species, difference, property, accident. They served
to classify ideas and beings.

21 4 catégories: the categories are the classes to which objects of
knowledge or thought may be reduced and by which these objects may
be arranged in a system for logical discussion. Aristotle made ten categories in logic, namely, substance, quantity, quality, relation, action, passion, time, place, situation, habit.

21 5 Barbara, etc.: the ridicule which Molière here casts upon the
scholastic and pedantic medieval system of logic, which still prevailed
to a large extent in his time, reaches its climax in the words "Barbara,
Celarent, Darii, Ferio, Baralipton." These form the first verse of a
mnemonic quatrain, which contains nineteen such words in all. Each
word represented one of the nineteen modes of regular syllogism according to the scholastic philosophers. Hence Molière has the double purpose of ridiculing scholastic methods and of creating a humorous scene
through the mystification of Jourdain. In these words the vowels
indicated the nature of the propositions of syllogisms, thus: **a** meant a
universal affirmative proposition; **e** a universal negative proposition;
i a particular affirmative proposition; **o** a particular negative proposition.

Hence Barbara meant a syllogism in which both premises and conclusion were universal affirmative propositions, thus:

> All men are mortal.
> All kings are men.
> Therefore all kings are mortal.

Celarent meant a syllogism with major premise universal negative, minor premise universal affirmative, and conclusion universal negative, thus :

> No created being is infinite.
> All men are created beings.
> Therefore no man is infinite.

Darii meant a syllogism with major premise universal affirmative, minor premise particular affirmative, and conclusion particular affirmative, thus :

> All geniuses are clever.
> Some geniuses are insane.
> Therefore some insane people are clever.

Ferio indicated a syllogism with major premise universal negative, minor premise particular affirmative, and conclusion particular negative, thus :

> No foreign-born citizen may be President.
> Sóme citizens are foreign-born.
> Therefore some citizens may not be President.

Baralipton (here only the first three vowels are taken) meant a syllogism with major premise universal affirmative, minor premise universal affirmative, and conclusion particular affirmative, thus :

> All whales are mammals.
> All mammals are vertebrates.
> Therefore some vertebrates are whales.

This last figure was so artificial that Aristotle did not use it at all in his system.

The other three verses in this memory-helping scheme were :

> Celarent, dabitis, fapesmo, frisesomorum,
>
> Cesare, camestres, festino, baroco ; — darapti,
>
> Felaptom, disamis, datisi, bocardo, ferison.

21 7 **rébarbatifs** : 'harsh,' 'unpleasant,' 'repellent,' 'repulsive,' 'barbaric.' Molière probably chose this word because of the similarity of its sound to *Barbara* above.

21 18 **il n'y a morale qui tienne** : 'ethics (*morale*) are of no use.'

21 19 **quand il m'en prend envie** : 'when I want to,' 'when I feel like it.'

21 29 **tourbillons** : 'whirlwinds,' 'whirlpools.' The allusion is to Descartes's theory of astronomy : "La matière du ciel, où sont les planètes, tourne sans cesse en rond, ainsi qu'un tourbillon qui aurait le soleil à son centre." This theory was displaced by Newton's theory of attraction.

22 1 orthographe : in the seventeenth century Louis XIV and the nobility generally took the greatest liberties with spelling. Therefore the fact that Jourdain wishes to learn spelling is an additional proof of his ignorance of what constituted or interested a nobleman.

22 8 nature des lettres : in the grammar lesson of the *maître de philosophie* Molière quotes almost textually from a recent book by the academician Géraud de Cordemoy, whom Bossuet had chosen as lecturer or reader to the dauphin. This book was " Discours physique de la parole," Paris, 1668. Cordemoy's passages are in turn literal translations of a fifteenth-century treatise by Martius Galeotus, once professor at Bologna, whom Louis XI brought to France, where he died in 1448. Indeed Molière seems to have taken the passages about the vowel O from Galeotus rather than from Cordemoy. The L. Moland edition gives the quotations from Cordemoy that concern us. It should be noted that the lesson applies only to the simple French vowels as they occur in *pâté, thé, ici, côte,* and *du* respectively.

22 29 I, O : some actors heighten the humor here by making these sounds resemble the braying of an ass. Indeed the awkward imitation of the teacher by Jourdain reminds one of La Fontaine's fable (Book IV, Fable V) *L'Âne et le Petit Chien,* wherein the ass thinks to enter into his owner's graces by doing what the little dog does :

> Dans cette admirable pensée,
> Voyant son maître en joie, il s'en vient lourdement,
> Lève une corne tout usée,
> La lui porte au menton fort amoureusement,
> Non sans accompagner, pour plus grand ornement,
> De son chant gracieux cette action hardie.

22 32 la belle chose que de savoir quelque chose : an ellipsis. We should expect *c'est une belle chose* or *quelle belle chose* etc. Translate, ' what a fine thing it is to know something ! '

23 7 comme si vous faisiez la moue : ' as if you were making a pout.'

23 15 celles-ci : Jourdain means the vowels.

24 27 me donnez : now *donnez-moi.* See note to **3** 10.

24 31 prose : the astonishment of Jourdain may have been suggested by the similar simplicity of Eugène Maurice de Savoie, comte de Soissons, who was still living when this play was produced. He died in 1673. Mme de Sévigné refers to this in her letter of June 12, 1680, to Mme de Grignan (Lettre 818 in Vol. VI, p. 449, of the Grands Écrivains edition): "Comment, ma fille, j'ai donc fait un sermon sans y penser! J'en suis aussi étonné que M. le comte de Soissons, quand on lui découvrit qu'il faisait de la prose." See also note to **34** 28. — **sans que j'en susse rien**: this use of the elegant imperfect subjunctive by Monsieur Jourdain, instead of a simpler form like *sans le savoir* or *sans rien savoir*, seems like an intentional affectation. Jourdain evidently is trying to show off before his teacher. Compare **43** 23.

25 3 **Mettre que**: has somewhat the value of an imperative. The phrase is an ellipsis, the thought of the *maître de philosophie* running back to the *mettre* in Jourdain's preceding phrase, *Je voudrais donc lui mettre* (**24** 32).

25 13 **pour voir**: 'for example.' See note to **35** 1.

25 14 **dont**: *dans lesquelles*. See note to **12** 19.—**on les peut mettre**: *on peut les mettre*, 'one may arrange them.' See note to **3** 21.

25 27 **tout du premier coup**: 'at the very first shot.'

25 29 For similar humorous scenes with doctors of philosophy as the butt of satire, see scenes iv, v of Molière's "Le Mariage forcé."

26 12 **Je m'allais mettre**: see note to **3** 21.

26 15 **après votre habit**: 'at work upon your suit.'

27 3 **je le donne en six coups** etc.: i.e. 'I'll give the most intelligent tailors six chances to my one, and yet I will surpass them in such a piece of work (= *le*).' Note especially the conceit of the word *éclairés*, 'enlightened.'

27 6–16 **en enbas, en enhaut**: Livet thinks that the repetition of *en* in each phrase is either a misprint or a bourgeois use of the day which Molière is ridiculing. The reference is to flower adornments on the coat, but it is not entirely clear whether "up" and "down" refer to the stem and flower of the adornment itself, or to the position of the adornment on the coat, that is, whether on the skirts of the coat or higher up. The most probable meaning seems to be that in *fleurs en enbas*, the flowers are upside down, the stems being above; *en enhaut* would then mean the normal position. To have the flowers upside down may have been an eccentric fashion of the day; hence Jourdain's unfamiliarity with it, and his satisfaction when he learns that people of quality have adopted this style. The actor's gesture at this place is to point the thumb down and then up, which still further suggests the relative position of flower and stem.

27 15 **voilà qui est donc bien**: 'then it is all right so.' See note to **3** 15.

27 21–25 The tailor's remarkable praise of his workmen is not without modern parallels. The present editor has seen an advertisement of a tailor declaring that he had "a cutter who is a consummate artist."

27 23 **monter une rhingrave :** 'to make a pair of wide knee breeches.' The *rhingrave* was intended for riding horseback, and hence was large and loose. A German prince from the Rhine region (German 𝔑𝔥𝔢𝔦𝔫= 𝔤𝔯𝔞𝔣, hence *rhingrave*) is said to have introduced this style into France sometime previously.

27 33 **en . . . lever un habit :** 'to cut out a suit from it.'

28 1 **le lever avec le mien :** 'to cut it out of the same cloth as my suit.'

28 9 **dansants :** frequently, as here, the present participle in Molière's day agreed with the subject. Quite as frequently, however, it did not. The present rule of nonagreement was not accepted by the Académie Française until the year 1679, and even then was not well established.

28 17 **pour voir :** *pour faire voir* or *pour qu'ils voient*. Molière uses the infinitive much more freely than is now generally permitted. This use is characteristic of his very direct style.

28 22 **Voilà ce que c'est de se mettre :** Molière frequently omits the *que* which is now necessary before *de* in such constructions. Translate, 'that's what it means to dress.'

29 7 **Altesse :** 'Highness,' a title for rulers and princes of the blood royal. Note that the tailor apprentice does not actually go so far as to call M. Jourdain by this title ; hence the meaning of the latter's *Il a bien fait* in line 11 is 'he did well not to call me "Altesse." '

29 9 **la :** *Votre Grandeur.*

ACTE III

30 1 **que j'aille :** *pour que j'aille*. See note to **6** 10. — **mon habit :** Jourdain's costume in the third act is a luxurious medley of green and yellow, an immense wig, a great tuft of plumes on his hat, and a sword hung to a gorgeous crossbelt.

30 5 **que :** *pour que*. See **6** 10 and **30** 1.

31 5 **je ne saurais me tenir de rire :** 'I can't help laughing.'

31 13 **voilà qui :** see note to **3** 15.

31 21 **Encore :** has here the idiomatic touch of the German 𝔰𝔠𝔥𝔬𝔫 𝔴𝔦𝔢𝔡𝔢𝔯, 'what! again!'

31 23 **me laissez rire :** now *laissez-moi rire*. See note to **3** 10.

32 25 **de peur d'y manquer :** 'without fail,' 'for fear of losing out';

the *y* seems to refer to *carême-prenant* above, although it may not refer to any definite antecedent at all.

32 26 dont : ' by which.' See note to **12 19.**

33 3 est presque sur les dents : ' is almost exhausted' or ' done up.'

33 5 notre servante : the *notre* expresses ridicule and contempt. See **3 18.**

33 18 prérogatives : this seems rather an unusual word for a person of Jourdain's limited education. We are tempted to believe that he is not quite sure of its meaning. Compare **5 30,** and see note.

33 26 pour renfort de potage : a popular saying ; literally, ' as an addition to the soup ' ; figuratively, ' as a climax of folly,' ' to complete things.'

33 30 vous faire donner le fouet : ' to get a whipping.'

33 31 l'avoir . . . savoir : another instance of Molière's free use of the infinitive ; see note to **28 17.** We should now expect *Plût à Dieu que je l'eusse . . . et que je susse.*

34 1 rendre la jambe . . . mieux faite : a popular proverbial expression meaning ' to be of greater profit,' used sarcastically here ; it should be noted that the costume of men in those days with its knee breeches emphasized the value of a well-developed calf.

34 19 Des chansons : literally ' songs,' but really here in the meaning ' nonsense.' Jourdain's reply seems to show that he takes his wife's answer literally.

34 28 tout ce qui n'est point vers n'est point prose : because this statement is nonsense, and despite the fact that it is in the original edition of 1671, many later editions, beginning with that of 1674, have changed to *tout ce qui n'est point vers est prose.* The standard edition, by Despois-Mesnard in the Grands Écrivains series, although it accepts the text of 1671, has a noncommittal note as follows (Vol. VIII, p. 106) : " Y a-t-il une faute dans l'original ? Est-ce Molière qui a voulu que M. Jourdain s'embrouillât ici tout a fait ? " Owing to this indecision subsequent editors have hesitated between the two readings. Livet, Mangold, Monval, Albert, Thirion, and a few others have adopted the original reading of 1671 ; the remainder have preferred the " correction " of 1674. The present editor believes that the reading *n'est point prose* is the correct one. See his article in *Modern Philology* for January, 1913, a summary of which follows : Every time that M. Jourdain attempts to repeat a phrase or an action in which he receives instruction, he makes a mess of it ; he cannot dance, fence, or even make a bow as he is told. Just a few lines below he tries to describe the pronunciation of U, and in so doing mixes the description of U with that of E, besides saying, "bring the *upper* jaw near the *lower*" (!) instead of the *lower* near the *upper*. In Act IV, scene vi, he hears the flowery compliments of Covielle: *votre cœur soit toute l'année comme un rosier fleuri*, and *que le ciel vous donne la force des lions et la prudence des serpents*; in Act V, scene iii, he remembers these vaguely enough to misquote them in a ludicrous manner, thus: *je vous souhaite toute l'année votre rosier fleuri*, and *je vous souhaite la force des serpents et la prudence des lions*. This latter complete inversion of the original is on a par with Harpagon's distortion of the ancient saying told him by Valère (Act III, scene i, of "L'Avare") into *il faut vivre pour manger et non pas manger pour vivre*.

Thus, in every instance Jourdain is unable to repeat correctly what he hears or to perform that which he is taught. If therefore the "correction" to *est prose* is to remain, we shall have the only case in the comedy in which Jourdain says or does anything correctly. The fact that the reading *n'est point prose* gives us nonsense is no argument for its elimination, unless we are to make sense of the remaining nonsense uttered by Jourdain. Molière intended to show that he is mentally incapable of doing or saying the simplest things that he is told, and if we are prepared to admit that a nonsensical misquotation is more humorous than a correct quotation, we should prefer the original *n'est point prose* to any subsequent correction. Surely Molière, ever alive to that which was most humorous, did not wish to lose the opportunity here afforded.

34 29 voilà ce que c'est d'étudier : see note to **28 22**.

35 1 pour voir : Livet, in his edition and also in his "Lexique de la langue de Molière," Vol. III, p. 809, says that this *voir* is the Old French adverb *voir*, from Latin *verum*. If this be true, the meaning would be 'really' or 'truly.' Littré, however, quotes under the verb *voir* (26) the passage from "L'Avare," V, ii, *Dépeignez-la un peu pour voir*; and editors have generally agreed that *pour voir* is from the verb *voir*, and has the meaning *pour exemple*. See the similar use in **25 13** and **35 30**; see also the "Lexique" of the Grands Écrivains edition, Vol. XIII, p. 613.

35 7 l'étrange chose que d'avoir : see note to **22 32**.

35 8 approches la mâchoire d'en haut de celle d'en bas : 'bring the *upper* jaw near the *lower*.' Compare this ludicrous description of U with that given by the *maître de philosophie* in **23 1–9**, and with the description of E in **22 18–19**. Jourdain has made a sorry mixture of the two. Compare the note to **34 28**.

35 13 C'est bien autre chose : 'it's quite another (finer) thing.'

35 17 **De quoi est-ce que tout cela guérit** : 'what's the use of all that?' 'of what use is all that?' Perhaps Nicole thinks that it all sounds like the cabalistic conjuring of disease by sorcerers.

35 23 **vous tient fort au cœur** : 'is much on your mind,' 'is a sore point with you,' 'is your bugbear.'

35 30 **pour voir** : see note to **35** 1.

35 32 **Diantre soit la coquine** : 'the devil take the hussy!'

36 2 **tierce . . . quarte** : the fencing master had taught him the quarte movement before the tierce; see **15** 13–18. Hence he thinks that the movements should always proceed in that order. Compare his similar stupidity at **34** 28.

36 3 **que** = *d'attendre que*, 'to wait for me to parry.'

36 8 **votre bourgeoisie** : the *votre* is contemptuous. See note to **3** 18.

36 10 **Çamon** : 'yes, indeed,' 'upon my word,' an old affirmative expression; the *mon* is probably derived from Latin *munde*, 'surely.' Compare its use in Chrétien de Troyes's "Cligès" (verse 905) : *Ce ne faz mon*, 'I surely do not do that,' where *mon* strengthens the negative. See, further, Livet's edition and his "Lexique de la langue de Molière."

36 11 **vos nobles** : the *vos* is contemptuous. See note to **3** 18. — **vous avez bien opéré** : 'you've done a nice piece of work' (ironical).

36 18 **que l'on voie** : the subjunctive here seems to English readers rather unnecessary. It is often used, however, in French to describe what is merely in the mind or in the desire of the speaker, but is not stated as a fact. Translate here, 'that people should see' or 'for people to see,' *not* 'that people see.'

37 5 **il ne manquera pas d'y faillir** : a proverbial expression; 'he'll do nothing of the sort' (literally, 'he will not miss failing in this'), 'he won't fail to break his promise.'

37 13 **Il ne nous faut plus que cela** : 'that is all we needed,' i.e. 'this is the climax.'

37 14 **il me semble que j'ai dîné** : 'I am satiated with eating,' 'my appetite is gone,' 'it makes me ill,' "I hate the sight of him" (Trollope).

37 17 **Mon cher ami, monsieur Jourdain** : this form of address is most condescending and snobbishly contemptuous.

37 23 **comme elle peut** : 'the best she may.'

38 2 **Il le gratte par où il se démange** : a popular expression; literally, 'he scratches him where he itches,' i.e. flatters his weaknesses. *Démanger* is no longer a reflexive verb, and even in Molière's day *lui démange* would have been more common; see the note on page 112 of the

Despois-Mesnard edition, and compare the modern *la main lui démange*, 'his hand itches,' and similar examples in Littre's "Dictionnaire."

38 12 mettez: a formula of the time to invite one to put on one's hat. Hats were then worn in the house without impropriety, their elegance making them very ornamental and handsome. In the presence of social superiors, especially of the nobility, however, the hats were removed; hence the ceremoniousness of this scene. Nobles alone were privileged to keep the hat on at all times.

38 21 J'aime mieux . . . qu'importun: contemporary authorities show that this expression was extremely bourgeois and common, lacking entirely that elegance which Jourdain doubtless thinks it possesses. Levi's edition calls attention to the use of such a phrase in "Merry Wives of Windsor," I, i: "I'll rather be unmannerly than troublesome."

39 11 un petit mémoire: Jourdain has a precise memorandum of all these sums, and carries it on his person drawn up exactly to the last denier. He is still the shopkeeper's son and the bourgeois when it is a question of money accounts.

39 12 louis: according to the calculation that follows, a *louis* (*louis d'or*) and a *pistole* were each equal to eleven *francs*; a *franc* or *livre* was equal to twenty *sous*, and a *sou* was equal to twelve *deniers*. If we bear in mind that the purchasing value of money at this time was five times as great as it is now, we shall see how very considerable were the following amounts:

line 12. 200 louis
line 14. 120 louis
line 16. 140 louis
          ⎯⎯⎯
line 18. 460 louis × 11   = 5,060 livres
line 22. To the feather dealer   1,832 livres
line 25. To the tailor   •   2,780 livres
line 28. To the merchant   4,379 livres 12 sous 8 deniers
line 32. To the saddler   1,748 livres 7 sous 4 deniers
                                 ⎯⎯⎯⎯⎯⎯⎯⎯⎯⎯⎯⎯⎯⎯⎯⎯⎯⎯⎯⎯
                                 15,799 livres 19 sous 12 deniers
page **40** line 2.   •   = 15,800 livres
Dorante then (**40** 4) borrows
     200 pistoles or louis × 11 = 2,200 livres
                                  ⎯⎯⎯⎯⎯
page **40** line 5.   Grand total 18,000 livres

39 27 Il est vrai: compare note to **4** 3.

39 28 septante-neuf: 'seventy-nine.' Modern French uses *soixante-dix-neuf*, but *septante* is still heard for *soixante-dix* in parts of southern

France, in Belgium, and in French Switzerland. *Septante, huitante, nonante* were regularly used in the seventeenth century.

39 30 Note the comic repetition of the small end of the largest sum in the calculation; this is another instance of the *dialogue en écho*. See note to **19** 7–23.

40 3 **est juste**: the reading *et juste* of the editions of 1674 and 1682 has much in its favor.

40 6 **au premier jour**: 'at the first opportunity.'

40 19 **qu'**: *avant que* or *jusqu'à ce que*, 'before,' 'until.' See note to **6** 10.

40 29 **J'ai force gens**: 'I know many persons.'

40 31 **ferais tort**: 'should wrong' or 'should offend.'

40 33 **Je vais quérir votre affaire**: 'I'll go get what you want.'

41 3 **Que faire**: 'what else can I do?'

41 10 **J'ai la tête** etc.: this popular expression seems to vary in meaning with its context. Usually it is scarcely more than a nonsensical, evasive answer, and at most means that nothing is the matter. Here, however, it is stronger, and is a refusal to answer civilly or to continue the conversation. It seems almost to approximate 'mind your own business.'—et si: *si* is here equivalent to *pourtant, néanmoins*. It is an old word, obsolete except in proverbial expressions such as this, which always have a tendency to retain archaic words or phrases.

41 12 **que je ne la vois point**: *que* is equivalent to *car* here; 'since,' 'for.' See note to **6** 10.

41 16 **se porte**: Molière is not averse to puns; compare the famous one on *grand'mère* and *grammaire* in "Les Femmes savantes." Here Madame Jourdain uses *se porte* literally in answer to its idiomatic use by Dorante: 'How goes it with her (How is her health)? She goes on her two legs.'

41 18 **le ballet . . . fait**: *fait* means here 'play,' 'act.' This suggestion of Dorante that Madame Jourdain and her daughter go to see the royal entertainment is far more amusing than it at first appears, since it would have been impossible for a bourgeois to have secured entrance. Hence it really is a fine piece of irony like the rest of Dorante's remarks to Madame Jourdain, and must have created much amusement at the court performances.

41 20 **fort envie de rire nous avons**: such inverted repetitions were a form of emphasis much in vogue among the people. Moland's edition gives several interesting cases.

41 24 **Tredame**: popular euphemistic contraction of the oath *Notre Dame*, 'Holy Virgin'; *dame* is a still further contraction. Madame Jourdain's anger is now increased by Dorante's reference to her age.

42 5 **divertissement royal :** compare note to **41** 18.

42 7 **vous baise les mains :** this is a formula for declining or refusing with thanks ; here, of course, there is an ironical touch.

42 10 **ballet :** this is the *Ballet des Nations* at the end of the comedy. The *repas* is that in the first scene of Act IV. — **cadeau :** in the seventeenth century this word meant a pleasure party, treat, or entertainment with a banquet given to ladies and usually in the open air ; a sort of elegant picnic.

42 12 **pour cause :** 'for a certain good reason,' i.e. that they may not be overheard.

42 15 **mîtes :** the past definite tense is now practically never heard in conversation ; its present use is literary.

42 28 **une confusion la plus grande :** we should now expect the definite article before *confusion*, but Molière felt free to use either the definite or the indefinite.

43 8 **fîtes :** see note to **42** 15.

43 9 **j'avais commerce :** ' I visit as a friend.'

43 23 **fisse :** this again is rather an elegant use of the imperfect subjunctive and has the value of a conditional. Jourdain seems to be showing off once more, this time to Dorante. Compare *susse* in **24** 31.

44 10 **quelque anguille sous roche :** ' some mischief on foot,' ' some secret mystery under way,' ' some snake in the grass ' ; literally, ' some eel under the rock.'

44 25 **il me vienne trouver :** see note to **3** 21. — **pour faire ensemble** = *pour que nous fassions ensemble.* See note to **28** 17.

45–53 **Scènes viii-x :** note the clever use of the lover's quarrel and reconciliation that now ensues. Molière has similar and, some editors think, better scenes in " Le Tartuffe " (Act II, scene iv) and " Le Dépit amoureux " (Act I, scene v, and Act IV, scenes iii, iv) ; those of the latter play resemble most closely the scenes in " Le Bourgeois gentilhomme." Molière always treats true lovers sympathetically, realizing no doubt the dramatic value of such treatment and its appeal to the average audience. He is always on the side of the lovers, and opposed to arbitrary and selfish control of their affections ; he is the consistent champion of the right of the young girl to choose her husband, and always opposes the marriage that is based upon selfish motives. In his plays, otherwise so full of realism, this forms a conspicuous exception in favor of the ideal.

45 2 **ambassadrice de joie :** this expression seems at first somewhat too literary and elegant for Nicole, as also the inverted construction in

line 17 below : *allons de cette belle histoire informer ma maîtresse*. There
is perhaps a comic touch in having Nicole ape the language of her
betters. However, Livet has shown in his edition, page 273, that *ambassadrice* was commonly used.

45 4 tes traîtresses paroles : normally we should expect the adjective
to follow the noun. Compare note to **4** 22.

45 16 quelle mouche les a piqués : 'what has roused them up so?'
literally, 'what fly has stung them?'

45 Scène ix : it should be noted how Covielle's amusing material-
istic parodies contrast with his master's more elegant language in this
scene. Each is a foil to the other; sometimes the comic element is
enhanced by Covielle's utter inability to do more than approve his
master's sentiments.

45 18 un amant le plus fidèle etc. : there is more justification here for
the *un* than for the similar use of the *une* in **42** 28, because of the *un
amant* just before it. The one repeats and emphasizes the other.

45 24 elle fait tous mes soins : 'she is the object of all my attentions,'
'the one care of my life.' Note the humor in the frequent repetition of
elle in this passage.

46 15 d'assidus hommages : the normal position of *assidus* would be
after the noun. This is another instance of Molière's free usage.
Compare note to **4** 22.

46 20 à la chérir : 'in cherishing her.' Such infinitive constructions
are very common in Molière.

46 22 à tourner : 'while turning.' See note to **46** 20.

46 26, 28 châtiments, soufflets : in several editions designed for English-
speaking students these words have changed places, though there is
no warrant whatsoever for such a change. In these editions Cléonte
says, *C'est une perfidie digne des plus grands soufflets*, and Covielle
answers, *C'est une trahison à mériter mille châtiments*. The standard
Despois-Mesnard edition of Molière, Vol. VIII, p. 128, has no such
reading even as a variant. Moreover, the whole nature and tone of
this dialogue requires that Cléonte use the elegant word *châtiments*,
leaving to the servant the inelegant paraphrase *soufflets*. This is a good
instance of how an error once made can be perpetuated. See the present editor's article in *Modern Philology* for January, 1913.— **à mériter
mille soufflets** : 'worthy of a thousand blows.' We should now expect
qui mériterait.

47 5 ensemble = *avec elle*. *Ensemble* is ordinarily used with a plural
subject; its use here with a singular subject is very exceptional.

47 7 lui donne . . . dans la vue : 'pleases her eye,' 'strikes her fancy.'

47 11 où = *auquel*. Molière often uses *où* for some form of *lequel*. See note to **12 19**.

47 13 pour mon compte : 'for my part.'

47 15 Donne la main : 'lend a hand,' 'help.'

47 18 peinture : the following description of Lucile is thought by most critics to be that of Molière's wife, who played this part.

47 22 lui : 'in her.'

48 4 ont je ne sais quel charme : 'have an indescribable charm.'

48 11 joies . . . ouvertes : 'boisterous joy,' "ever-gaping hilarity."

48 22 Le moyen : 'how is that possible?'

48 24 à la haïr, à la quitter : equivalent to *en la haïssant, en la quittant*, or to a conditional clause. Compare note to **46** 20.

48 25 toute belle, toute pleine d'attraits, toute aimable que je la trouve : 'however beautiful . . . I may find her.' Note that in each of these cases the spelling *toute* is kept, although modern French requires that when *tout* is used adverbially before feminine adjectives, it shall be spelled *toute* only before those beginning with a consonant or *h* aspirate, but shall remain *tout* before a vowel or *h* mute. To-day *toute aimable* would be written *tout aimable*.

49 8 Que voilà qui est scélérat : 'how rascally that is!' See note to **3 15**.

49 9 Que cela est Judas : 'how like Judas (i.e. how treacherous) that is!' In *Judas* the *s* is silent.

49 12 on : usually *on* is an indefinite pronoun, but occasionally in ironical or veiled speech, as here, it indicates a definite person. A remarkable use of *on* in this veiled, but really definite, sense is found in Molière's " Le Tartuffe," Act IV, scene v.

49 13 prendre la chèvre : a popular expression meaning 'take offense,' 'grow angry with the sudden, capricious impatience of the goat.' Compare *se cabrer*, which means 'rear up,' 'prance about,' 'fly into a passion,' 'get skittish,' 'fire up,' etc. Both *chèvre* and *cabrer* are derived from Latin *capra*, 'goat.' Compare *caprice* and its derivatives in French and English, also English " caper."

49 14 On a deviné l'enclouure : 'they have guessed what the trouble is.' *Enclouure* means the soreness due to a nail's (*clou*) having penetrated beyond the hoof into the flesh when an animal is shod. The resulting limping of the animal forces an investigation of the cause.

49 25 Queussi, queumi : this is a popular phrase in the dialect of villages near Paris, and means 'the same with me,' 'ditto here,' or the like. The probable origin is *quel soi, quel moi*. The obsolete English "ka me, ka thee" may have some connection with this expression.

50 8 Point d'affaire : 'not at all,' 'I 'll have nothing to do with you.'

50 24 c'en est fait : 'it 's all settled,' 'it 's all over.'

50 26 Plus de commerce : 'no more acquaintance with you,' "no more dealings" (Levi).

51 16 Point d'affaire : see note to **50 8**

51 30 je n'en ferai rien : 'I 'll do nothing of the sort.'

52 29 Ne m'en donnes-tu point à garder : a popular expression meaning 'impose upon,' 'humbug.'

52 33 qu'avec . . . de choses : 'how many storms in my heart' etc.

53 1 que facilement . . . aime : 'how easily we allow ourselves to be persuaded by those we love !'

53 6 prenez vite votre temps : 'profit quickly by the opportunity.'

53 12 faire une demande : the usual custom in France is for a third party, some relative or intimate friend of the suitor, to ask for the hand of the lady. The absence of this conventional formality here is in line with Molière's advocacy of simplicity and directness in matters of love.

53 13 pour m'en charger moi-même : 'to undertake it myself.'

53 17 gentilhomme : compare Littré, who quotes the "Dictionnaire de l'Académie": "En France, sous l'ancien régime, on appelle *noble*, celui qui, étant anobli, *commence* la noblesse de sa famille ; ceux qui *naissent de lui* ont le titre de *gentilshommes*. Un ancien gentilhomme se nomme homme de condition, et un gentilhomme d'une famille illustrée, homme de qualité. Tout gentilhomme est noble, mais tout noble n'est pas gentilhomme ; le prince fait des nobles, mais le sang fait des gentilshommes." Thus Jourdain will be contented with nothing less than a nobility of at least one generation, since he insists not merely upon the rank of *noble*, but upon that of *gentilhomme*. In reality his ambitions are much higher, since he wishes a marquis for a son-in-law, and even threatens to make his daughter a duchess! Note also that his models are *gens de qualité*, the highest class of the nobility.

53 19 tranche le mot aisément : 'speaks out readily.'

53 20 aucun scrupule : the assumption of nobility without legal right was so prevalent that Colbert in 1667 issued an edict requiring all who called themselves nobles to present their proofs. This is of interest as justifying Molière and later writers in their attacks upon the false nobles, a type therefore very common in French comedy. The nobility of Dorante in this play, for instance, is exceedingly doubtful.

54 6 où = *auquel*. See note to **12 19**.

54 9 **Touchez là, monsieur. Ma fille n'est pas pour vous :** 'shake hands, sir ; you can't have my daughter.' This phrase has since become proverbial to mean an abrupt refusal with an effort to retain the friendship of the person so denied. The humor consists in the apparent acquiescence which turns out to be a complete refusal. Molière probably saw this trick in Chevalier's one-act comedy (1662) " Les Galants ridicules ou les amours de Guillot et de Ragotin," end of scene vi :

GUILLOT

J'aime votre fille Angélique.

LE DOCTEUR

Quoi ? c'est l'objet de vos souhaits ?
Touchez, vous ne l'aurez jamais.

See the Grands Écrivains edition of Molière, Vol. VIII, p. 143.

54 15 **de la côte de Saint-Louis :** 'from the rib of Saint Louis.' Saint Louis was Louis IX, king of France, born 1215, died 1270. This is a proverbial expression meaning of very remote and distinguished ancestry.

54 17 **je vous vois venir :** 'I see what you are coming to,' 'what you are driving at.' This is still a common expression in French.

54 18 **que :** *d'autre part* or *d'autre chose* would now be necessary before this *que*.

54 20 **Voilà pas le coup de langue :** 'is n't that slander for you ?' *Ne* ought really to precede. Molière uses *ne voilà pas ce que je vous ai dit* in " George Dandin," Act III, scene viii, and in other comedies. Occasionally we find also *ne voilà-t-il pas.* The omission of *ne* is therefore very exceptional. A *coup de langue* is what might be expected of a backbiting, shrewish, termagant woman.

54 23 **Peste soit de la femme :** 'plague take the woman !'—**Elle n'y a jamais manqué :** 'she never missed a chance to bring that up,' 'to harp on that story.'

54 24 **mais pour le mien :** from this passage it appears that Jourdain had never been a merchant himself and that he does not wish to believe that his father had ever been. Hence Covielle in Act IV, scene v, can the more readily convince him.

55 7 **Dieu m'en garde :** 'God preserve me from it,' 'God forbid.'

55 9 **où** = *à laquelle.* See note to **12** 19.

55 13 **S'il fallait qu'elle me vînt visiter :** 'if she should happen to come to visit me.'

55 17 **qui fait tant la glorieuse :** 'who puts on such airs,' 'who swaggers around so.'

55 18   **qui était** = *laquelle était.* See note to **12** 19.

55 19   **jouer à la madame :** 'to play ladies with us.'

55 21   **la porte Saint-Innocent:** Livet's edition, p. 238, quotes from Furetière's dictionary to the effect that in popular speech, one said *la porte de Paris* for *l'apport de Paris.* The word *apport*, now obsolete, meant 'market place.' Hence *la porte Saint-Innocent* might mean 'the market place of Saint Innocent.' Livet even asks, "Ne faudrait-il pas écrire 'l'apport des Saints-Innocents'?" There were a church, a cemetery, and a fountain "des Saints-Innocents," located in the market quarter, and some editors say that *la porte Saint-Innocent* means the gate to the cemetery of that name. Between these two interpretations editors have hesitated; to us the explanation suggested by Livet seems the more probable, and it was adopted by the editors of Molière in the Grands Écrivains series as a "correction or addition"; see Vol. XI, p. 309.

55 23   **l'on . . . si riches :** note that *on* may take an agreement in the plural, if the sense is clearly plural.

55 24   **à être** = *tout en étant* : one of the frequent cases where Molière uses an infinitive although now the participle is usually preferred. Compare note to **46** 20.

56 8   **l'exemple :** i.e. the example of those who successfully pretend to be noble.

56 9   **Vous moquez-vous :** 'are you joking?' 'are you foolish?' 'do you really mean it?'

56 18   **jouer :** 'to play a trick on,' 'to fool.'

56 24   **qui vient le mieux du monde ici :** 'which comes in here most opportunely.'

56 25   **notre ridicule :** see note to **4** 19.

57 1   **chercher tant de façons :** 'to be so particular.'

57 2   **donner . . . dans toutes les fariboles :** 'to swallow all the nonsense.'

57 11   **et être né** = *et* (or *pourvu*) *que je fusse né*, 'provided I had been born.' This is another instance of Molière's free use of the infinitive (see note to **28** 17), and is particularly interesting since he has just used the subjunctive *qu'il m'eût coûté.*

57 17   **comme cela que :** this is a redundancy of servants' language, equivalent to 'so so, that,' 'as how as,' 'the likes of this, that.' It is used by children and by uneducated or embarrassed people.

58 8   **à recevoir** = *en recevant.* Compare note to **46** 20.

58 17   **dont :** 'from which.' See note to **12** 19.

58 19   **y :** refers to *au mariage* above, i.e. 'you ought to be married already.'

58 21 À quoi tient-il : ' what prevents ? '

58 24 les deux plus raisonnables personnes du monde : this is an unusual position for the superlative adjective, and therefore it becomes
very emphatic. *Plus raisonnables* is placed as an equivalent of *meilleures*,
which normally precedes the noun. We have here another instance of
Molière's freedom from restraint.

58 25 personnes . . . ils : note that although *personne* is normally
feminine, *ils* in line 26 refers to it. We should now expect *elles*, but in
the seventeenth century the masculine agreement is frequently found,
especially when there are several words intervening. See *personne* in the
" Lexique de la langue de Molière " (Grands Écrivains, Vol. XIII, pp.
268–269).

58 28 l'expérience que vous avez faite : ' your previous experience.'

58 30 j'en reviens toujours là : ' I come back to the same view of this
matter,' ' I cannot get away from this opinion.'

59 4 que vous ne vous incommodiez : this use of *que* for *sans que* is no
longer possible. Indeed a simpler construction *sans vous incommoder*
would probably be preferred now. See note to **6** 10.

59 9 faites . . . tant valoir : ' value so highly.'

59 17 la troisième : the third bow (see page 14, Act II, end of
scene i).

59 18 sait son monde : ' knows how to treat his guests politely,' ' knows
how to behave in polite society ' (ironical here).

59 19 ce m'est une gloire : *c'est une gloire pour moi.* See note to **4** 4.

59 24 que : *que* often repeats a previous conjunction, in this case *si*
in line 23.

60 13 gardez-vous-en bien : ' be very careful not to.'

60 28 grâces : ' acts of graciousness,' ' favors.'

ACTE IV

62 8 de vous faire = *en vous faisant* or *s'il vous fait.* Compare note
to **46** 20.

62 10 que : repeats *comme.* See note to **59** 24.

62 12 des incongruités de bonne chère, et des barbarismes de bon goût :
' gastronomic improprieties and sins (or offenses) against good taste.'

62 18 pain de rive à biseau doré : a loaf baked on the edge (*rive*) of the
oven and not touching the other loaves. The overlapping crust (*biseau*)
of such a loaf, being equally exposed to the heat, becomes golden-brown
(*doré*).

62 22 **veau de rivière :** 'Normandy veal'; *de rivière* refers to the fact that the calves were reared in Normandy along the banks of the Seine river. Their meat was considered superior.

63 3 **soupe à bouillon perlé :** a rich soup which, when mixed with cold water, forms pearl-like bubbles of its fatty substances. — **soutenue :** 'accompanied' (probably in the same dish).

63 4 **dindon :** it seems from contemporary evidence that only certain parts of the turkey were considered great delicacies.

63 16 **dégoûté :** 'fastidious,' 'difficult to please.'

63 21 **merveilleusement . . . admirablement :** long, sonorous adverbs were very popular in the fashionable speech of the day.

63 29 **chansons à boire :** 'drinking songs.' These were then a popular form of musical entertainment and many eminent composers wrote the music for them. Thus Lulli composed the first one that follows, as well as many others; the second song was probably written by Lecerf de la Vieuville. See the music in Livet's edition, pp. lxxiv ff.

64 3 **vous vous prêtez des armes :** 'you become allies.'

64 7 **Qu'en mouillant . . . d'attraits :** *que* goes with *d'attraits*, 'how many charms etc.'

65 16 **je le quitte :** 'I give it up,' 'I abandon the game.' The *le* is here very indefinite and has no real antecedent.

65 17 **en main :** 'ready.'

65 19 **touchez :** the old custom was for each guest to help himself with his own spoon from the main dish. The foolish Jourdain takes all that Dorimène touches without taking; being a lady she had the right to choose first. The use of separate spoons for serving was only just beginning at this time. See the "addition" in the Grands Écrivains edition (Vol. XI, p. 309); also pp. 240–241 of the Livet edition.

65 20 **ravit . . . ravir :** Jourdain does not lose the opportunity to use the same word that Dorimène employed, but in a different sense. She had meant by it merely 'charms' or 'pleases'; he uses it in the sense of 'ravish,' 'steal.'

65 24 **monsieur mon mari :** polite sarcasm tinged with bitterness.

65 26 **un théâtre là-bas :** this refers probably to the preparations for the Turkish ceremony which Covielle had mentioned in Act III, end of scene xiv (pp. 56–57). It seems less likely that the reference is to the *Ballet des Nations*, which closes the play; this latter is referred to as a *ballet* in Act V, beginning of scene ii. — **à faire noces :** 'fit for a wedding.'

66 1 **comme :** modern *comment*.

66 4 **quelles fantaisies sont les vôtres :** 'what are you dreaming of?'

66 8 seulement: see note to **16 6**.

66 9 mieux regarder aux choses que vous dites: 'to be more careful of the things you say.'

66 18 Je n'ai que faire de lunettes: 'I have no need of spectacles.'

66 21 prêter la main: 'to help.'

66 26 Allez: is here an expression of anger, 'shame on you.'

66 27 vous vous moquez: means here 'it is not right of you,' 'you can't mean it,' 'you wrong me.'

67 5 qui me tient = *ce qui me retient*. See note to **3 15**.

67 15 déguisé: the disguise of Covielle is that of a traveler returned from the Orient; he has an Oriental garment and a long beard.

67 20 que = *lorsque* or *quand*. See note to **6 10**.

68 4 monsieur votre père: according to De Callières, "Des mots à la mode," quoted by Livet, p. 241, this form of address was reserved for princes; hence Jourdain's surprised repetition of it: *monsieur mon père*. In addition to this fact, we have to note here another instance of Molière's use of the *dialogue en écho*. See note to **19** 7–23.

68 28 Depuis avoir: would now be *depuis que j'ai*. *Depuis* may no longer be used with an infinitive, *après* having taken its place in part.

69 5 quelle = *laquelle ?* or *quelle nouvelle ?*

69 9 le va voir: see note to **3 21**.

69 14–24 Le fils du Grand Turc: another instance of *dialogue en écho*. See note to **19** 7–23.

69 17 Comme = *lorsque*. The *que* in line 18 is used instead of repeating *comme* (see note to **59** 24), but its meaning is rather *puisque*. — **je le fus voir**: this use of *être* in the meaning of 'to go' is now rare. For the position of *le*, see note to **3 21**. For the use of *fus*, see note to **42 15**.

69 20 Acciam croc etc.: a large part of the "Turkish" used by Covielle and Cléonte is taken from Rotrou's comedy "La Sœur," Act III, scenes v, vi; some is really Turkish or Arabic, but the rest is mere nonsense, resembling the use of jargon in the famous medieval farce of "Maître Pierre Pathelin." Molière's troupe often presented "La Sœur," which had been first printed in 1647. The use of this jargon affords Molière many opportunities for the *dialogue en écho*, the comic effect of which is greatly heightened by the strangeness of the words.

69 25 Comme: is here 'when.' See note to **69 17**.

70 11 pour achever mon ambassade: this phrase is here parenthetical in nature; otherwise we might expect *pour que j'achève mon ambassade*.

70 13 mamamouchi: this word, created by Molière, has since passed into the French language to mean (1) a man disguised as a Turk in carnival time; (2) a person, particularly an official, puffed up with conceit. Littré declares that the word comes from the Arabic *mā menou schi*, 'good-for-nothing.' Livet's edition suggests *baba*, 'father,' plus *mouchir*, 'a pasha of the highest rank.' See also the Introduction, p. xxiv. — qui = *ce qui*. See note to **3** 15.

70 17 Paladin : Coville's education is not sufficient to enable him to explain this word; hence he cleverly avoids doing so.

70 21 pour lui en faire mes remerciements : 'so that I may give him my thanks for this.'

70 23 Comment ! le voilà qui va venir ici : 'what are you thinking of! He is coming here.'

70 29 Tout ce qui : 'the only thing that.'

70 30 qui s'est allé mettre : *qui est allée se mettre*. See also note to **3** 21.

71 5 Ambousahim etc : the first part of this is apparently nonsense. *Salamalequi* is the ordinary Arabic salutation, *salâm* 'peace,' *aleik* 'upon thee.' The last word sounds in scholarly Arabic like English *alike*, in popular Arabic like English *a lake*. Addressing several men it would be *aleikum*; addressing a woman it would anciently have been *aleiki* as given by Molière, but this was obsolete before Molière had any chance to hear it. Note that *alequi* recurs twice as the ending of words which Coville is to interpret as blessings, **71** 12, **82** 11. Compare also the French *salemalec* and English "salaam," a very low, abject bow. The use of "so long" as words of salutation in parting is said by the Century Dictionary under "so-long" to be a perversion of "salaam."

71 7 votre cœur . . . rosier fleuri : Jourdain later attempts to quote this compliment and that in *que le ciel . . . serpents* below (line 13), and, as usual, gets them completely muddled (see Act V, scene iii). — **soit :** for use of the subjunctive, see note to **10** 19.

71 18 Bel-men : for Turkish *bilmen*, 'I do not know.'

72 12 Je vous le donnerais etc : 'I should have to give you many chances to guess.'

72 18 la bête : if the meaning here of *bête* is 'fool,' the reference is to Jourdain; if, however, *bête* has its literal meaning of 'animal,' we have merely a humorous reference of Coville to himself. The latter seems the more consistent, since Coville's answer is apparently to Dorante's last words, *puisque tu l'entreprends*.

72 21 pour faire place à : 'to make room for.'

72 23 La Cérémonie turque : see the Introduction, pp. xxii ff., for an account of the history of this burlesque.

72 25 **dansants :** see note to **28** 9.

72 26 **dont :** 'with which.' See note to **12** 19.

73 3 **le Muphty :** a mufti is a Mohammedan jurisconsult; the "Grand Mufti" of Constantinople, now better known as the Sheikh-ul-Islam, is the head (under the Sultan) of the Mohammedan religion. In the court performances only, the rôle of the Muphty was played by the celebrated composer Lulli, who had written the music of the songs and of the interludes. He appeared under the stage name Chiacheron, and pleased, Louis XIV so well by his acting that he received the important post of *secrétaire du roi.*

73 6 **levant . . . ailes, se prosternent, se relèvent :** three of the six postures which are alternately assumed in the regular form of prayer which all Mohammedans go through at the call of the muezzin.

73 7 **comme si c'était :** we should now expect *c'étaient.*

73 8 **chantants :** see note to **28** 9.— **Alli, Alla :** doubtless an echo of the Mohammedan confession of faith, whose first and most familiar half, *lâ ilâh' illa 'llâh' '* (there is) no god but God,' is usually distorted in one way or another by Europeans unfamiliar with Arabic. Of course the name *Allâh* 'God' recurs in other connections in the elaborate prayer. The name of Ali, Mohammed's son-in-law and in Persian belief the first of his successors who had a legitimate right, would be a sacred exclamation to a Persian but not to a Turk; it is not probable that we have here an echo of this name.

73 10 **ekber :** Arabic for 'most great,' usually transliterated *akbar*; 'is' should be understood with it. The cry "God (is) most great," usually given in English as "God is great," is a leading formula of Mohammedan praise, and is repeated (the worshiper standing erect) at two points in the course of the regular prayer.

73 12 **rasé :** it is rather strange that Jourdain is represented here as shaved, since Mohammedans traditionally have a high regard for the beard; in the sixteenth century a sultan of Turkey was rebuked by a mufti for shaving off his beard. — **auquel :** refers to *le Bourgeois ; il* refers to *le Muphty.*

73 14 **Se ti sabir,** etc.: 'if you know, you answer; if you know not, be silent, be silent. I am Muphty; you, who are you? You do not understand; be silent, be silent.'

These and similar subsequent verses are in part in the so-called Frank language (*lingua franca*), a species of international language created for commercial and diplomatic use around the Mediterranean. Formerly this was spoken along the south and east coasts, but now its use has been greatly restricted, and it is confined to sailors and the rougher elements of harbor cities. During the days of piracy in the Barbary States it was used as the means of communication between the pirate captors and their Christian slaves, especially in Algiers and Tunis. With the French conquest of Algiers (1830) and Tunis (1881) the use of the *lingua franca* yielded gradually to French and Arabic. The *lingua franca* differs in details in accordance with varying localities; in general, however, it may be described as a mixture and a crisscross or blend of Italian, Spanish, French, and other Romance idioms with Arabic and touches of other eastern tongues. In Molière's phrases the chief elements are Spanish and Italian. He uses similar language for comic effect in scene viii of " Le Sicilien." The *lingua franca* is known also as the *sabir* language, probably because of the frequent use of *sabir* in the phrase *mi no sabir*, ' I do not know.' Hugo Schuchardt, however, in an interesting article in the *Zeitschrift für romanische Philologie*, 1909 (Vol. XXXIII, pp. 441–461), declares that the name *sabir* comes from Molière's use in the phrase above, *se ti sabir*. A characteristic of this artificial language is the use of an infinitive for nearly all verbal inflections and a corresponding simplification of all other grammatical forms, somewhat after the manner in which nurses talk to babies. In this it also resembles the way in which Chinese or aboriginal tribes first learn to talk any European tongue.

73 22 **font retirer:** an instance of the ellipsis of the reflexive pronoun after *faire*. The verb is really *se retirer*, but in the seventeenth century the reflexive object of an infinitive depending upon the main verbs *faire, laisser, voir, entendre, écouter, regarder, sentir*, and *mener* was often omitted.

73 24 **Dice, Turque,** etc.: ' say, Turks, who is this man ? '

73 25 **Anabatista:** ' Anabaptist,' ' Baptist.'

73 26 **Ioc:** (pronounced *Yok*) Turkish or Tatar for ' no.'

73 27 **Zuinglista:** a follower of the reformer Ulrich Zwingli (1484–1531) of Saint Gall in Switzerland.

73 29 **Coffita:** a Copt or Copht (an Egyptian Christian of the Monophysite sect); their sacred books are in the Coptic language, which is derived from ancient Egyptian.

74 2 **Ussita:** a Hussite, a follower of John Huss (1373–1415), the Bohemian reformer. — **Morista:** it is uncertain whether this means a Moravian or Moor. The latter seems the more probable; the Moors remaining in Spain after the overthrow of their kingdom were called Moriscos. — **Fronista:** this seems to mean a contemplative, profound

thinker (Greek φροντιστής), but there is apparently no religious sect of this name. If we could assume illegible handwriting on Molière's part, and consequent misprinting of this name, it is a bare possibility that the "Fronista" might be a Fohist, i.e. a Buddhist (*Fo* being Chinese for Buddha).

74 5 Star pagana: 'is he a pagan?'

74 7 Luterana: a follower of Luther.

74 9 Puritana: a Puritan, member of the English Protestant sect, many of whom were forced by persecution to emigrate to New England.

74 11 Bramina: a Brahmin or Brahman, a Hindu priest. — **Moffina**: apparently there is no such sect. — **Zurina**: no such sect is known; perhaps the word is suggested by Zurich, the Swiss city.

74 14 Mahametana: a Mohammedan.

74 15 Hey valla: (Arabic *î wallâh*, the *î* being pronounced like English *e*, and the *w* as in English) 'yes, by Allah (God).' The ordinary Arabic for "yes" is *na'am* or *na'im*, but *î* is used for "yes" with strong exclamatory force.

74 16 Como chamara: 'what is his name?' Compare Italian *come*, 'how,' and *chiamare*, 'to call.'

75 5 Mahameta etc.: 'To Mohammed for Jourdain, I pray evening and morning. Wish to make a Paladin of Jourdain, of Jourdain. Give the turban and give the scimitar, With the galley and the brigantine, To defend Palestine. To Mohammed for Jourdain, I pray evening and morning.' Is it a mere coincidence that Jourdain bears the name of the chief river of Palestine?

75 16 Star bon Turca Giourdina: 'is Jourdain a good Turk?'

75 18 Hu la ba ba etc.: as written this is nonsense, but Auger declares that when somewhat transposed and changed it resembles the Turkish *Allah baba, hou, allah baba,* 'God my father, God, God my father.' Trollope's comment on this suggestion of Auger is that it is "prodigiously ingenious!" It is, however, hardly credible.

76 6 jusques à mettre = *jusqu'à ce qu'il mette*. Another instance of Molière's use of the infinitive. See note to **28 17**.

76 14 Hou: Arabic disjunctive nominative pronoun 'He,' used so much with reference to God in some manifestations of Mohammedan religion (especially by the howling dervishes in their whirling dances) that certain Mohammedans have come to regard it as a sacred word. In the eighteenth century the use of this word in the play was considered a profanation by the Turkish ambassador Saïd Effendi.

76 15 assistants, inclinants : agreement of present participles. Compare, however, immediately below (line 17) *en chantant . . . et continuant.* See note to **28** 9.

76 22 Ti non star furba : 'you are not a rogue?'

76 24 Non star forfanta : 'you are not a braggart (coward, rascal)?'

76 26 Donar turbanta : 'give the turban.'

77 1 Ti star nobile, etc. : 'you are noble, 't is no fable ; take the saber.'

77 4 mettants : agreement of present participle. See note to **28** 9.

77 7 Dara, dara, bastonara, etc. : 'give, give, the beating.'

77 11 Non tener honta etc. : 'have no shame ; this is the last insult.'

77 17 sautants, dansants et chantants : agreement of present participles. See note to **28** 9.

ACTE V

78 2 momon : 'challenge to a game of dice,' carried by carnival masqueraders to the parties challenged, who were usually ladies. The challenge often took the form of an enormous ball of cord, which was meant to represent a purse containing the stakes. It was carried in silence, hence perhaps the association with English " mum " (see the Despois-Mesnard edition of Molière, Vol. I, p. 188, note 4 to verse 1221 of " L'Étourdi " ; also the note in the L. Moland edition, which gives several interesting cases of the use of this word). Madame Jourdain believes that her husband has put on the costume of the bearer of such a challenge.

78 11 votre : contemptuous. See note to **3** 18.

78 17 paladin : see **70** 17. Jourdain quotes Covielle.

78 18 baladin : note the pun with *paladin* above.

78 23 Mahameta per Giourdina : see **75** 5 ff.

79 20 voici justement le reste de notre écu : once a commercial expression, used probably at the completion of a satisfactory bargain ; it became proverbial, meaning 'this is the last straw (the finishing stroke),' 'this caps the climax,' and was especially used, as here, when undesirable company arrived. Dorimène's return seems strange after her treatment by Madame Jourdain ; hence Dorante's arguments to justify it.

79 28 J'en fais beaucoup de cas : 'I think very highly of him.'

79 29 bonne fortune : i.e. in his love affair, 'good fortune in securing the wife of his wishes.'

80 1 ballet : this is the *Ballet des Nations*, which comes at the end of the fifth act.—**qui nous revient :** 'which is to our advantage' (see Littré's " Dictionnaire," s.v. *revenir*, No. 26).

80 2 **laisser perdre**: we are tempted to see in this construction another case of the omission of the reflexive object of an infinitive after *laisser*. See note to **73** 22.

80 3 **mon idée**: compare the text at **44** 2–5.

80 13 **fût**: we should rather expect *soit*. Compare note to **3** 19.

80 16 **mon bien** etc.: this is a rather grandiloquent speech for a man who is apparently penniless and whose character as a liar and a parasite upon Jourdain is clear. It is Jourdain who pays the bills.

80 24 **révérence à la turque**: a profound bow or salaam, the right hand being extended toward the ground and then brought back toward the lips and thence upon the forehead.

80 25 **la force des serpents** etc.: Jourdain mixes this compliment badly. Compare note to **71** 7.

81 1 **votre rosier fleuri**: another idiotic misquotation. Compare note to **71** 7. See also note to **34** 28.

81 2 **de prendre part** = *de ce que vous prenez part*. Molière preferred the infinitive as more direct. Compare note to **28** 17.

81 4 **pour vous faire**: 'so that I may make to you.' Compare note to **53** 13.

81 18 **Le voilà**: in strict syntax we should expect *la voilà*, since the reference is to *Son Altesse turque*, and *Altesse* is feminine.

81 19 **pour lui donner la main**: 'that she may give him her hand in agreement.' Ambiguity might have been avoided by using the subordinate clause *pour qu'elle lui donne la main*.

81 26 **Strouf, strif**, etc.: nonsensical syllables to represent Jourdain's frantic attempts to talk Turkish.

82 10 **Alabala crociam** etc.: these words of Covielle are the merest nonsense; those of Cléonte, however, are, with the exception of *ourin*, Arabic. The sense of the first portion of Cléonte's speech is essentially that given by Covielle below (line 13), although, if the *a* in *tubal* is long, the meaning has all the vulgarity of Rabelais. The context, and also Molière's fondness for an occasional broad jest, seem to favor this latter assumption.

82 13 **arrouse**: for modern *arrose*, from *arroser*, 'to water.' The form was already archaic in Molière's day, and its use here was clearly intended to heighten the comic effect of the dialogue.

82 15 **Je vous l'avais bien dit**: "did n't I tell you?" (Levi.)

83 1 **qui se peut souhaiter**: *qui peut se souhaiter*. See note to **3** 21. Modern French requires the subjunctive after a superlative, unless what is stated is an absolute, undeniable fact. In the seventeenth century, however, this rule was not completely established (see Haase, " La Syntaxe française du XVIIe siècle," pp. 186–187). We may, therefore, have here a relic of the older usage with the indicative ; or Jourdain may wish to affirm beyond denial what he says, and hence uses the indicative. A third possibility is that Molière wishes to have Jourdain make a grammatical error purposely, just as, inversely (see notes to **24** 31 and **43** 23), he makes Jourdain occasionally use rather elegant language to show off when he is with his teacher or with Dorante.

83 4 **touchez-lui dans la main :** ' give him your hand,' ' take his hand.'

83 8 **Je n'en ferai rien :** see note to **51** 30.

83 18 **voilà qui :** see note to **3** 15.

83 28 **assemblage :** some editors translate this merely ' union ' or ' gathering of persons.' The Despois-Mesnard edition, however (Vol. VIII, p. 204, note 1), shows that Madame Jourdain's tone is one of scorn and anger, and hence that the interpretation should be in the sense of ' strange union ' or ' ridiculous marriage.' This edition also cites several other instances of this use in Molière (see Vol. XII, pp. 86–87 ; see also the Livet edition, p. 277).

84 6 **Je n'ai que faire :** compare note to **66** 18.

84 17 **qui nous fait intéresser dans :** the infinitive here is in theory reflexive, *nous intéresser*. In the seventeenth century, however, the reflexive object pronoun of an infinitive was often omitted when the main verb was *faire, laisser*, etc. See note to **73** 22. Perhaps in this particular instance the *nous* before *fait* made a second *nous* before *intéresser* seem less necessary.

85 7 **Je n'ai que faire :** compare note to **66** 18.

85 20 **Ne faites que m'écouter :** ' only listen to me.'

85 31 **comme cela :** ' if that 's the case.'

85 33 **Ne faites pas semblant de rien :** the *pas* is now redundant ; ' pretend to know nothing of our scheme.'

86 11 **c'est que :** an ellipsis ; the meaning is ' I will tell you.' Some such expression as *je n'ai qu'une chose à vous dire* has been omitted.

86 14 **faire accroire :** ' hoodwink.'

86 19 **Tandis qu'il viendra et qu'il dressera** = *en attendant qu'il vienne* etc. *Tandis que* in this usage is archaic.

86 22 **C'est fort bien avisé :** ' that 's a very good idea.'

86 28 **à Rome :** as if so wonderful a thing should be published at the center of the Christian world.

87 **Ballet des Nations :** this was also incorporated with some changes, in 1672, in " Les Fêtes de l'Amour et de Bacchus," a pastoral opera given by the Académie Royale de Musique. In common with most editions that insert this Ballet at all, the present editor has preferred to follow the earlier version adopted by the Despois-Mesnard edition. It was felt wisest to incorporate the Ballet because of its historic connections with the play, connections fully recognized in all the elaborate revivals in France, which have almost invariably reproduced it.

87 14 **Aho! l'homme aux libres**, etc.: in Gascon dialect. The French equivalent is: 'Hé, l'homme aux livres, qu'on m'en baille (donne). J'ai déjà le poumon usé : Vous voyez que chacun me raille ; Et je suis scandalisé De voir aux mains de la canaille Ce qui m'est par vous refusé.'

88 4 **Eh cadédis**, etc.: in French this would be: 'Hé! parbleu, monsieur, voyez qui l'on peut être! Un livret, je vous prie, au baron d'Asbarat. Je pense, morbleu! que le fat N'a pas l'honneur de me connaître.'

88 8 **Mon'-sieur le donneur de papieir**, etc.: 'Monsieur le donneur de papier, Que veut dire cette façon de vivre ? Quant à moi, je m'écorche tout le gosier À crier Sans que je puisse avoir un livre ; Parbleu, ma foi, monsieur, je pense que vous êtes ivre ! '

88 14 **franc et net**: 'to speak plainly.' Adjectives used adverbially were very common in the seventeenth century.

88 28 **Lantriguet**: according to the best editors, this is the Breton name for Tréguier in Brittany, and is mentioned merely to typify an extremely provincial and petty locality. The prefix *lan* means 'church' or 'cloister.' Tréguier has since become more famous as the birthplace of Ernest Renan. The explanation of O. Schulze in Vol. IV, pp. 78–80, of the *Zeitschrift für französische Sprache und Literatur*, that *Lantriguet* is a misprint for *d'entre le guet*, and that the whole line means 'the watchmen,' is interesting but not convincing.

89 3 **jeteur de vers**: 'wretched poet,' 'rimester.' Scheffler suggests that he threw the librettos out over the heads of the spectators. — **manque au capital**: 'lacks essential qualities.'

89 4 **L'entend fort mal**: 'understands his business very ill.'

89 27 **Bentré ! jé suis à vout**, etc.: 'Ventre ! (i.e. ventrebleu!) je suis à bout. — J'enrage, Dieu me damne ! — Ah ! qu'on a soif dans cette salle-ci ! — Je meurs ! — Je perds la tramontane. — Ma foi ! moi, je voudrais être hors d'ici.'

90 2 **perdre la tramontane**: literally, 'to lose the North Star,' hence 'to be quite bewildered.' *Tramontane* came to mean 'North Star' from the fact that in the Mediterranean the North Star appears beyond the mountains.

90 16 **ni :** here means ' or.'

91 12 **Sé que me muero de amor,** etc. : the translation of this stilted and affected Spanish is as follows : ' I know that I am dying for love, and I seek pain. Though dying of desire, I die with such good grace that all that I suffer is less than that which I am willing to suffer, since no rigor may surpass my desire. I know that I am dying for love, and I seek pain. Fate caresses me with such anxious pity that it assures me of my life in the danger of death. To live after such a blow is the miracle of my health. I know, etc.

Ah ! what madness with such rigor to complain of love, of the fair boy who is all gentleness. Ah ! what madness ! Ah ! what madness !

Grief torments him who gives himself up to grief, and no one dies of love except him who knows not how to love.

Love is a sweet death, when love is returned ; if we rejoice in love to-day, why wishest thou to disturb love ?

Let the lover rejoice and listen to my counsel, for when one loves, all that one needs is to find the way.

Come, come, festivals ! Come, dancing ! Joy, joy, joy ! Grief is only an idle tale.'

93 2 **Di rigori armata il seno,** etc. : ' Having armed my breast with rigor, I revolted against love ; but I was vanquished in a twinkling when I gazed into two beautiful eyes. Ah ! how little a heart of ice resists a shaft of fire !

But my torment is so dear, and my wound is so sweet, that my pain is my happiness and my cure would be tyranny. When love is more intense, how much more does it please and give joy ! '

93 14 **Scaramouches :** a type of buffoon in Italian comedy represented by a Neapolitan adventurer ; despite his boastfulness he was easily frightened. His costume was black. — **Trivelins :** gymnastic buffoons in older Italian comedy, who delighted the spectators by wonderful and dangerous feats of agility.

93 15 **Arlequin :** another kind of gymnastic clown in Italian comedy ; he wore a variegated costume. The Arlequin rôle in " Le Bourgeois gentilhomme " was played by the celebrated Dominique Biancolelli. See the L. Moland edition, p. 131, for an account of his life. — **représentent une nuit :** this was a show, often in pantomime, representing the ordinary events of night, such as observation of the sky, dreams, attacks, scaling of walls, serenades, etc., etc.

93 19 Bel tempo che vola etc. : ' The fair hour that flees away, carries with it pleasure. In the school of love, one learns how to seize the moment. As long as the age of bloom (which, alas, flees so quickly) smiles at us, let us sing, let us rejoice in the fair days of youth, for a lost blessing is nevermore recovered. A beautiful eye which enchains a thousand hearts, makes its wounds sweet, its grief joyful. But when age grown cold pines away, the benumbed soul no longer has any flame. Let us sing, etc.'

95 20 l'assistance : means here the players and spectators on the stage.

VOCABULARY

The heavy figures refer to pages, the light figures to lines. The sign ∞ is used for the word in heavy type at the beginning of the paragraph

à *prep.* to, at, in; by, **10** 17; with, **16** 22; for, **44** 3; toward, **47** 11; *sometimes indicates emphatic possession, as* **nos occupations à vous et à moi 4** 1, our occupations, yours and mine; **songer** ∞ think of; ∞ **la turque** in the Turkish manner. *This preposition had in the 17th century a much larger use than now, having many of the modern functions of* **dans, par, pour, de, avec, sur, envers,** *etc.; it was particularly frequent before the infinitive in cases where now we expect* **en** *with the present participle*

abaisser *v.* lower; **s'**∞ degrade *or* humble oneself

abord *m.* approach, meeting; **d'**∞ *adv.* at once, first

absence *f.* absence

abuser *v.* deceive, mislead

accabler *v.* overwhelm

accepter *v.* accept

accommoder *v.* suit, adapt; **s'**∞ adapt oneself

accompagner *v.* accompany

accord *m.* agreement, harmony; **demeurer d'**∞ agree; **tomber d'**∞ come to an agreement

accorder *v.* grant; **s'**∞ harmonize, become harmonious

accroire *see* faire

accueil *m.* welcome, reception

acheter *v.* purchase

achever *v.* complete, finish

acquérir *v.* acquire; **s'**∞ acquire, gain over; **acquis** gained, won

acquitter *v.* acquit, discharge; **s'**∞ pay one's debts

acte *m.* deed, act

acteur *m.* player, actor

action *f.* action

adieu *m.* farewell; *adv.* good-by, farewell

admirable *adj.* wonderful

admirablement *adv.* wonderfully

adresser *v.* address, direct; **s'**∞ address, speak to

affaire *f.* business, affair, thing; **point d'**∞ not at all, I 'll have nothing to do with you; **belles** ∞**s** fine business, mess

affecter *v.* put on, affect

affilé *adj.* glib, well-hung, sharp (*of the tongue*)

affront *m.* insult, affront

afin : ∞ **de** *prep.* (*with infinitive*) to, in order to; ∞ **que** *conj.* (*with subjunctive*) that, in order that

âge *m.* age ; **en ∾** of an age

agir *v.* act

agiter *v.* move, stir

agréable *adj.* pleasant, charming

aider *v.* help

aile *f.* wing

ailleurs *adv.* elsewhere

aimable *adj.* lovable, lovely

aimer *v.* love ; **∾ mieux** prefer ; **j'ai-merais mieux mourir** I 'd rather die

ainsi *adv.* thus

air *m.* air, wind, appearance, melody, tune ; **d'un ∾** in such a way that ; **bon ∾** stylish appearance ; **homme du bel ∾** man of fashion, fop, dandy, dude ; **∾ à boire** drinking song

aise *adj.* glad, happy

aise *f.* ease, joy, leisure

aisé *adj.* of easy carriage, graceful, supple

aisément *adv.* easily

ajuster *v.* arrange, compose, prepare ; rig out, **72** 7 ; **s'∾** adjust oneself, conform, humor, **85** 25

alarme *f.* anxiety, uneasiness

Alcoran *m.* the Koran, sacred book of the Mohammedan faith

aller *v.* go ; fit, become *or* suit (*of clothing*) ; *often of mere auxiliary force suggesting an immediate future, as* **vous l'allez entendre** you shall hear it ; **∾ mieux 7** 22, be better ; **allons ! come ! allez ! begone ! allez** *in* **66** 26 *is an expression of anger, a vigorous* what ! **s'en ∾** go away ; **allez-vous-en 28** 23, keep on, continue ; *Molière uses* **s'en aller** *with an infinitive where now* **aller** *is used*

alliance *f.* match, marriage

allonger *v.* lengthen, extend

allumé *adj.* lighted

almanach *m.* almanac

alors *adv.* then

alternativement *adv.* alternately

amadouer *v.* coax, cajole, flatter, appease, tame

amande *f.* almond

amant *m.* lover

amasser *v.* amass

ambassade *f.* embassy

ambassadrice *f.* messenger, ambassadress

âme *f.* soul ; **ma chère ∾** my beloved

amener *v.* bring

ami *m.* friend

amitié *f.* friendship, love

amour *usually f. in Molière's day* (*see Livet's " Lexique de la langue de Molière," Vol. I, p. 105*), love, love affair

amoureux -euse *adj.* loving, in love ; **l'∾ empire** the empire of love ; **l'amoureuse loi** the law of love

amoureux *m.* lover

amuser *v.* amuse, trifle with, deceive, put off with idle promises, waste one's time

an *m.* year

ancien -enne *adj.* former, ancient

animal *m.* (*pl.* **animaux**) animal, creature, fool

année *f.* year

annoncer *v.* announce

anoblir *v.* confer nobility upon

apaiser *v.* appease

apercevoir *v.* see, perceive ; **s'∾** perceive, become aware of

appeler v. call; **s'∽** be named, be called; in **appelez-moi 30 5, moi** is ethical dative

applaudir v. applaud

applaudissement m. applause, approbation

appliquer v. apply

apporter v. bring

apprendre v. teach, tell, learn

apprêt m. preparation

approbation f. approval

approche f. approach

approcher v. bring together; **s'∽ de** come near to

appuyer v. lean; press, **23** 21; help, support, **79** 26

après prep. after; adv. afterwards; **∽ que** conj. after

après-dînée f. the time after dinner, afternoon or evening; now usually **après-dîner**

arc-en-ciel m. rainbow

ardent adj. loving

ardeur f. passion

argent m. money

armé adj. fortified, armed

armée f. army

armes f. pl. arms, military service; **maître d'∽** fencing master; science **des ∽** art of swordsmanship

arracher v. pull off

arranger v. arrange

arrêter v. stop, engage, hire; **s'∽** stop

arrière m. back part; **en ∽** adv. back, backwards

arriver v. come, happen

arrogance f. haughtiness

art m. art

article m. item, article

articulation f. articulation

artifice m. craft, artifice; **feu d'∽** fireworks

assaisonner v. season, flavor

assemblage m. union, number; symphony, **3** 3 (speaking of musical instruments)

assembler v. put together, construct

asseoir v. seat; **s'∽** sit down

assez adv. enough, quite

assidu adj. unceasing, assiduous

assistance f. audience

assistant m. aid, assistant

assorti adj. selected, harmonious, matching, proper

assuré adj. bold, courageous

assurément adv. surely

assurer v. make certain, assure

attachement m. affection, inclination

attendre v. wait, await, wait for, expect; **s'∽ à** expect, wait for

attirail m. parade, procession, crowd, mob; peculiar to Molière in its application to persons

attitude f. posture, pose

attrait m. charm, attraction

attrayant adj. attractive, alluring, enticing, winsome

au contraction of **à + le** (the article)

aucun -e adj., pron. any; **ne . . . ∽** no, none, not any, no one, nobody

audace f. boldness, audacity

au-dessus de prep. above, superior to

aujourd'hui m., adv. to-day, now

auparavant adv. first, beforehand

auprès de prep. near, with

aussi adv., conj. besides, also, too; **∽ . . . que** as . . . as

aussitôt *adv.* immediately; ∾ **que** *conj.* as soon as

autant *adv.* as much, as many

autoriser *v.* authorize

autour de *prep.* around, about

autre *adj.*, *pron.* other; ∾ **chose** anything else; l'une et l'∾ both of you; d'∾ **sorte** otherwise; ∾s **59** 7, other things; **autres** *sometimes emphasizes a plural subject pronoun, as in* **28** 7

autrefois *adv.* formerly

aux *contraction of* à + **les** (*the article*)

avancer *v.* come forward, advance; **avancez!** forward! (*in fencing, an order to step forward with the right foot when thrusting*)

avant *adv.*, *prep.* before, ahead; en ∾ forward; ∾ **que de** *prep.* (*with infinitive*) before, *equivalent to* **avant de** *in modern French*; ∾ **que** *conj.* (*with subjunctive*) before; ∾ **qu'il soit (fût) peu** before long

avantage *m.* advantage

avantageux -euse *adj.* advantageous

avec *prep.* with, in addition to

aventure *f.* chance, adventure, hazard, coincidence, incident

aveugler *v.* blind

avis *m.* opinion

avisé *adj.* thought out, advised

aviser *v.* apprise, advise; s'∾ venture, presume, take into one's head

avoir *v.* have, obtain, get; il y a there is, there are; *in expressions of time* il y a *means* ago; **qu'y a-t-il?** what's the matter? ∾ **besoin de** need; ∾ **raison** be right; ∾ **soin** be careful; ∾ **honte** be ashamed; ∾ **peur** be afraid; **auraient à souhaiter 4** 7, ought to wish; ∾ **à faire à** have dealings with; **qu'avez-vous?** what's the matter with you? ∾ **beau faire, dire, donner,** *etc.*, do, say, give, *etc.*, in vain

avouer *v.* confess, declare

babillard *adj.* chattering

bagatelle *f.* trifle; *as exclamation,* nonsense!

bailler *v.* give, give blows, strike; *obsolescent and somewhat inelegant in Molière's time*

bâiller *v.* yawn

baiser *v.* kiss; ∾ **les mains** decline with thanks

baisser *v.* lower; se ∾ bend down

baladin *m.* professional dancer in a theater (*but not necessarily in an unfavorable sense*), mountebank

ballet *m.* ballet, a dance of elegance and dignity

banc *m.* seat

banquet *m.* banquet

barbarie *f.* rudeness, coarseness, barbarity

barbarisme *m.* offense. *See* **incongruité**

bas, basse *adj.* low, base; *adv.* (*as stage direction*) in a low tone; d'en ∾ lower

bas *m.* bottom

bas *m.* stocking; ∾ **de soie** silk stocking; *only people of rank and wealth were permitted to wear silk stockings, wool being the ordinary material*

basse *f.* bass voice, bass notes

bassesse *f.* vulgarity; low social station

baste *interj.* (*from Italian* **basta** enough, stop!) enough of that! zounds!

bastonara *f.* beating

bâti *adj.* rigged out, **30** 14; fitted, **47** 22; **bien** ∽ well shaped; **mal** ∽ ill shaped, ugly

bâton *m.* stick

bâtonner *v.* beat

battement *m.* stamping, thumping (*of the right foot in fencing*)

battre *v.* beat; **se** ∽ fight

beau, bel, belle *adj.* beautiful, fine, decent; **tout beau** gently, steady! **avoir beau faire, dire, donner,** *etc.*, do, say, give, *etc.*, in vain

beaucoup *adv.* much, many, a great deal

beau-père *m.* father-in-law

beauté *f.* beauty

beaux-arts *m. pl.* fine arts

bélître *m.* beggarly fellow, good-for-nothing, rascal; ∽ **de pédant** beggarly pedant, "pedantic blockhead"

belle *f.* beautiful woman, beauty

berger *m.* shepherd

bergère *f.* shepherdess

besogne *f.* work, business

besoin *m.* need; **avoir** ∽ **de** have need of, need

bête *f.* beast; stupid person, fool, **34** 7

bévue *f.* blunder

biais *m.* method, direction, way, bias

biau *dialectic form for* **beau** *adj.* fine, *Moriarty's edition suggests*

the translation "foine." *Compare* **carriaux**

bien *adv.* indeed, well, very; much, many; all right, **27** 15; on good terms, **43** 15; **eh** ∽ well! **je voudrais** ∽ I should really like; **ou** ∽ or else; **il faut** ∽ it is quite necessary; **savez-vous** ∽ do you happen to know? **Bien** *often adds an idiomatic touch of emphasis which it is difficult to render*

bien *m.* good, good fortune, happiness, **59** 24; welfare, substance; wealth, *especially when plural*

bilieux -euse *adj.* passionate, choleric, ill-tempered

billet *m.* note

bis (*sound the* **s**) *adv.* twice, repeated

blanc, blanche *adj.* white, tender, bleached

blesser *v.* wound

bocage *m.* grove

boire *v.* drink; **pour** ∽ as a tip; **air à** ∽ drinking song

bois *m.* forest

bon, bonne *adj.* good; ∽ **bourgeois** well-to-do tradesman, worthy fellow; **bonne bourgeoisie** plain bourgeoisie, the citizen class

bonheur *m.* happiness

bonnet *m.* cap; ∽ **de nuit** nightcap

bonté *f.* kindness

botte *f.* thrust; **pousser** *or* **porter la** ∽ lunge, thrust

bouche *f.* mouth, (*in poetry*) lips

boue *f.* mud

bouger *v.* stir, move; **pas** *is often omitted with the negative of* **bouger** *as with* **pouvoir, savoir, oser, cesser**

bougie *f.* wax candle

bouillon *m.* bubble, broth, soup

bouquet *m.* nosegay, bouquet

bourgeois *m.* citizen, tradesman, commoner, *belonging to the middle class of French society. Often it refers directly to M. Jourdain*

bourgeoisie *f.* middle class (*of French society*), trading *or* merchant class

bourle *f.* (*from Italian* burla jest, *whence also* burlesque) hoax, farce, practical joke

bourreau *m.* hangman, executioner

bourse *f.* purse

bout *m.* end, tip; être à ∽ to be exhausted; en venir à ∽ to succeed

bras *m.* arm

brigantina *f.* brigantine sail; brigantine, *a small ship in use in the Mediterranean*

brillant *adj.* bright, brilliant, sparkling

broche *f.* spit (*for roasting meat*)

brouillamini *m.* (*probably related to* brouiller mix) confusion, uproar, disorder, *especially of sounds*; "higgledy-piggledy"

bruit *m.* noise; que de ∽ what a racket!

brûler *v.* burn, be eager

brusquement *adv.* quickly, abruptly

brutal *m.* vulgar person

burlesque *adj.* ludicrous, ridiculous

but *m.* aim, purpose

c' *see* ce *pron.*

çà *interj.* here! come now!

cadeau *m.* pleasure party; *see note to* **42** 10

cadence *f.* time (*in dancing*); en ∽ in time, keep time!

camisole *f.* jacket, waistcoat, *the garment now called* gilet; *a short jersey or doublet with sleeves, worn over or under the shirt*

campagne *f.* country (*as distinct from city*), campaign; en ∽ under way

canaille *f.* common crowd

cantonné *adj.* quartered (*a term of heraldry*); at the four corners, flanked, covered, **63** 4

capable *adj.* capable

capacité *f.* ability

capital *m.* essential, main thing; manquer au ∽ forget the important thing

capricieux -euse *adj.* full of caprice

caquet *m.* cackle (*figurative for* tongue), gossip, chatter, scandal; ∽ bien affilé very glib *or* sharp tongue

car *conj.* because, for

carême-prenant *m.* Shrovetide, Mardi gras, carnival time, *the three days preceding Ash Wednesday, especially Tuesday*; masquerader, masker, clown

caresse *f.* favor, kindness

caresser *v.* receive appreciatively, make much of

carré *m.* breast (*of mutton*)

carriaux *dialectic form for* **carreaux** *m. pl.* floor tiles. *Compare* biau

carrosse *m.* coach

cas *m.* case, circumstance; en tous cas in any event; faire ∽ esteem

cause *f.* reason, cause

causer *v.* cause, talk, chatter

ce, c' *pron.* (*with the verb* être) it;
c'est, ce sont it is, they are; c'est
là 8 33, that is; c'est que the fact
is; ce *is frequently the grammatical subject of* être, *and the real or
logical subject follows a* que *later
in the sentence, as in* 4 4, 4 17, 4 27,
*etc.; in translating it is smoother
to begin with the logical subject* (*see
note to* 4 4); ∞ que (*object*), ∞ qui
(*subject*) what, something which;
∞ que c'est what it is; tout ∞ que
all that; de ∞ que 85 1, because

ce, cet, cette, ces *adj.* this, these,
that, those

céans *adv.* here within, in this
house *or* place; *a word already
obsolescent in Molière's time and
used only by old people and the
lower classes*

ceci *pron.* this

céder *v.* yield

cela *pron.* that, this

celui, celle, ceux, celles *pron.* the
one *or* ones, this, that, these,
those

cendre *f.* ashes

cent *adj.* hundred

cent *m.* a hundred

cependant *adv.* yet, nevertheless

cérémonie *f.* ceremony

certain *adj.* certain; *before nouns
it is rather indefinite, after nouns
it is absolute in the sense of real
certainty*

ces *see* ce *adj.*

cet, cette *see* ce *adj.*

chagrin *m.* grief, trouble, concern,
affliction, vexation, worry

chaleur *f.* heat

chambre *f.* bedchamber; robe de
∞ dressing gown

changement *m.* change

changer *v. tr.* change; ∞ de *intr.*
change

chanson *f.* song; ∞s! nonsense!
∞ à boire drinking song

chant *m.* song, singing

chanter *v.* sing; *in* 21 22 *familiarly
for* say *or* teach

chanteur *m.* public singer, street
singer, "ballad monger"

chaos *m.* confusion, chaos

chapeau *m.* hat

chapitre *m.* chapter, subject, text,
question

chaque *adj.* each, every

charge *f.* position, office

charger *v.* load, intrust; ∞ de coups
belabor

charité *f.* charity, goodness

charmant *adj.* delightful

charme *m.* charm, attraction

chasser *v.* hunt, dismiss, drive
away

châtiment *m.* punishment, chastise-
ment

chatouillant *adj.* tickling, flattering,
delightful

chatouiller *v.* tickle, delight, please

chef-d'œuvre *m.* masterpiece

chemin *m.* road, way

chêne *m.* oak

cher, chère *adj.* dear

chercher *v.* seek, fetch

chère *f.* cheer (*of provisions for a
feast*), fare

chérir *v.* love tenderly, cherish

cheval *m.* (*pl.* chevaux) horse

chèvre *f.* goat

chez *prep.* with, at one's house, home, *or* place of business; **de ∽ lui** of his house

chicorée *f.* chicory, endive

chien *m.* dog

chimère *f.* extravagant fancy, whim

choisir *v.* choose

chose *f.* thing, matter, affair; *in* **autre ∽** anything else, something else, *it is masculine because used vaguely as a sort of pronoun*

-ci *adv.* here; *added to nouns preceded by demonstrative adjectives it gives the latter the distinct meaning* this; **par∽ par-là** here and there

ciel *m.* heaven

cimeterre *m.* scimitar

cinq *adj.* five

civil *adj.* polite, engaging

civilité *f.* good breeding, courtesy

clair *adj.* clear; *adv.* clearly

clairement *adv.* clearly

Climène *f. conventional name for a woman who is beloved. Molière uses the name about a dozen times in his plays. It is usually applied to a shepherdess*

cœur *m.* heart, courage, pluck; **de très grand ∽** very heartily

cohue *f.* throng, noisy crowd

coiffé *adj.* with the head covered, having the hair dressed

coiffer *v.* dress the hair; **se ∽** cover one's head

coin *m.* corner

colère *f.* anger, wrath; **se mettre en ∽** get angry

collège *m.* school, boarding school, college

collet *m.* neckband, turndown collar, ruff; *in the more fashionable shapes it came down over the shoulders*

combien *adv.* how much, how many

comédie *f.* comedy, play

comédie-ballet *f.* a comedy interspersed with dancing and music

comète *f.* comet

commandant *adj.* dominant, strong, commanding

commandement *m.* command

commander *v.* command, order, dominate; *with direct object of the thing commanded and indirect object of the person ordered, as in* **12** 24

comme *adv.* as, like; (*for modern* **comment**) how, **14** 21, **66** 1, *etc.;* as it were, **22** 31; such as, **4** 4; **∽ il faut**, proper, fashionable, *or adverbially*, in proper, fine, *or* fashionable style; *conj.* when, **69** 25

commencement *m.* beginning, rudiment

commencer *v.* begin

comment *adv.* how, what do you mean; why, **37** 24; **∽ cela? ∽ donc?** how is that?

commerce *m.* acquaintance, friendly relations; *see notes to* **43** 9, **50** 26

commettre *v.* commit

commission *f.* errand

compagnie *f.* company

comparer *v.* compare

compliment *m.* compliment

composer *v.* write, compose, form, arrange

composition *f.* composition

comprendre *v.* understand, appreciate; include, class, **18** 31

compte *m.* account

compter *v.* account

comte *m.* count (*a title of nobility*)

concevoir *v.* conceive

conclure *v.* be conclusive, prove, conclude; ne conclut rien proves nothing, is no precedent

condition *f.* social rank, station, profession, quality

conduire *v.* manage

conduite *f.* behavior

confidence *f.* confidence; faire (une) ∽ tell a secret

confondre *v.* confuse, overwhelm, confound

confus *adj.* embarrassed

confusion *f.* tumult, embarrassment

conjurer *v.* entreat, conjure

connaissance *f.* knowledge

connaître *v.* know, be acquainted with, recognize; de nous faire ∽ to make ourselves known; se ∽ aux choses have knowledge of things, be a judge *or* connoisseur; se ∽ en étoffes be acquainted with, *or* a good judge of, stuffs (fabrics)

consentir *v.* agree to, consent

conséquence *f.* logical conclusion

conserver *v.* keep, maintain, treasure up

considération *f.* esteem, importance

considérer *v.* have consideration for, esteem, consider

consister *v.* comprise, consist of

consonne *f.* consonant

constance *f.* fidelity, constancy

content *adj.* satisfied

conter *v.* tell; humbug (*with an untruth*)

continu *adj.* sustained, continued

continuel -elle *adj.* continual

continuer *v.* keep up, continue

contorsion *f.* writhing, contortion

contrat *m.* contract

contre *prep.* against; se mettre en colère ∽ vous get angry with you

contre-sens *m.* wrong meaning; à ∽ at the wrong time

conversation *f.* conversation

convier *v.* invite

coquin *m.* rascal, scamp

coquine *f.* hussy, wench

corps *m.* body, matter

côte *f.* rib, side

côté *m.* side, direction, way; de ce ∽ in this direction, on this side; de ∽ et d'autre on both sides; de tous les ∽s on all sides

coup *m.* blow, stroke, shot, deed, trial, trick

cour *f.* court

courage *m.* courage, heart

courir *v.* run, hasten

couronné *adj.* crowned

cours *m.* course

coûter *v.* cost, be hard, difficult

couvrir *v.* cover; se ∽ put on one's hat

crever *v.* burst, die

crier *v.* shout, cry

croire *v.* believe

croquer *v.* be crisp, crackle

crotter *v.* cover with mud *or* dirt

croûte *f.* crust

cruel -elle *adj.* cruel; *m. f.* cruel one

cuisine *f.* kitchen

cuisinier *m.* cook, caterer

cuisse *f.* thigh

cuistre *m.* college servant, clown-ish *or* vulgar pedant, snob

curieux -euse *adj.* curious

curiosité *f.* peculiar thing, curiosity

d'abord *adv.* first, at once

dadais *m.* booby, ninny, awkward simpleton, donkey

dame *f.* lady

Damis (s *silent*) *m.* an imaginary name for a typical epicure or bon vivant

damner *v.* damn

dans *prep.* in, within, into; *often used for modern* à

danse *f.* dance, dancing

danser *v.* dance. *See note to* **28** 9

danseur *m.* dancer

davantage *adv.* more; ∽ que more than (= *modern* plus que)

de *prep.* of, out of, with, about, from; as, **37** 6; by, **67** 16; in, *as* ∽ ce côté **3** 11, in this direction, on this side, *and after superlative expressions, as in* **8** 15; to, *as* le chemin ∽ son cœur **43** 24, les approcher l'une ∽ l'autre, que dites-vous ∽ mes livrées ? on, *as* se repaître ∽ gloire **4** 16; for, *as* recevoir ∽s choses **4** 24, paye ∽ toutes nos fatigues, fâché ∽s coups, la demande ∽ ma fille ; concerning, **18** 3, *where it is used for* sur ; ∽ cette façon thus ; ∽ ce que **85** 1, because; *sometimes untranslatable, as* quelque chose ∽ nouveau **3** 16, deux mailles ∽ rompues **26** 18, *and in partitive*

constructions, as par ∽ chatouil-lantes approbations **4** 22. *As is seen by these examples,* de, *like* à, *had a larger use than it now has*

débiteur *m.* debtor

debout *adv.* standing

déchirer *v.* tear up

déclaration *f.* declaration

découvrir *v.* discover

décrépit *adj.* broken-down

dedans *adv.* therein ; inside ; in it, **8** 4; *compare* là-∽ ; en ∽ inwards, *i.e.* " in tierce," **16** 7 (*see notes to* **15** 13, **15** 18)

défaut *m.* defect, fault

défendre *v.* protect, defend, forbid

défier *v.* challenge

dégoûté *adj.* fastidious, hard to please

dégoûter *v.* disgust

degré *m.* stage, degree

déguisement *m.* disguise

déguiser *v.* hide, disguise, distort, change the nature of

dehors *adv.* out; en ∽ outside, out-wards, *i.e.* " in quart," **16** 7

déjà *adv.* already

délicat *adj.* delicate, delicious, re-fined, dainty

délicatesse *f.* subtlety, nicety, deli-cacy

demain *adv.* to-morrow

demande *f.* question, proposal ; for-mal request for a lady's hand in marriage, *made then, as some-times now in rural districts, by a friend or relative of the suitor,* **53** 12; belle ∽ what a question to ask !

demander *v.* ask, ask for

démanger *v.* itch

démarche *f.* step

démesuré *adj.* enormous, exceedingly great

demeurer *v.* dwell, remain ; ∽ d'accord agree

démonstratif -ive *adj.* conclusive ; raison démonstrative logical *or* conclusive reasoning

démonstration *f.* proof

denier *m. a small copper coin ; formerly of silver, and, still earlier, of gold ; in Molière's time twelve deniers equaled a* sol (sou)

dent *f.* tooth

dépêcher *v.* hasten, dispatch ; se ∽ hurry

dépendre *v.* depend, be dependent

dépense *f.* expenditure

dépenser *v.* spend

dépit *m.* spite, anger ; en ∽ de in spite of

déplaire *v.* displease ; sans vous ∽ may it not displease you, " if you will excuse my saying so "

depuis *prep.* from, since ; ∽ peu a short time ago ; ∽ quatre jours four days ago ; *sometimes used before infinitives for modern* après, *as in* 68 28 ; ∽ que *conj.* since (*of time*)

déraciner *v.* uproot, loosen, pull up

dernier -ère *adj.* latter, last

dérobé *adj.* stolen

derrière *adv., prep.* behind ; par ∽ behind

derviche *m.* dervish, a monk of the Moslem faith

des (*contraction of* de *and the plural article* les) of the, some ; *often untranslatable*

dès *prep.* (*of time*) from . . . on ; ∽ le matin since morning ; ∽ aujourd'hui from to-day

descendre *v.* descend, be descended

déshabillé *m.* suit for house wear

déshonorer *v.* dishonor

désir *m.* desire

désordre *m.* disorder, discord

dessein *m.* plan

dessous *adv.* under

dessus *adv.* on it, on them, thereon ; la lèvre de ∽ the upper lip ; *prep.* on, above

dessus *m.* treble, soprano, *or* tenor voice ; ∽ de violon first violin

détestable *adj.* detestable

détour *m.* deviation, evasion, "beating about the bush "

détourner *v.* turn aside

deux *adj.* two ; tous ∽ both together ; nous dire . . . à tous ∽ to say to both of us ; ∽ à ∽ two by two

deuxième *adj.* second

devant *adv.* before ; par ∽ in front ; *prep.* in the presence of, in front of

deviner *v.* guess ; ∽ l'enclouure guess where the shoe pinches

devoir *v.* owe, ought, must, be one's duty to, have to ; *often it merely has a future meaning, as* qui doit commencer ce matin, who is to begin this morning

devoir *m.* duty, respect ; rendre nos ∽s pay our respects

diable *m.* devil; **au ∾ l'impertinent** the devil take the insolent fellow

dialogue *m.* duet (*now obsolete in this meaning*), dialogue

diamant *m.* diamond

diantre *m.* devil, deuce; *euphemistic for* **diable**

dicton *m.* popular saying, gallant expression

Dieu *m.* God; **mon ∾** heavens!

différent *adj.* various, different

digne *adj.* worthy

dignité *f.* dignity, distinction, high rank

dindon *m.* turkey

dîner *v.* dine

dire *v.* say, speak about, tell, recite; **vouloir ∾** mean, signify; **ainsi dites** so called; **dire** *was often used in Molière's time where we now expect* **parler,** *as* **vous n'avez qu'à ∾ 27** 18

discernement *m.* insight, good judgment

discourir *v.* discourse

discours *m.* talk, remark, speech, words

disposer *v.* dispose

disputer *v.* quarrel

dissension *f.* discord

distinguer *v.* distinguish, differentiate

distrait *adj.* absent-minded

divers *adj.* various, different

divertissement *m.* diversion, festivity, entertainment of which plays, music, and dancing were features

diviser *v.* divide

dix-huit *adj.* eighteen

docte *adj.* scholarly, learned

doigt *m.* finger; a small quantity (*of wine; compare the English* "*thimbleful.*" *It probably meant a small glass*)

donc *adv., conj.* then, therefore

donner *v.* give, strike, place, touch; **∾ la main à** aid, help; **∾ à rire** give cause for laughter; **se ∾ pour** pass oneself off for; **∾ leçon** *in* **15** 2 *is equivalent to* **∾ la leçon;** **faire ∾ le fouet 33** 30, get a whipping

donneur *m.* giver

dont *pron.* whose, of whom, of which; in which, **25** 14; by which, **12** 19; from which, **58** 17. *This word had then a larger and freer use than now*

doré *adj.* golden

dos *m.* back

doucement *adv.* gently

douceur *f.* comfort, sweetness

douleur *f.* grief

doute *m.* doubt; **sans ∾** certainly

douter *v.* (*takes* **de** *before its object*) doubt; **se ∾** suspect

doux, douce *adj.* sweet, gentle, soft, fine; **tout ∾** gently!

douze *adj.* twelve

drap *m.* cloth

dresser *v.* straighten, hold erect (*for* **redresser**); draw up

droit *adj.* right, erect, straight

droit *m.* right

drôle *adj.* queer, funny

drôlerie *f.* nonsense, tomfoolery, drollery, funny "thingumbob," **5** 27 du (*contraction of* de + le *the article*) of the, some; *often untranslatable*

duchesse *f.* duchess

dupe *f.* dupe, a person easily deceived

eau *f.* water

ébaubi *adj.* amazed, speechless

éblouir *v.* dazzle

ébranler *v.* shake

écarté *adj.* apart

écarter *v.* spread apart, open, distend, put aside

écho *m.* echo

éclair *m.* lightning, lightning flash

éclaircir *v.* clear up, explain, enlighten

éclairé *adj.* enlightened, cultured, intelligent

éclat *m.* brightness, outburst, exposure, publicity, scandal

éclatant *adj.* striking

éclater *v.* shine forth, burst forth, sparkle

écolier *m.* pupil, student

écorcher *v.* rub the skin off, flay

écouter *v.* listen

écrire *v.* write

écu *m.* crown (*a coin*)

effacé *adj.* out of the way, not exposed

effet *m.* effect; **fera plus d'∾** encore will be still more effective; **faire son ∾** be successful, effective

effronterie *f.* boldness, impudence

effroyable *adj.* frightful

égal *adj.* equal; **rien d'∾** anything equal

élargir *v.* widen; **s'∾** enlarge, make bigger, stretch

élégance *f.* elegance

élément *m.* element

élève *m. f.* pupil, scholar

elle *pron.* (*as conjunctive*) she, it; (*as disjunctive*) she, her, it

éloigner *v.* send off; **s'∾ de** deviate from, be averse to

embarras *m.* perplexity, mix-up

embarrasser *v.* inconvenience, embarrass; **s'∾** perplex *or* busy oneself

embéguiner *v.* infatuate; **s'∾** become infatuated *or* smitten

embellir *v.* make more beautiful, embellish

emmener *v.* lead away, bring, take along

émouvoir *v.* move, excite; **s'∾** become excited

empêcher *v.* prevent, avoid, help; **s'∾** help it

empire *m.* sway, control; **l'amoureux ∾** the sway of love

emporter *v.* carry away; **l'∾ sur** be superior to, far surpass; **s'∾** get angry

empressement *m.* eagerness, earnestness, anxiety

emprunt *m.* loan, the act of borrowing

emprunter *v.* borrow

en *pron.* any, one, some of it, of them, its, for it, therefrom; therewith, *as* **j'∾ demeure d'accord**; *it sometimes refers to a very indefinite antecedent or even to none at all, as in* **17** 27, **52** 29, **58** 30. *In modern use* en *very* *rarely refers to persons, but in Molière's time it was often so used, as in* dis m'∽ **47** 17, *about her*

en *prep.* in, on, into; *with present participles*, while; *usually the subject of the participle is the same as that of the main verb, but occasionally not, as* ∽ la voyant **47** 30, *when one sees it*; ∽ tête *in one's head*; ∽ bergers *like shepherds*; ∽ Turc *dressed like a Turk*; ∽ hommes *like men*; mâchoire d'∽ bas *lower jaw*; mâchoire d'∽ haut *upper jaw*. **En** *is often used for modern* à

encens *m.* praise, flattery, incense

encore *adv.* in addition, also, yet, still, again, more; *with the indefinite article*, another; mettez ∽ add; ∽ une fois once more

endormir *v.* put to sleep, lull

endroit *m.* place

enfant *m. f.* child

enfin *adv.* finally, at last, in short, "once for all"

enflammer *v.* inflame

enflé *adj.* swollen

engageant *adj.* winning, prepossessing, attractive, engaging

engager *v.* engage; s'∽ oblige, bind, *or* compromise oneself

enharnacher *v.* deck, rig out; se faire ∽ make a guy *or* fool of oneself by dressing ridiculously

enivrer (*note that* en *is here nasal*) *v.* intoxicate; s'∽ become intoxicated

enjôler *v.* wheedle, decoy, fool; *related to English "enjail," and used first of caged birds which attract others to a like fate*

enjôleur *or* **enjôleux** (*the latter being the popular and careless pronunciation of words in* -eur, *especially at the end of a phrase*) *m.* cajoler, wheedler, humbug, sponge, parasite

enjouement *m.* merriment, liveliness, joviality

ennemi (*note that* en *is not nasal here*) *m.* enemy

enrager *v.* be indignant, enraged, mad

enseigner *v.* teach

ensemble *adv.* together

ensuite *adv.* next

entendre *v.* hear, understand

enthousiasme *m.* emphasis, power

entier -ère *adj.* complete

entièrement *adv.* completely, entirely

entre *prep.* between, among; d'∽ eux of them

entre-baiser : s'∽ *v.* kiss each other

entrée *f.* entrance

entreprendre *v.* undertake

entrer *v.* enter; *note that* dans (*or another preposition*) *is commonly used to give the complete equivalent of* enter; *see also* ∽ sous l'amoureuse loi **11** 4

entretenir *v.* support; s'∽ converse

entr'ouvrir *v.* open a little, open halfway

envie *f.* desire, envy

envieux -euse *adj.* jealous, envious

envoyer *v.* send; ∽ **promener** give walking papers to, get rid of by sending away; ∽ **quérir** send for

épanoui *adj.* expansive, uncontrolled, boisterous, blossoming, full-blown

épaule *f.* shoulder

épée *f.* sword

épouser *v.* marry

épouvantable *adj.* frightful

épouvanter *v.* frighten

équipage *m.* costume, outfit, train, retinue, equipage

équipé *adj.* rigged out; *a popular expression for* habillé

érudition *f.* learning

escogriffe *m.* tall ugly good-for-nothing, lout, lubber, clown, monster, hulk

Espagnol -e *m. f.* Spaniard

esprit *m.* mind, intelligence, brains, wit

essai *m.* trial, attempt

essuyer *v.* wipe; endure (*new in this meaning in the 17th century*)

estime *f.* esteem

estimer *v.* esteem

estropié *adj.* crippled; *in* 14 16 *apparently equivalent to* awkward, *as if hanging loosely*

estropier *v.* maim, cripple

et *conj.* and; *in Molière's time often used before relative pronouns where now it is not admissible, as in* 79 26

état *m.* state, nation, country

étendre *v.* extend, stretch, amplify, develop, spread

éternel -elle *adj.* eternal

étoffe *f.* goods, material, cloth

étonné *adj.* amazed, astonished

étouffer *v.* strangle, choke

étrange *adj.* strange, peculiar, indescribable, extraordinary

étrangler *v.* strangle

être *v.* be; *as an auxiliary verb it is used to form the compound tenses of passive verbs, intransitive verbs of motion, as* aller, venir, partir, *etc., and reflexive verbs;* est-ce que *introduces a question;* qu'est-ce que c'est que? *what is?* soit agreed, all right; ∽ à belong to; c'est que *the fact is;* c'est-à-dire *that is to say;* ce l'est *in* 49 17 *is equivalent to* c'est cela it is so; je le fus voir 69 18, I went to see him

étriller *v.* thrash, beat (*literally,* curry)

étroit *adj.* close, tight-fitting, narrow

étudier *v.* study; ∽ dans = *modern* étudier

eux *pron. pl. m.* (*disjunctive*) them, they

éveillé *adj.* awake

éviter *v.* avoid

exact *adj.* precise, accurate, exact

exagérer *v.* boast, amplify, praise to excess, emphasize, exaggerate

excellence *f.* excellence

excuse *f.* excuse; faire ∽s ask pardon, make excuses

excuser *v.* pardon

exécuter *v.* carry out, perform

exécution *f.* carrying out, execution

exemple *m.* example; par ∽ for instance

exercer *v.* practice

exercice *m.* drill, exercise

expérience *f.* experiment, trial, experience

expliquer *v.* explain

exposer *v.* expose

exprimer *v.* express

exquis *adj.* delightful, exquisite

extravagance *f.* foolish *or* extravagant conduct

extravagant *m.* mad *or* foolish person

extrémité *f.* extremity

fable *f.* fable

fâché *adj.* sorry, vexed

fâcheux -euse *adj.* annoying, painful, deplorable, vexatious, cruel

facilement *adv.* readily, easily

façon *f.* way, manner, preparation, fuss; **de la belle ∽** in proper fashion; **de ∽ que** so that, in such a way that; **∽ de vivre** conduct

fagoter *v.* bundle up, dress up frightfully like a scarecrow

faiblesse *f.* weakness

faillir *v.* miss, fail; *this verb is now less used than in Molière's day*

faire *v.* do, act, make, arrange, cause; **∽ vivre** give a livelihood, *but in* 10 26, give life to; **∽ voir** show; **∽ paraître** show; **vous ∽ entendre** let you (have you) hear; *often used as an auxiliary verb to express the idea of making another person do something, as* **que je lui ai fait composer** which I had him compose; *often repeats a previous verb, like* do *in English, a usage very common in 17th-century French, as in* 4 10, 8 19, 28 11; form, be, 45 24; **se ∽** 84 29, take place; **se fait** 3 3, is played; **il s'est fait** 56 23, there was played (made); **s'en puisse ∽** can be made; **∽ une confidence** tell a secret; **∽ accroire** hoodwink; **faire** *is often used without an object of the thing done, as in* 14 32, 15 4; **avoir à ∽ à** (= **avoir affaire à**) have dealings with; *of weather conditions, as* **qu'il fait beau!** how beautiful the weather is! *or* what fine weather! *in many other idiomatic expressions which have been explained in the notes*

fait *adj.* settled, finished, over with; dressed, **37** 29; **bien ∽** well-built, well-formed, healthy, good-looking, of importance; **tout à ∽** very, completely

fait *m.* deed, doings, fact, result, business, affair

falloir *v.* be necessary *or* needed; *since this verb is impersonal, a far better translation is usually made of it by changing to a personal construction with* must, have to, should, need, ought, *etc., as* **il faut à votre fille** your daughter needs; **comme il faut** properly, fashionably, in a proper *or* right way; **il faut bien** 10 15, it is quite necessary; **l'ordre qu'il faut** the necessary order

famille *f.* family

fantaisie *f.* whim, caprice, fancy

faribole *f.* stuff and nonsense, trifle, ridiculous idea

fat *m.* coxcomb, fop, puppy

fatigue *f.* labor, fatigue

fatiguer *v.* weary, tire, harass, wear out

faute *f.* fault; ∞ **de** for lack of

faveur *f.* favor

feindre *v.* feign, pretend

feinte *f.* deception, feint

félicité *f.* happiness

féliciter *v.* congratulate

femme *f.* wife, woman

fendre *v.* split

fer *m.* iron

ferme *adj.* steady, firm, steadfast

fermer *v.* close; bring up the rear of, **73** 3

féroce *adj.* wild, ferocious, fierce

festin *m.* banquet, feast

festiner *v.* banquet, treat, entertain

feu *adj.* late (*deceased*); ∞ **votre père** your late father

feu *m.* (*pl.* **feux**) fire; *the plural is often used poetically for* love; ∞ **volant** will-o'-the-wisp, shooting star, flaming meteor; ∞ **d'artifice** fireworks

feuillage *m.* foliage

feuillet *m.* leaf (*of a book*)

fidèle *adj.* faithful

fieffé *adj.* arrant, downright, past master in

fièvre *f.* fever

figure *f.* figure, appearance from head to foot, symbol; arrangement of the terms *or* propositions of a syllogism, **21** 5

figurer *v.* figure, represent; **se** ∞ picture to oneself, imagine

fille *f.* daughter, girl

fils *m.* son, boy

fin *adj.* subtle, clever, fine

fin *f.* end; **à la** ∞ at last

finir *v.* end

flamme *f.* flame, love, passion

flanqué *adj.* flanked

flatter *v.* flatter

fleur *f.* flower, flower ornament

fleuret *m.* foil (*for fencing*)

fleuri *adj.* in bloom, covered with flowers

flûte *f.* flute player

foi *f.* faith, fidelity, word of honor, constancy

fois *f.* time (*in such uses as "first time," "second time," etc.*); **encore une** ∞ once more

fol, folle *see* **fou**

folie *f.* folly

fond *m.* bottom; **à** ∞ thoroughly

force *f.* vigor, strength, force; **à** ∞ **de** because of, by dint of; **à toute** ∞ absolutely, most strongly

former *v.* form; **se** ∞ be formed

fort *adj.* strong; *adv.* very; wide, **22** 16; tight, **26** 6; much, **36** 10; well, **68** 11

fortune *f.* happiness, prosperous *or* lucky suit (*in love*)

fortuné *adj.* lucky, fortunate

fou, fol, folle *adj.* foolish, mad

foudre *f.* thunderbolt, lightning bolt

fouet *m.* whip, switch

fourbe *m.* cheat

fourrer *v.* thrust

fracas *m.* uproar

franc, franche *adj.* frank, honest, out-and-out

franc *adv.* frankly, openly

franc *m.* *a coin of the same value as the* **livre** *and equivalent to about twenty cents*

français *adj.* French

franchement *adv.* frankly, honestly

franchise *f.* liberty, freedom, frankness

frapper *v.* strike

fratras *m. the reading in the original edition,* **fatras** *in some later editions, and* **fracas** *in others,* **90** 11; *this last is probably the best;* **fatras** *means* confused mass, **fracas** *means* uproar

fréquent *adj.* frequent

fréquenter *v.* associate with

fripon *m.* cheat, rascal

friponne *f.* jade, hussy

frôler *v.* graze, touch lightly

froncer *v.* frown, knit one's brows

frotter *v.* rub, scrub, polish

fuir *v.* shun, flee from *or* away

fumet *m.* flavor

funeste *adj.* fatal

furieusement *adv.* frightfully, terribly, awfully, furiously. *In the affected, or précieuse, society of the day long and superlative adverbs were much in vogue; they were considered the mark of aristocratic breeding. This particular word was a great favorite*

gagner *v.* overcome, gain, win over

galamment *adv.* elegantly

galant *adj.* stylish, smart, elegant, gallant, courtly; ∼ **homme** thorough gentleman

galanterie *f.* fine manners, aristocratic bearing, elegance, love-making, gallantry

galera *f.* galley

galère *f.* galley

galimatias *m.* twaddle, rigmarole, rubbish, gibberish

garçon *m.* boy, waiter, apprentice; ∼ **tailleur** tailor's apprentice

garde *f.* guard; **en garde** on guard (*the position of defense*)

garder *v.* keep; **gardez-vous-en bien** be very careful not to do it; **Dieu m'en garde** God preserve me from it, God forbid

garnir *v.* adorn, trim

gâter *v.* spoil, ruin

gauche *adj.* left

gauche *f.* left hand *or* side

gendre *m.* son-in-law

gêner *v.* hinder

généreusement *adv.* nobly, generously

généreux -euse *adj.* noble, generous

génie *m.* genius

genou *m.* (*pl.* **genoux**) knee

gens *m. f. pl.* people; *f. when adj. precedes, m. when it follows, as in* **16** 21, **32** 9, **68** 17, *yet in* **35** 19 **tous ces** ∼ (*because* **ces** *is the same form for both genders*); ∼ **de qualité** people of rank. *or* quality; **honnêtes** ∼ people of culture and refinement; **jeunes** ∼ young men

gentil -ille *adj.* pretty

gentilhomme *m.* nobleman, squire

gentiment *adv.* nicely, gracefully, neatly, prettily

Giourdina *m.* Jourdain

gladiateur *m.* public fighter, prize fighter, gladiator, swashbuckler

gloire *f.* honor, fame, great dignity, glory; *a rather vague word in the 17th century*

glorieux -euse *adj.* illustrious, glorious, proud, haughty

gosier *m.* throat, windpipe

gourmandé *adj.* dressed, larded, stuffed, made appetizing

goût *m.* taste

goûter *v.* taste, enjoy

gouvernement *m.* government, administration, governing

gouverner *v.* arrange, govern, administer

grâce *f.* grace, charm, graciousness, favor, mercy; ∽ *or* ∽s thanks; de ∽ in mercy's name, I pray you

grand *adj.* large, great, tall; ∽e qualité high rank; **Grand Turc** Sultan of Turkey

granda dama *f.* great lady. *Compare* **grande segnore**

grand'dame *f.* great lady, grand lady, lady of fashion

grande segnore *m.* great lord. *Compare* **granda dama**

grandeur *f.* greatness; **Grandeur** *a title*, Grace, Highness, *now an ecclesiastical title only, but formerly also applied to higher nobles who had not the title of "Altesse" or "Excellence"*

grand'maman *f.* grandma, grandmother

grand-père *m.* grandfather

gratter *v.* scratch; *see note to* **38** 2

gravement *adv.* seriously, gravely

grêle *f.* hail

grimace *f.* grimace

grisette *f.* woman of humble social station, *but not necessarily a word of disparagement. Probably*

the name arose from the gray (**gris**) *color of the usual clothing of women of lowly station;* **grisette** *was also the name of a gray fabric*

gros, grosse *adj.* large (*in all dimensions*), fat, stout

grosseur *f.* size, bulk

grouiller *v.* shake (*the head from old age*), tremble

guère *adv.* but little, not much; ne . . . ∽ scarcely, hardly

guérir *v.* cure; ∽ l'esprit relieve the mind

guerre *f.* war

gueux, gueuse *adj.* beggarly

gueux *m.* beggar

habile *adj.* clever

habiller *v.* dress

habit *m.* costume, suit; *the word often includes in Molière's time shoes, stockings, and hat, and does not mean, as it does now, merely* coat

hai *interj.* (*exclamation of satisfaction*) ah!

haine *f.* hatred

haïr *v.* hate, despise

halle *f.* market

hanche *f.* hip

hanter *v.* frequent, associate with, haunt

harmonieux -euse *adj.* harmonious

hasard *m.* chance, hazard

hasarder *v.* risk, chance

hausser *v.* hold up, raise

haut *adj.* high; à ∽e voix in a loud voice; ∽e capacité great ability

haut *m.* top, summit

hautbois *m.* oboe player

haut-de-chausses *m.* knee breeches; *now an obsolete word. Stockings were originally called* **bas-de-chausses**, *but are now called only* **bas**

haute-contre *f.* counter-tenor, *a voice higher than an average tenor, but with less volume; the "contraltino" of the Italians*

hautement *adv.* highly, greatly; l'emporte ∽ far surpasses

hauteur *f.* height

hé *interj.* hey! I say! ∽ bien! well!

hélas *interj.* alas!

héros *m.* hero

hésiter *v.* hesitate

heure *f.* hour, time; de bonne ∽ early; à cette ∽ now; tout à l'∽ (*of past time*) just now, (*of future time*) soon, at once

heureusement *adv.* fortunately, happily, luckily

heureux -euse *adj.* happy

histoire *f.* history, story, business, affair, (*in contemptuous sense*) folly

holà *interj.* hello there! ho! hi!

hommage *m.* respect, homage

homme *m.* man; *in* **3** 19 *used disrespectfully;* son ∽ **16** 9, his man (= opponent); honnête ∽ man of honor, education, and good breeding, perfect gentleman, nobleman

honnête *adj.* honorable, honest, polite; ∽ homme *see* homme

honneur *m.* honor

honorable *adj.* full of honor, honorable

honorer *v.* honor

honte *f.* shame; avoir ∽ be ashamed

honteux -euse *adj.* shameful, disgraceful

horreur *f.* dread, horror

hors *prep.* outside, out

huit *adj.* eight; ∽ jours a week

humble *adj.* humble

humblement *adv.* humbly

humeur *f.* humor, mood, disposition, ill humor

ici *adv.* here

idée *f.* idea, thought, conception

ignorance *f.* ignorance

ignorant -e *m. f.* ignoramus, dunce

il *pron.* he, it, there; *with many impersonal verbs it is best left untranslated, as* ∽ nous le faut we need, tout ce qu'∽ vous plaira all that you want; ∽ y a there is, there are; ∽ n'est rien there is nothing; ∽ est homme (= c'est un homme) **65** 17, he is a man; *etc.*

image *f.* image

imaginer *v.* imagine; s'∽ fancy

imiter *v.* follow the example of, imitate

immédiatement *adv.* directly

impatience *f.* eagerness

impertinence *f.* impropriety, incivility, silliness, stupidity, blunder, inconsistency, incongruity

impertinent *adj.* improper, insolent, foolish, repulsive, speaking out of season

impertinent -e *m. f.* insolent person

importance *f.* importance

importun *adj.* obtrusive, troublesome

importun -e *m. f.* intruder, bore

impossible *adj.* impossible

imposteur *m.* swindler

imposture *f.* deceit, hypocrisy, imposture

impudemment *adv.* insolently, impudently

impudent *m.* insolent fellow

incivil *adj.* impolite, uncivil, unmannerly

inclination *f.* fondness

incliner *v.* bend; **s'∾** bow

incommodé *adj.* inconvenienced, annoyed

incommoder *v.* inconvenience, embarrass (*financially*)

incongruité *f.* impropriety, offense, incongruity

inconstance *f.* fickleness

inconstant *adj.* fickle

inconvénient *m.* disadvantage, drawback

indienne *f.* dressing gown with very large sleeves

indigne *adj.* unworthy

infâme *m.* infamous person, wretch

infidèle *m. f.* faithless one

infidélité *f.* faithlessness

infiniment *adv.* infinitely

informer *v.* inform

ingrat *adj.* ungrateful

ingrat -e *m. f.* ingrate

injure *f.* insult

inquiéter *v.* make anxious, worry

insensiblement *adv.* imperceptibly, insensibly

insinuer *v.* insinuate; **s'∾** steal in, ingratiate oneself

insolemment *adv.* insultingly, insolently

insolence *f.* insolence

insolent -e *m. f.* insolent person

inspirer *v.* suggest, inspire

instruire *v.* inform, instruct

instrument *m.* musical instrument

intéresser *v.* interest; **s'∾** take an interest; *with* **dans** *of things*, *with* **pour** *of persons*

intérêt *m.* interest, self-interest, selfishness, greed

intermède *m.* interlude, intermezzo (*played between the acts*)

interprète *m.* interpreter

introduire *v.* introduce

inutile *adj.* useless

inventer *v.* devise, invent

invention *f.* device, invention

inviter *v.* tempt, invite

invocation *f.* prayer, invocation

invoquer *v.* invoke

italien -enne *adj.* Italian

Italien -enne *m. f.* Italian

ivre *adj.* drunk, intoxicated

jalousie *f.* jealousy

jamais *adv.* never, ever; **ne . . . ∾** never

jambe *f.* leg

jardin *m.* garden

jargon *m.* unintelligible sounds, jargon

je *pron.* I

jeter *v.* throw; **se ∾** hurl oneself, fall upon

jeudi *m.* Thursday

jeune *adj.* young

joie *f.* pleasure, joy

joindre *v.* join

joli *adj.* pretty

Jordina *m.* Jourdain

joue *f.* cheek

jouer *v.* play, play a trick on, fool

joueur *m.* player

jouir *v.* enjoy; *requires* **de** *before its object*

jour *m.* day, life; opportunity, **40** 6; **huit ∾s** a week

jugement *m.* good judgment

juger *v.* judge

jurer *v.* swear

jusque *or* (*poetic*) **jusques** *prep.* clear to, as far as, until; **jusqu'à 17** 27, to the extent of

juste *adj.* just, right, becoming, well-fitting, exact

justement *adv.* precisely, exactly

justifier *v.* justify

l' *contraction of* **le** *or* **la**, *the article and pronoun, before words beginning with a vowel or* **h** *mute; see* **le**

la *feminine article,* the; *in the phrase* **de ∾ sorte** *it has demonstrative value,* in that way; *also feminine personal pronoun,* her, it; *see* **le**

là *adv.* there; *when added to nouns or demonstrative pronouns it emphasizes the meaning* that; **par-ci par-∾** here and there; **par ∾** thereby, that way

là-bas *adv.* down there, over there, yonder

lâcheté *f.* cowardice

là-dedans *adv.* in it, in there, therein

là-dessus *adv.* on this subject, thereupon

laid *adj.* unseemly, improper, ugly

laisser *v.* let, allow, leave, let alone; *for a peculiar idiom, see note to* **53** 1

lait *m.* milk; **vache à ∾** milch cow

langage *m.* language; manner of speech, **34** 21

langue *f.* tongue, language

languir *v.* pine away, linger, languish

laquais *m.* servant, lackey, footman

laquelle *see* **lequel**

larme *f.* tear

las, lasse *adj.* weary

latin *m.* Latin

le, la, l', les *article,* the; *direct object personal pronoun,* him, her, it, them; *sometimes idiomatic, so, or even untranslatable, as* **je vous le disais 39** 5, I told you so; **il nous le faut 4** 4, we need; **je le donne en six coups 27** 3, I give six trials; **comme vous le savez 38** 23, as you know; **ce l'est** it is; **comme vous le pensez** as you think; *etc.*

leçon *f.* lesson

lequel, laquelle, lesquels, lesquelles *pron.* who, which, whom

les *see* **le**

lettre *f.* letter

leur *indirect object personal pronoun,* them, to them; *also possessive adjective,* their, *and, when preceded by the definite article, possessive pronoun,* theirs

lever *v.* raise; (*in tailoring*) cut out

lèvre *f.* lip

liaison *f.* connection, relation

libéralité *f.* generosity

liberté *f.* freedom, liberty

lieu *m.* spot, place; **au ∽ de** instead of

ligne *f.* line

lion *m.* lion

lire *v.* read

livre *m.* book; **∽ du ballet** libretto, *containing the words of the songs and the description of the dancing*

livre *f.* pound; *also a coin of the same value as the* **franc** (*see* **franc**); *a livre was formerly worth a pound weight of silver, but its value rapidly decreased; eleven livres equaled in Molière's day one* **louis** *or* **pistole**

livrée *f.* livery

livret *m.* booklet, libretto; *it was printed in quarto size by Ballard and given to the spectators; little more than our modern program*

logique *f.* logic

logis *m.* house, home, lodging

loi *f.* rule, law

loin *adv.* far

loisir *m.* leisure

l'on *see* **on**

long, longue *adj.* long

longe *f.* loin (*of meat*)

longtemps *adv.* a long time

lorsque *conj.* when

louange *f.* praise

louer *v.* praise

louis *m.* *a gold coin, of the same value as the* **pistole**; *equivalent to eleven livres or francs in Molière's day; originally its value was ten francs and later twenty francs; also called* **Louis d'or**;

coined first in 1640 in the likeness of Louis XIII and named for him

lugubre *adj.* mournful

lui *conjunctive personal pronoun, indirect object of verbs,* him, her, it, to him, to her; *also disjunctive personal pronoun,* him, it; *used in the 17th century to apply to things, as in* **5** 11, *now usually limited to persons; emphatic subject,* he

lumière *f.* light; **les ∽s** enlightenment, intelligence, intellectual capacity, culture

lune *f.* moon

lunettes *f. pl.* spectacles

m' *see* **me**

ma *see* **mon**

mâchoire *f.* jaw; **∽ d'en bas** lower jaw; **∽ d'en haut** upper jaw

madame *f.* (*pl.* **mesdames**) madam, lady

mademoiselle *f.* (*pl.* **mesdemoiselles**) Miss, young lady

magnifique *adj.* gorgeous, splendid

Mahomet *m.* Mohammed

mahométan *adj.* Mohammedan

maille *f.* stitch, mesh

main *f.* hand

maintenant *adv.* now, at present

mais *conj.* but

maison *f.* house, household

maître *m.* master, teacher; **∽ tailleur** master tailor; **∽ de musique** music teacher; **∽ à danser** dancing master; **∽ d'armes** fencing teacher; **∽ de philosophie** teacher of philosophy

maîtresse *f.* mistress, sovereign

mal *adv.* ill, badly ; *used often as a kind of negation*

mal *m.* (*pl.* **maux**) sickness, pain, ill, evil ; **faire ∾** hurt, harm ; **vouloir du ∾ à** (*the origin of the modern* **en vouloir à**) be angry with

malaisé *adj.* difficult

malavisé *adj.* ill-advised, misinformed, ill-judging, impertinent

malheur *m.* misfortune, ill

malheureusement *adv.* unhappily, unfortunately

malitorne *m.* clumsy lout, booby, awkward fellow

mamamouchi *m.*, *see note to* **70 13**

mander *v.* inform (*usually in writing*)

manger *v.* eat

manière *f.* sort, manner ; **de la belle ∾** prettily ; **de ∾** in such a way that ; **de la ∾ que** just as

manque *m.* lack

manquement *m.* failure, mistake, blunder (*now obsolete in this meaning*), some slight sin of omission

manquer *v.* fail, fail in one's duty, miss

maraud *m.* rascal, blackguard

marchand *m.* tradesman, purveyor, merchant ; cloth merchant, **39 29**

marche *f.* march

marcher *v.* walk, march

mari *m.* husband

mariage *m.* marriage

marié *adj.* united, blended

marier *v.* give in marriage ; **se ∾** marry

marin *adj.* marine

marque *f.* sign, mark

marquer *v.* show, point out, mark

marquis *m.* marquis

marquise *f.* marchioness, wife *or* widow of a marquis

mascarade *f.* trick, masquerade

masque *m.* mask (*either the mask itself or its wearer*)

matière *f.* subject, matter

matin *m.* morning ; **le ∾** mornings, in the morning

maudit *adj.* accursed, cursed

maudit -e *m. f.* accursed *or* cursed one

mauvais *adj.* bad

me, m' *pron.* me, to me, myself, for me

médiocre *adj.* ordinary, commonplace

médisance *f.* slander, calumny

méditer *v.* plan, meditate

mégarde *f.* inadvertence

meilleur *adj.* better ; **le ∾** best

mélancolique *adj.* gloomy, in bad humor

mélange *m.* medley

mêler *v.* mingle, mix, join *or* add ; **se ∾** undertake, busy oneself with, meddle ; **mêlez-vous de vos affaires** mind your own business

même *adj., adv.* same, very, even ; **de ∾** likewise ; *added to* **moi, vous,** *etc.*, self, *as* **moi-∾** myself

mémoire *m.* memorandum

ménage *m.* housework, household, house

mener *v.* lead ; **∾ par la main** lead by the hand (*the polite way at that time of escorting a lady*)

menton *m.* chin

menuet *m.* minuet (*a dignified dance, of short steps or movements, originating in Poitou*)

mépris *m.* scorn, disdain

méprisable *adj.* contemptible, despicable

mépriser *v.* scorn, disdain, despise

mercredi *m.* Wednesday

mère *f.* mother

mérite *m.* worthiness, merit

mériter *v.* deserve, merit

merveille *f.* wonder, marvel; **à ∽** wonderfully well, marvelously, admirably

merveilleusement *adv.* wonderfully, marvelously

merveilleux -euse *adj.* wonderful, fine, marvelous

mes *see* **mon**

mesdames *see* **madame**

mesdemoiselles *see* **mademoiselle**

messieurs *see* **monsieur**

métal *m.* (*pl.* **métaux**) metal

météore *m.* meteor

métier *m.* trade, occupation

mets *m.* dish (*of food*)

mettre *v.* put, place, put on (*of clothing, the hat, etc.*); set to work, **26** 15; **mettant le sabre à la main** drawing their sabers; **∽ la paix entre** pacify; **se ∽** be put on (**28** 6), dress (**28** 23); **se ∽ en tête** put *or* get into one's head; **se ∽ en colère** get angry; **mettez-vous là 55** 26, *a free and easy invitation to take a seat;* **se ∽ à genoux** kneel

mie *f.* darling, dearest love

mien, mienne *pron.* (*usually preceded by the definite article*) mine

mieux *adv.* better, more; **le ∽** the best; **le ∽ du monde** most opportunely

mignon -onne *m. f.* darling, pet

mijaurée *f.* foolishly affected woman (*an affected, yet coarse, coquettish, and conceited woman*)

milieu *m.* center, middle, midst; **au ∽ de** in the midst of

mille *adj.* thousand

mille *m.* a thousand

minéral *m.* (*pl.* **minéraux**) mineral

misérable *adj.* wretched, beggarly

miséricorde *f.* mercy; *as interj.* mercy on me!

mode *f.* fashion, style; **à la ∽** fashionably, in style

modération *f.* moderation

modérer *v.* restrain

moi *pron.* I, me, to me, myself

moi-même *pron.* myself; **de ∽** of my own accord

moins *adv.* less; **le ∽** the least; **au ∽** at least, surely, without fail

mon, ma, mes *poss. adj.* my

monde *m.* world, society, people; **tout le ∽** everybody; *the phrase* **du ∽** *strengthens superlatives, as* **le plus propre du ∽,** *and is best translated often by mere emphasis*

monnayé *adj.* paid in cash, coined, "minted," taking the form of money

monseigneur *m.* your lordship, your excellency; *now an ecclesiastical title, but formerly more generally used for dukes, peers, highest judges, archbishops, and bishops*

monsieur *m.* (*pl.* **messieurs**) sir, the gentleman, Mr.

monter *v.* mount, go up

montrer *v.* show, point out, teach

moquer: se ∞ *v.* not care for, jest, mock at

morale *f.* ethics

morbleu *interj.* (*euphemism for* **mort Dieu** God's death) zounds (*contracted from* God's wounds). *Compare* **parbleu**

morceau *m.* (*pl.* **morceaux**) piece, morsel; **bons** ∞x titbits, fine cooking

mort *f.* death

mortel -elle *adj.* deadly, fatal, mortal

mot *m.* word

mouche *f.* fly, gadfly

moue *f.* wry face, pouting

mouiller *v.* moisten, wet

mourir *v.* die

mouton *m.* sheep; mutton, **62** 21; *in* **8** 4 *the meaning may also be* mutton *or* lamb

mouvement *m.* motion, movement, action, impulse, passion

moyen *m.* means, way; **le** ∞? how is it possible?

muet -ette *adj.* dumb, mute

multitude *f.* crowd

muphty *m.* mufti, *an interpreter of the Moslem faith; in Molière's time he was thought to be the chief of the Mohammedan religion, but the usual title of the head of the Mohammedan faith was "Grand Mufti"; he is now better known as the "Sheikh-ul-Islam." Strictly speaking a mufti is now a Mohammedan jurisconsult*

musicien -enne *m. f.* singer

musique *f.* music, band; **concert de** ∞ (= **concert**) concert

naître *v.* be born

nation *f.* nationality, nation

nature *f.* nature

naturel -elle *adj.* likely, probable, natural, pertaining to nature

ne *adv.* not, no; *usually with* **pas, point,** *etc., but occasionally it is a sufficient negative alone, as with* savoir **8** 3, pouvoir **9** 5, bouger **30** 6; *also in* si *clauses, where* si . . . ne *means* unless, *and in* il y a huit jours que je ∞ vous ai vu **42** 13, il n'y a morale qui tienne **21** 18; *also in* **59** 4, *where* que = sans que, *and in such expressions as* dire . . . qu'elle n'abusera de sa vie **45** 7, *or* je ne sais qui me tient que je ∞ vous fende la tête **67** 5; *occasionally omitted in Molière's time, as* voilà pas le coup de langue **54** 20; *often redundant and untranslatable in the second member of a comparison, as* mieux qu'il ∞ fait, plus . . . que n'est le tigre; ∞ . . . aucun no, none; ∞ . . . de sa vie (= ∞ . . . jamais) never; ∞ . . . guère scarcely, hardly; ∞ . . . jamais never; ∞ . . . ni . . . ni neither . . . nor; ∞ . . . pas no, not; *in* ∞ faites pas semblant de rien **85** 33 *the* pas *is unnecessary;* ∞ . . . point not, *is more emphatic than* ∞ . . . pas; ∞ . . . plus no more, no longer, not any more; ∞ . . . que only; ∞ . . . rien nothing. *In the 17th century the infinitive is often* *placed between the two words of its negative, instead of having both these precede it, as they do now*

nécessaire *adj.* essential

neige *f.* snow

nenni (*pronounced nă-ni*) *adv.* no, not at all, by no means; *an archaic form, indicating in* **30** 19 *the rustic origin of Nicole*

net, nette *adj.* clean, clear; *adv.* plainly; **franc et** ∽ to speak plainly

nettoyer *v.* clean

neuf *adj.* nine

neuf, neuve *adj.* new

nez *m.* nose; **rire au** ∽ laugh in one's face; **lui dire à son** ∽ tell him to his face

noble *adj.* noble

noble *m.* a noble, member of the nobility

noblesse *f.* nobility, nobility of rank

noce *f.* wedding

noir *adj.* black. *Black was the usual color of the clothes of the bourgeoisie, the nobles alone being accustomed to dress in bright colors. The disappearance in modern times of this gaudiness in men's attire is one of the indications of the spread of democracy*

nom *m.* name

non *adv.* no, not; ∽ **pas** *emphatic negative;* **pourquoi** ∽ why not? **non** *is not used with verbs* (*see* **ne**)

nonchalance *f.* carelessness, indifference

nos *see* **notre**

notaire *m.* notary public

notre *poss. adj.* (*pl.* **nos**) our; *in popular speech it often means* my, *as in* **33** 5

nous *pron.* we, us, to us

nouveau, nouvel, nouvelle *adj.* new, novel, another, recent

nouvelle *f.* news

nuit *f.* night; **bonnet de** ∽ nightcap

obéir *v.* obey

obéissance *f.* obedience

obéissant *adj.* obedient

objet *m.* object

obligation *f.* obligation; **avoir** ∽ to be under obligation

obligeant *adj.* obliging, courteous

obligé *adj.* grateful

obliger *v.* oblige, place under obligation

obstination *f.* stubbornness

obstiné *adj.* stubborn

obtenir *v.* secure, obtain

occasion *f.* opportunity, occasion

occupation *f.* occupation

œil *m.* (*pl.* **yeux**) eye; **beaux yeux 7** 24, *a common poetic expression to symbolize beauty*

officieux -euse *adj.* kind, obliging, officious (*in a good, not an ironical, sense*)

offrir *v.* offer

oignon *m.* onion

oiseau *m.* (*pl.* **oiseaux**) bird

ombre *f.* shadow, shade, protection

on, l'on *indefinite pron.* one, some one, they, we, you, people; *an expression with* **on** *is frequently translated as passive, as* ∽ **voit un élève** a pupil is seen

onde *f.* waves, water, sea; ∽ **noire** the black gulf (*the river Styx that bounded Hades; symbolic of death*)

opéra *m.* masterpiece, **63** 3

opération *f.* operation

opérer *v.* produce results, manage, get effects

opiniâtre *adj.* obstinate; *as noun,* headstrong person

opiniâtreté *f.* obstinacy, persistency

opposer *v.* oppose; **s'**∽ object

opposite *m.* opposite, contrary; **à l'**∽ **de** opposite, in a level line with

ordonner *v.* plan, arrange, order

ordre *m.* order

oreille *f.* ear

ornement *m.* adornment

orthographe *f.* spelling

ôter *v.* remove, take away; **s'**∽ move away

ou *conj.* or; ∽ . . . ∽ either . . . or

où *adv.* where; when, **26** 5; whither, to which, **47** 11; **d'**∽ whence; **par** ∽ **38** 2, where. *Molière uses* **où** *often where now we usually find some form of* **lequel**

ouais *interj.* (*indicating surprise*) well well! gracious! upon my word!

oublier *v.* forget

ouf *interj.* (*exclamation of relief after an ordeal*) oh!

oui *adv.* yes

ouï *past participle of the obsolete verb* **ouïr,** hear, *which is now found only in the past participle and the present infinitive;* ∽ **dire** heard it said

outrage *m.* insult

outre *prep.* besides, in addition to

ouvert *adj.* open, unobstructed

ouverture *f.* opening; overture, opening or introductory music

ouvrage *m.* work

ouvrir *v.* open

pagana *m.* pagan

page *m.* page, boy servant

pain *m.* bread

pair *m.* equality, peer; **de** ∽ on an equality

paix *f.* peace

paladin *m.* a knight of medieval times, a knight of Charlemagne, *then extended to mean* a chivalrous person

palais *m.* palate

Palais-Royal *m. a palace in one of the fashionable districts of Paris in Molière's day, where also his theater was located*

pantoufle *f.* slipper

par *adv.* (*intensive particle*): ∽ **trop 90** 13, far too much, excessively

par *prep.* by, through; ∽**-ci** ∽**-là** here and there; ∽ **là** thereby, by that; ∽ **où** by what, where; ∽ **la ville** through the city; ∽ **exemple** for instance; ∽ **derrière** behind; ∽ **devant** before, in front; ∽ **terre** on the ground *or* floor. **Par** *had a much freer use than to-day, standing for modern* **pour**, à cause de, *or* par suite de, *as* (*for* pour) ∽ **deux raisons 59** 1, for two reasons

paraître *v.* appear; **faire** ∽ show

parbleu *interj.* (*euphemism for* **par Dieu**) egad! zounds! *Compare* **morbleu**

parce que *conj.* because

par-dessous *adv.* below, under

par-dessus *adv., prep.* above, over, on top of

pardon *m.* pardon

pareil -eille *adj.* such, like, alike

parent *m.* relative; ∽s parents

parer *v.* adorn, parry; se ∽ adorn oneself

parfait *adj.* perfect

parfaitement *adv.* perfectly

parisien -enne *adj.* Parisian

parler *v.* speak, talk; *often used transitively, as* **ce que je parle avec vous**; **ne m'en parlez point** it's useless to argue over it, don't dispute it; **apprendre à ∽** teach manners

parler *m.* speech, talk, manner of speaking

parmi *prep.* in the midst of, among

parole *f.* word; **tenir ∽** keep one's word

part *f.* part, share; **à ∽** aside; **de ma (votre) ∽** in my (your) name, from me (you); **des deux ∽s** on both sides; **prendre ∽** take an interest

parti *m.* suitor, suitable match

particulier -ère *adj.* particular

particulier *m.* individual; **en ∽** privately

particulièrement *adv.* intimately, fully, especially

partie *f.* portion

partir *v.* start, set out, leave, depart

partout *adv.* everywhere, all around

pas *adv.* no, not; *see* **ne**

pas *m.* step; **de ce ∽** instantly; **sur ses ∽** in his way

passable *adj.* satisfactory, tolerable

passer *v.* spend, pass; **passe, passe** (*subjunctive*) let that pass, never mind that; **se ∽** occur; **se ∽ de** do without

passion *f.* emotion, passion

passionné *adj.* ardent, passionate

pâte *f.* dough, paste

patience *f.* patience

pauvre *adj.* poor; *used often as a term of endearment*

payer *v.* pay

pays *m.* country

paysan -anne *m. f.* peasant

pédant *m.* pedant; **bélître de ∽** good-for-nothing pedant; *see* **bélître**

peine *f.* trouble, difficulty, sorrow, anxiety

peintre *m.* painter

peinture *f.* picture, painting

penché *adj.* leaning, resting, supported

pendant *prep.* during; **∽ que** *conj.* while

pendard *m.* hangdog, good-for-nothing, scoundrel

pendarde *f.* hussy, gallows bird

pensée *f.* thought

penser *v.* think, expect

perçant *adj.* piercing

percer *v.* pierce, stab

perdre *v.* lose, destroy; **laisser ∽** allow to be lost, miss

perdrix *f.* partridge

père *m.* father

perfide *m. f.* perfidious one

perfidie *f.* treachery, perfidy

perlé *adj.* resembling pearls, pearly

perpétuellement *adv.* continually, constantly

perruque *f.* wig. *Wigs had been fashionable since about 1629. The favorite color was blond; hence in part the word "blondin," applied to young gallants who wore wigs of this color*

persil *m.* parsley

personnage *m.* character, personage

personne *f.* person; girl, **47** 23. *Although* **personne** *is feminine, Molière uses a masculine plural pronoun to refer to it in* **58** 26 (*see note to* **58** 25)

persuader *v.* win over, persuade

peser *v.* weigh; ∽ **sur les bras** oppress me, weigh upon me

peste *f.* plague, pestilence

petit *adj.* little, small, slight, short, petty, narrow

peu *m.* little; **un** ∽ a little, somewhat; *often with the value of* please, *as in* **45** 10; **avant qu'il soit (fût)** ∽ before long; **fort** ∽ **de chose** a mere trifle; **à** ∽ **de chose près** almost

peur *f.* fear; **avoir** ∽ be afraid; **de** ∽ **d'y manquer** *see note to* **32** 25

peut-être *adv.* perhaps

Philis (*sound the* **s**) *f.* Phyllis, *a conventional name in poetry*

philosophe *m.* philosopher; ∽ **de chien** dog of a philosopher, lowdown philosopher. *Molière frequently ridicules the conceit and*

irritability of the "*philosophe*" of his day, these qualities being especially characteristic of the men trained to argue in the schools of that time

philosophie *f.* philosophy, science; **maître de** ∽ teacher of philosophy. *It was a broadly inclusive term in those days*

physique *f.* physics. *Note the wide domain of physics at that time. It included physics, chemistry, astronomy, anatomy, and other sciences, and was used in opposition to metaphysics*

pièce *f.* piece, fragment; dish, **62** 16, *and apparently* **67** 6

pied *m.* foot; **de** ∽ **ferme** *see note to* **15** 14; ∽ **à** ∽ step by step

pierre *f.* stone

pigeonneau *m.* young pigeon, squab

pimpesouée *f.* affected *or* pretentious (*and often* stupid) woman, one affectedly modest, "stuck-up minx "

pinceau *m.* brush

piquer *v.* sting

pis *adv.* worse; **tant** ∽ so much the worse

pistole *f.* pistole; *French name given to a Spanish or Italian gold coin of the same value as a* **louis**, *which, in Molière's day, was eleven francs or livres. It was also coined in France. There were also pistoles equal to ten livres, but the calculation in Act III, scene iv, only permits a value of eleven livres. See the note to* **39** 12

place *f.* seat, place; à sa ∿ **46** 23, for her; faire ∿ make room

placer *v.* locate, place

plaindre *v.* pity; se ∿ complain

plaire *v.* be pleasing, please, delight; **s'il vous plaît** if you please, please; **plaît-il?** what is it? **plût au ciel** would to heaven; **plût à Dieu l'avoir** would to God I had it

plaisant *adj.* amusing, absurd, foolish

plaisir *m.* pleasure, delight; service, favor, good office, **38** 30

plancher *m.* floor

plante *f.* plant

plein *adj.* complete, full

pluie *f.* rain

plumassier *m.* dealer in plumes *or* feathers, *which were worn extensively on men's hats at that time. Nobles alone had the right to wear a "panache," or plume*

plume *f.* feather, plume, pen

plupart *f.* majority; la ∿ most

plus *adv.* more; ne . . . ∿ no more, no longer; le ∿ most; *before numerals,* ∿ de more than

plusieurs *adj., pron.* several

plutôt *adv.* rather

poignet *m.* wrist

poing *m.* fist

point *adv.* no, not, not at all; ne . . . ∿ not (*more emphatic than* ne . . . pas); ∿ de vers no verses; ∿ du tout not at all; ∿ d'affaire **50** 8, all to no purpose, not at all

pointe *f.* tip, point

pointu *adj.* pointed, peaked

Poitevin *m.* inhabitant of Poitou (*a former province in western France; chief city Poitiers*)

politique *m.* statesman, politician

porte *f.* door, gate

porter *v.* carry, wear, bring; ∿ la botte thrust, lunge (*in fencing*); ∿ du respect (= porter respect) be respectful; ∿ son esprit influence, incline his mind; se ∿ be (*in respect to health*)

posséder *v.* possess

possession *f.* possession

posture *f.* position, posture

pot *m.* jar, bottle, pot (*of wine*)

potage *m.* soup

poudre *f.* powder, dust

poumon *m.* lungs

pour *prep.* for, to, in order to, as for; regarding, because of, **17** 26; in favor of, **46** 30; *often with an infinitive in Molière it is equivalent to a modern causal clause and is more vigorous, as in* **9** 10; *sometimes equivalent to a purpose clause, as* ∿ voir **28** 17 = ∿ qu'ils voient; ∿ quand for the time when; *often equivalent to* comme *in the quality of, as in* **68** 13; ∿ voir *see note to* **35** 1

pourpoint *m.* doublet, *an old form of upper garment for men*

pourquoi *adv., conj.* why

pourtant *adv.* however, nevertheless

pourvoir *v.* provide for; settle in matrimony

pourvu que *conj.* provided that

pousser *v.* thrust, push, strengthen, force, grow; ∿ la botte lunge (*in fencing*); ∽ **en quarte, en tierce** (*in fencing*) thrust in quart, in tierce (*see notes on* **quarte 15** 13, **tierce 15** 18)

poussière *f.* dust

pouvoir *v.* may, can, be able; *with the negative of this verb* **pas** *is often omitted* (*see* **bouger, savoir**)

pouvoir *m.* power

précieux -euse *adj.* precious

précipitation *f.* haste

préférence *f.* precedence, choice, superiority

premier -ère *adj.* first; **d'être des** ∽**s** to be among the first

premièrement *adv.* first, firstly, in the first place

prendre *v.* take, catch, contract, conceive, employ; **il me prend envie** I wish; ∽ **garde** look out, be careful; **prends-y bien garde** be very careful you don't; ∽ **la peine** be so good as; ∽ **part** show an interest

préparé *adj.* ready

préparer *v.* make ready, arrange

prérogative *f.* privilege

près *adv.* near; **à peu de chose** ∽ almost, nearly

présence *f.* presence

présent *m.* gift, *usually one of considerable value*

présenter *v.* present, offer; **se** ∽ appear

presque *adv.* almost

prêt *adj.* ready

prétendre *v.* aspire, lay claim to, try, intend

prêter *v.* lend; ∽ **l'oreille** *or* ∽ **silence** listen; **se** ∽ **des armes** be allies; ∽ **la main** assist

preuve *f.* proof

prévenir *v.* anticipate, forestall, warn, prevent

prier *v.* request, beg, pray; **je vous en prie** I beg of you

prince *m.* prince

principe *m.* beginning, foundation, principle, law

pris *adj.* taken; **bien** ∽ well-shaped, graceful, well-proportioned, elegant, slender

prix *m.* value, cost, price, prize

procéder *v.* arise, have an origin, proceed

produire *v.* produce; **se** ∽ **4** 18, show one's talents as an artist, play

proférer *v.* utter

profession *f.* profession; **faire** ∽ **de** profess

profiter *v.* profit; ∽ **de** profit by *or* from

profusion *f.* extravagant expenditure, lavishness

prologue *m.* prologue

promener *v.* take for a walk; **se** ∽ walk up and down; **envoyer** ∽ give walking papers to, get rid of by sending away

promettre *v.* promise

prompt *adj.* quick, prompt

promptement *adv.* quickly

prononcer *v.* pronounce, articulate; **se** ∽ be pronounced

propos *m.* talk; **à** ∽ by the way; **tout à** ∽ in the nick of time, very opportunely; **à tout** ∽ on every occasion

propre *adj.* clean, proper; suitably *or* elegantly dressed, **37** 25; suitable, suited

proprement *adv.* in style, properly

propriété *f.* property, quality

prose *f.* prose

prospérité *f.* good fortune

prosterner *v.* prostrate; **se ∾** prostrate oneself, bow down

province *f.* province, region

prudemment *adv.* wisely, prudently

prudence *f.* prudence, wisdom

puis *adv.* then

puisque *conj.* since

puits *m.* well

pupitre *m.* desk

pur *adj.* pure, mere

qualité *f.* quality, moral *or* temperamental characteristic, rank; **gens de ∾** people of rank *or* quality

quand *conj.* when; *with the conditional tense,* even if; **pour ∾** for the time when

quarante *adj.* forty

quartaine *adj.* occurring every fourth day, quartan; **fièvre ∾** (*now also* **fièvre quarte**) quartan fever (*one that returns every fourth day*)

quartier *m.* quarter, district, part

quatre *adj.* four

quatre-vingt(s) *adj.* eighty, fourscore

que *relative object pron.* whom, which, that; *interrogative pron. and adv.* what, how, how much; why, **23** 10; **qu'il est doux !** how sweet it is ! **∾ . . . de 23** 24, how much

que *conj.* that; until, **3** 10; *often a preceding verb of wishing is omitted, as in* **32** 2; **est-ce ∾** *a phrase introducing questions;* **qu'est-ce que c'est ∾** what; *often used in place of other conjunctions, as for* **pour ∾ 30** 1, in order that; *for* **car 41** 12, since; *for* **lorsque 67** 19, when; *for* **sans ∾ 59** 4, without; *for* **avant ∾ 6** 10, **40** 19, before, until; *often repeats a previous conjunction and has the same meaning as that conjunction, as in* **59** 24, **62** 10; *frequently untranslatable, as in* **est-ce ∾,** **qu'est ce que c'est ∾,** *and especially after* **ce +** *some form of* **être** *when* **que** *introduces the real, logical subject of the sentence, as in* **4** 5; *sometimes* **ce +** *a form of* **être** *is omitted, as in* **22** 33; *sometimes the* **que** *itself is omitted, as in* **28** 22; *untranslatable also in such conjunctive phrases as* **avant ∾ de** (*now* **avant de**), **sans ∾,** **jusqu'à ce ∾,** *etc., also in such phrases as* **∾ voilà,** **je crois ∾ oui,** **je suis sûre ∾ non;** *in comparisons of inequality,* than; *in comparisons of equality,* as; **ne . . . ∾** *semi-negation,* only

quel, quelle *interrogative adj.* what, which; *for* **lequel 69** 5, which, what

quelque *adj.* some, few; **∾ autre 40** 31, any one else; **∾ chose** *m.* something, anything; **∾ chose de nouveau, de vrai, de si bas,** *etc.,* something new, true, so low, *etc.*

quelquefois *adv.* sometimes

quelqu'un *pron.* some one, somebody

quereller *v.* pick a quarrel with, scold (*usually one's equals*) quérir *v.* fetch, seek; **envoyer** ∽ send for; *it is used only in the infinitive and after* **aller, venir, envoyer**; *now antiquated*

question *f.* question

qui *relative subject pronoun and interrogative subject and object pronoun,* who, whom, whosoever, which, that; one who, **7** 25; something which, **3** 15, **13** 1; what (= ce ∽), **67** 5, **83** 18; *in the 17th century* qui *did not need to stand close to its antecedent, and was used far more loosely than it is now*

quinze *adj.* fifteen

quitter *v.* abandon, leave, quit, jilt

quoi *pron.* what, what! *frequently used after prepositions and referring to indefinite antecedents;* ∽ **que** whatever, whatsoever; **en** ∽ **16** 13, wherein; **à**∽**5** 18 = ce à ∽

quoique *conj.* although

raccommoder *v.* repair, adjust, arrange

radoucir *v.* soften; lower the voice

ragaillardir *v.* liven up, enliven, put life into

railler *v.* rail; **se** ∽ **de** make fun of

raison *f.* reason, right; **avoir** ∽ be right; ∽ **démonstrative** logical reasoning

raisonnable *adj.* reasonable

raisonner *v.* reason, discourse, argue

ramage *m.* singing of birds

ramener *v.* bring back

rang *m.* row (*of objects*); rank, social position

ranger *v.* arrange; **se** ∽ take one's place in line

rapprocher *v.* bring together, draw near

raser *v.* shave

ravi *adj.* delighted

ravir *v.* please greatly, delight, captivate; ravish, seize with violence, steal away

ravissant *adj.* ravishing, delightful

ravissement *m.* delight, ecstasy, rapture

rebuter *v.* rebuff; **se** ∽ be discouraged

recevoir *v.* receive; receive an injury, **16** 4

recherche *f.* search, suit, courtship

récit *m.* recital

récompense *f.* reward

reconnaître *v.* recognize, acknowledge, be grateful for

reculer *v.* step back, draw back

redonner *v.* give back, give again

redoubler *v.* renew, repeat, redouble

redresser *v.* correct, redress, compensate

réduire *v.* reduce

refuser *v.* refuse

regagner *v.* return to, regain

régal *m.* entertainment, feast, treat; *see its synonym* **cadeau**

régaler *v.* reward, recompense, make ample atonement, entertain

regard *m.* look, glance

regarder *v.* look at, consider

règle *f.* rule; **dans les** ∽**s** according to rule

régner *v.* rule, reign

régulièrement *adv.* regularly

rejeter v. reject

réjouir v. rejoice; **se ∽** be glad, rejoice

réjouissance f. rejoicing, merry-making, lively dance

relevé adj. lofty; adorned, **62** 19; haughty, **55** 20; set off, strengthened, given a better taste, **63** 2

relever v. lift again, get up, set off; **se ∽** rise

religion f. faith, religion

remerciement m. thanks

remercier v. thank

remettre v. put or place again, remit; **remettez-vous** recover (after thrusting), fall back into position

remplir v. fill, fulfill

remuer v. move

rencontre f. meeting

rencontrer v. meet, find; **se ∽ 70** 33 (= **se trouver**), exist, occur

rendre v. give back, repay, render, return; **∽ mes petits services** be of service to you; **∽ nos devoirs** pay our respects; **se ∽** yield, surrender

renfort m. addition, strengthening, reënforcement

renoncer v. renounce

rente f. income, source of income

repaître v. feed, nourish; **se ∽ de** feed upon, delight in, revel in

repas m. meal, repast, banquet

répéter v. repeat

répliquer v. answer, answer back, retort

répondre v. correspond, answer, be answerable for

réponse f. answer

repos m. peace, rest

reposer v. place again; **se ∽** rest

représenter v. play (a drama), represent

reprise f. resumption, time; **à trois ∽s** three times in succession

reprocher v. reproach

résistance f. resistance

résolument adv. firmly, resolutely

résolution f. resolve

résoudre v. resolve, settle, decide; **se ∽** make up one's mind, resolve

respect m. respect

respirer v. breathe

ressembler v. be like, resemble

ressentiment m. resentment, dislike, anger

reste m. remainder, remains; **au ∽** besides, however, and now, by the way

retardement m. delay

retenir v. retain, remember; hinder

retirer v. retire, draw back; **se ∽** withdraw

retour m. return

retourner v. return, go back

réussir v. succeed

revenir v. return, come back; suit, satisfy, please

rêver v. dream, be absent-minded

révérence f. bow, salutation

révérer v. respect, reverence

revers m. reverse, disaster

richesse f. fortune, value, richness

ridicule adj. ridiculous; as noun, ridiculous man

rien m. nothing; note the emphatic use of un **∽** in **49** 26; **ne . . . ∽** nothing; **rien** often means anything, as in **18** 3, **27** 22, **46** 10

rigueur f. severity, tyranny, rigor

riposte *f.* quick answer, repartee

rire *v.* laugh; ∽ de laugh at

ritournelle *f.* (*from Italian* **ritornello** return) prelude, interlude *or* refrain (*being variations or repetitions of the song theme, played by the violins while the voices rest*)

rive *f.* edge

rivière *f.* river

robe *f.* gown, dress, robe; ∽ de **chambre** dressing gown

roche *f.* rock

roi *m.* king, *usually referring to Louis XIV*

rôle *m.* part (*in a play*), rôle

rompre *v.* break, break off

rond *m.* ring, circle

rosier *m.* rose bush

rosser *v.* thrash, belabor, drub

rossignol *m.* nightingale

rouge *adj.* red

rouvrir *v.* open again

royal *adj.* royal

ruiner *v.* ruin, impoverish

sabre *m.* saber, sword

sacrifice *m.* sacrifice

sage *adj.* wise, sensible

sagesse *f.* wisdom

salle *f.* room, hall, reception room, parlor; *often in the 17th century*, dining room

saluer *v.* greet, salute, bow to

sang *m.* blood

sans *prep.* without; ∽ **doute** doubtless, certainly

santé *f.* health

satire *f.* satire

satisfaire *v.* satisfy

satisfait *adj.* satisfied

saut *m.* jump, leap

sauter *v.* jump, leap

savant *adj.* learned, clever, skillful, masterly

savoir *v.* know, know how; *with the negative of this verb* **pas** *is often omitted* (*see* **bouger, pouvoir**); *in the conditional it is often equivalent to a mild* **pouvoir**, can, be able

savoir *m.* knowledge

scandalisé *adj.* troubled, irritated

scarcina *f.* scimitar, a curved Turkish sword

scélérat *adj.* wicked; *as noun*, rascal, scoundrel, wretch

scène *f.* scene, stage

science *f.* science, art

scrupule *m.* conscientious objection, scruple

se *reflexive pron.*, *used only with reflexive verbs*, himself, herself, itself, oneself, themselves, to himself, herself, *etc.*

seau *m.* (*pl.* **seaux**) bucket

sécher *v.* dry up, melt away, die

second *adj.* second

secret *m.* secret; sure method of success

seigneur *m.* lord, nobleman

séjour *m.* sojourn, abode, spot

sellier *m.* saddler, a maker of saddles, harnesses, and carriages

selon *prep.* in accordance with

semblant *m.* appearance

sembler *v.* seem, appear

sens *m.* judgment, sense, opinion

sensé *adj.* sensible

sentiment *m.* feeling, opinion, sentiment

sentir *v.* feel, appreciate ; savor of, smell, smack of ; have the scent of, know what is going on ; **se ∽** feel that one has

seoir *v.* be becoming, suit, become

séparer *v.* part, separate

sept *adj.* seven

sérieusement *adv.* seriously

sérieux -euse *adj.* serious, sober, not gay

sermonner *v.* lecture, sermonize

serpent *m.* serpent

serrer *v.* grip, seize, press ; **∽ fort** grip tight

servante *f.* maidservant

service *m.* service

servir *v.* help, serve ; **∽ de** serve as ; **se ∽ de** make use of

serviteur *m.* servant

seul *adj.* alone, sole, mere, single, only

seulement *adv.* only, even

sève *f.* sap, strength, strong body (*of wine*), taste

sexe *m.* sex

si *adv.* so ; yet, however, **41** 10 ; **∽ . . . que** so . . . as ; *conj.* if, whether ; **∽ . . . ne** unless

siècle *m.* century, age

sied *third sing. pres. indic. of* **seoir**

signe *m.* sign

silence *m.* silence

simple *adj.* innocent, credulous, simple

six *adj.* six ; **∽-vingts**, sixscore, one hundred and twenty

sœur *f.* sister

soi *pron.* oneself

soie *f.* silk

soif *f.* thirst ; **avoir ∽** be thirsty

soin *m.* anxiety, care, attention

soit *third sing. pres. subj. of* **être** very well, be it so ; *conj.*∽ . . . ∽ whether . . . or, either . . . or

soixante *adj.* sixty

sol *m.* sou, cent ; *first made of silver, then of copper ; twenty sols (sous) equaled one* **livre** *or* **franc**

solide *adj.* solid, substantial

somme *f.* sum

sommet *m.* top ; the highest part (end) of a hall, farthest from the stage

son, sa, ses *poss. adj.* his, her, its

son *m.* sound

songe *m.* dream

songer *v.* think ; **∽ à** think of ; **je ne songeais pas** I forgot

sonner *v.* sound, ring

sorte *f.* kind, sort, manner ; **de la ∽** in this *or* that manner, thus ; **de ∽ que** so that ; **d'autre ∽** otherwise

sortir *v.* go out, (*theatrical*) exit ; **∽ d'affaire** settle up

sot, sotte *adj.* foolish, silly, crazy ; *as noun*, fool

sottise *f.* foolish thing, foolishness ; ill-natured thing

sou *m.* cent ; *see* **sol**

souci *m.* care

soucier *v.* trouble ; **se ∽** care, mind

soufflet *m.* blow, box, slap

souffrir *v.* suffer, endure, permit, bear

souhait *m.* wish

souhaiter *v.* wish, desire

soûl (*the* l *is silent*) *m.* fill ; **tout mon ∽** all I want to, to my heart's content

soulier *m.* shoe

soumettre *v.* enslave, subject, submit, subdue

soupçon *m.* suspicion

soupe *f.* soup

soupir *m.* sigh

soupirer *v.* sigh

sourcil *m.* eyebrow; **froncer le** ∽ knit one's brows

sourd *adj.* deaf

soutenir *v.* maintain, sustain, support, reënforce

souvenir : se ∽ de *v.* remember

souvent *adv.* often; le plus ∽ **41** 28, more often than not

spectacle *m.* spectacle, display

stratagème *m.* trick, stratagem

stupide *m.* fool, stupid person, blockhead

style *m.* style; **du** ∽ **de** in the style of

subsister *v.* endure, last, live, subsist

sucer *v.* suck, drain; *in* **40** 26 *it is suggestive of the leech*

suffire *v.* suffice, be sufficient

suivre *v.* follow, attend

sujet -ette *adj.* subject, liable

sujet *m.* cause, subject, purpose, reason

superbe *adj.* magnificent

supplice *m.* torture, punishment

sur *prep.* on, upon, regarding

sûr *adj.* certain, sure

surprenant *adj.* surprising

surtout *adv.* above all, especially

sus (*sound final* s) *interj.* now then! come on! cheer up!

symphonie *f.* orchestra, assembly of instruments

t' *see* **te**

table *f.* table

tâcher *v.* try, endeavor

taille *f.* figure, stature, waist, cut

tailleur *m.* tailor, haberdasher; *in Molière's day tailors supplied also shoes, stockings, wigs, plumes, and other wearing apparel, but apparently only as agents for trades other than their own;* **garçon** ∽ tailor's apprentice; **maître** ∽ master tailor

taire *v.* say nothing about; se ∽ be silent

talent *m.* talent

tandis que *conj.* while, until, while waiting for

tant *adv.* so much, so many, so long; ∽ . . . **que** as much as, until

tante *f.* aunt

tantôt *adv.* soon, presently, by and by, just now

tapis *m.* rug, carpet

tarare *interj.* fiddlesticks! fiddle-deedee! pshaw! no!

tarder *v.* delay, tarry, be long (*in doing something*); il ne **tardera** **guère** he'll soon be here

taudis *m.* hovel, dirty place

te, t' *pron.* thee, to thee, you, to you

tel, telle *adj.* such; **un tel** such a one, so and so

témoignage *m.* proof, testimony

temps *m.* time, while, weather, season; **de tout** ∽ at all times; **tout le** ∽ **43** 30, all the time needed, plenty of time; **de** ∽ **en** ∽ from time to time

tendre *adj.* tender

tendrement *adv.* softly, tenderly, daintily

tendresse *f.* tenderness

tenir *v.* hold, keep; carry; endure, bear; have, 26 7; possess, 49 5; believe, maintain, insist, 4 17; **tiens!** *or* **tenez!** see here! ∽ **parole** keep one's word; **tient** 67 5 = **retient**

terre *f.* earth, ground, floor; **par** ∽ on the floor

tête *f.* head; **se mettre en** ∽ (**en** ∽ *would now be* **dans la** ∽) get into one's head

théâtre *m.* theater, stage

tigre *m.* tiger

tintamarre *m.* clatter, hurly-burly, hubbub

tirer *v.* draw, remove, shoot; ∽ **des armes** be skilled in arms (*especially with swords*); **se** ∽ draw away, withdraw, retire

titre *m.* title

tomber *v.* fall; ∽ **d'accord** agree, admit, acknowledge

tonnerre *m.* thunder

tort *m.* wrong, harm; **faire** ∽ do a wrong, offend; **à** ∽ **et à travers** at random, haphazard

tôt *adv.* soon

total *adj.* total, entire

touchant *adj.* striking, touching, attractive

toucher *v.* touch, move, concern, gratify, please

toujours *adv.* always, ever

tour *m.* turn, round

tourner *v.* turn, express; **se** ∽ turn around

tout, toute, tous, toutes *adj., adv.* all, any, whole, every; *used adverbially,* quite, exactly, very; **tous deux** both; **tout le monde** everybody; **tout ce que** everything that, all that; **tout à fait** quite, entirely, thoroughly; **de tout temps** at all times; **tout beau!** *or* **tout doux!** gently! look out! **tout du premier coup** at the very first shot; **point (pas) du tout** not at all; **tout à l'heure** right off, (*with a past tense*) just now; **tout comme** just as; **tout à vous** entirely at your service; **tout à propos** most opportunely, in the very nick of time; **à toute force** absolutely; **toute belle . . . que** however beautiful

tout *m.* everything

tracas *m.* worry, stir

trahison *f.* treason

train *m.* retinue

traîner *v.* drag, bring; bring in their train, 58 13

trait *m.* draft, swallow, arrow

traité *m.* treatise

traitement *m.* treatment

traiter *v.* treat

traître -esse *adj.* treacherous, traitorous

traître *m.* traitor

traîtresse *f.* traitress

trancher *v.* cut; ∽ **le mot** use the word readily *or* with authority

transporté *adj.* enraptured, elated

travail *m.* (*pl.* **travaux**) work, labor

travailler *v.* work, labor

travers *m.* breadth, whim; à ∾
 adv., *prep.* through, across; à
 tort et à ∾ at random, haphazard

tremblement *m.* vibration, thrill,
 trembling

trembler *v.* shake, tremble

trémousser *v.* stir; **se ∾** skip, frisk,
 flutter about

trente *adj.* thirty

très *adv.* very, very much

triompher *v.* exult, triumph

trois *adj.* three

troisième *adj.* third

tromper *v.* deceive; **se ∾** be mis-
 taken

trompeur -euse *adj.* deceitful

trop *adv.* too, too much, too many;
 par ∾ far too much, very

troubler *v.* disturb

troussé *adj.* arranged, fixed up,
 "tucked up"; *more often applied
 to cooked food*

trouvé *adj.* felicitous, happy, successful

trouver *v.* find, think, like; **je me
 trouve assez de bien** I find myself
 sufficiently wealthy; **se ∾** be

truchement *m.* interpreter

tu *pron.* thou; *used as the pronoun of affection, sometimes also
 of disdain and in speaking to
 inferiors*

tuer *v.* kill

turban *m.* turban

turc, turque *adj.* Turkish; **à la
 turque** in the Turkish manner

turc *m.* Turkish language; **Turc**
 Turk; **Grand Turc** Sultan of
 Turkey

un, une *indefinite article*, a, an;
 numeral, one; **l'un** one; **l'un(e)
 et l'autre** both

union *f.* harmony, union

universel -elle *adj.* world-wide, universal

usage *m.* custom

user *v.* wear out, make use of

utile *adj.* useful

utilité *f.* usefulness

vacarme *m.* din, turmoil, racket,
 hubbub

vache *f.* cow; **∾ à lait** milch cow

vain *adj.* vain, empty, useless

vaincre *v.* conquer, overcome

valet *m.* manservant, valet

valoir *v.* be worth, be of the same
 value as, be equal to; **∾ mieux**
 be worth more, be better; **il
 vaut mieux pour elle un honnête
 homme** an honorable man is better for her; **faire ∾** cause to appreciate, extol, *but in* **59** 9, set
 a value upon

varier *v.* vary, diversify

veau *m.* calf, veal

véhémence *f.* vehemence

velours *m.* velvet. *For a long time
 this was worn only by the nobility,
 because of its great cost*

velouté *adj.* (*of wine*) deep-colored,
 with fine mellow flavor, velvety

vendre *v.* sell

vengeance *f.* revenge, vengeance

venir *v.* come, happen; **∾ de +**
 infinitive, have just (done something); **∾ aux mains** come to
 blows; **venons à** now for; **en ∾
 à bout** succeed

vent *m.* wind

ventrebleu *interj.* (*euphemism for* **ventre Dieu** God's body) "odsbud," zounds

véritable *adj.* true

vérité *f.* truth; **à la ∾** in truth

verre *m.* glass

vers *prep.* toward

vers *m.* verse

verser *v.* shed, pour

vert *adj.* green

vert *m.* tartness, greenness (*of wine not yet completely made*)

vertigo *m.* whim, caprice, madness, folly

vertu *f.* virtue

veste *f.* jacket, coat, waistcoat; **portant la ∾ 71** *heading of scene vi,* carrying the flaps of the tunic, *a long Oriental robe worn over other garments*

vêtir *v.* clothe, dress

veuve *f.* widow

vie *f.* life, existence; **ne . . . de sa (ta) ∾** never again

vieux, vieil, vieille *adj.* old

vilain *adj.* ill-bred, improper, vulgar, ugly

vilaine *f.* wretched person, hussy, mean creature

village *m.* village

ville *f.* city

vin *m.* wine

vingt *adj.* twenty, score; **quatre-∾(s)** eighty; **six-∾s** one hundred and twenty; *counting by scores was then more common than now; compare* "*les Quinze-Vingts,*" *the name of a hospital in Paris for three hundred blind people, also the Biblical English* "*threescore years and ten,*" "*fourscore,*" *etc.*

violence *f.* violence, torture

violon *m.* violin, fiddler; **dessus de ∾** first violin

visage *m.* face

vis-à-vis de *prep.* opposite, facing

vision *f.* notion, hobby, vision, silly idea

visite *f.* visit

visiter *v.* visit

vite *adv.* quickly

vivre *v.* live; **façon de ∾** conduct; **vive!** long live!

vœu *m.* (*pl.* **vœux**) vow, prayer, desire

voici *prep., adv.* here is, here are; **le ∾** here he is

voilà *prep., adv.* there is, there are, that is, those are, behold; **∾ qui est bien** that is good; **le ∾ qui vient** there he comes, he is coming; **vous ∾** there you are; **que ∾** over there; **que ∾ qui est scélérat!** how rascally that is! **que ∾ de belles mains!** what beautiful hands! **∾ qui est fait** it's all over; **∾ pas le coup de langue** there's a glib backbiting tongue; **∾ ce que c'est de se mettre** that's what comes from dressing

voir *v.* see; **faire ∾** show, display; **voyons!** come! **je vous vois venir** I see what you are driving at, I know your intentions

voisinage *m.* neighborhood

voix *f.* voice, sound; vowel sound, *see* **voyelle**

vol *m.* theft

volant *adj.* flying; **feu** ∽ will-o'-the-wisp

voler *v.* fly, steal

volonté *f.* will

volontiers *adv.* willingly

votre *poss. adj.* (*pl.* **vos**) your

vouloir *v.* wish, want, will, be willing, try, expect, be firmly determined, insist; ∽ **bien** be quite willing; ∽ **dire** mean; ∽ **de mal à** be angry with, have a grudge against

vous *pron.* you, to you, yourself, yourselves; ∽-**même** yourself; **vous** *was the usual form of address in the 17th century even between husband and wife*

voyage *m.* travel, journey

voyager *v.* travel, journey

voyelle *f.* vowel, vowel sound

vrai *adj.* real, true

vraiment *adv.* truly

vraisemblance *f.* probability, likelihood, similarity to truth

vue *f.* sight; **sa** ∽ **43** 30, the sight of her

y *adv.* there, therein, thereto, for it, in it, to it, at it; **il** ∽ **a** there is, there are; *often very indefinite and hence difficult to translate*

yeux *plural of* œil

ANNOUNCEMENTS

INTERNATIONAL
MODERN LANGUAGE SERIES

FRENCH

GINN AND COMPANY Publishers

INTERNATIONAL
MODERN LANGUAGE SERIES

FRENCH — *continued*

Lazare: Les Plus Jolis Contes de Fées	$0.35
Lazare: Premières Lectures en Prose et en Vers	.35
Legouvé and Labiche: La Cigale chez les Fourmis (Van Daell)	.20
Lemaître: Morceaux Choisis (Mellé)	.75
Leune: Difficult Modern French	.60
Loti: Pêcheur d'Islande (Peirce)	.45
Luquiens: Places and Peoples	.50
Luquiens: Popular Science	.60
Maistre: La Jeune Sibérienne (Robson)	.35
Maistre: Les Prisonniers du Caucase (Robson)	.30
Marique and Gilson: Exercises in French Composition	.40
Maupassant: Ten Short Stories (Schinz)	.40
Meilhac and Halévy: L'Été de la Saint-Martin; Labiche: La Lettre Chargée; d'Hervilly: Vent d'Ouest (House)	.35
Mellé: Contemporary French Writers	.50
Mérimée: Carmen and Other Stories (Manley)	.60
Mérimée: Colomba (Schinz)	.40
Michelet: La Prise de la Bastille (Luquiens)	.20
Moireau: La Guerre de l'Indépendance en Amérique (Van Daell)	.20
Molière: L'Avare	.40
Molière: Le Bourgeois Gentilhomme (Oliver)	.45
Molière: Le Malade Imaginaire (Olmsted)	.50
Molière: Les Précieuses Ridicules (Davis)	.50
Musset, Alfred de: Selections (Kuhns)	.60
Pailleron: Le Monde où l'on s'ennuie (Price)	.40
Paris: Chanson de Roland, Extraits de la	.50
Picard: La Petite Ville (Dawson)	.40
Potter: Dix Contes Modernes	.30
Racine: Andromaque (Searles)	.40
Renard: Trois Contes de Noël (Meylan)	.15
Rostand: Les Romanesques (Le Daum)	.35
Rotrou: Saint Genest and Venceslas (Crane)	1.00
Sainte-Beuve: Selected Essays (Effinger)	.35
Sand: La Famille de Germandre (Kimball)	.30
Sand: La Mare au Diable (Gregor)	.35
Sévigné, Madame de: Letters of (Harrison)	.50
Van Daell: Introduction to French Authors	.50
Van Daell: Introduction to the French Language	1.00

GINN AND COMPANY Publishers

NOUVEAU COURS FRANÇAIS

By André C. Fontaine, Boys' High School, Brooklyn, N.Y.

272 pages, illustrated, 90 cents

This new book in first-year French combines the best features of the grammatical and the natural methods. Advocates of class drill in the spoken language in addition to written work will find the book very satisfying. The exercises for translation into French are conversational in tone, and questions in French, which form a part of each lesson, offer abundant opportunity for oral work. Much of the grammar is given entirely in French.

The reading matter includes a concise résumé of French history ; a description of Parisian life and geography ; discussions of the metric system and of the government, the agriculture, the industry, the commerce, and other social and economic features of France.

The grammar is presented in a sane and practical manner, with special emphasis on the proper use of the French past tenses. The idiomatic expressions of everyday life receive particular attention, and frequently used literary quotations, with their origin and modern application, are cited and explained. In short, the book is eminently adapted to the acquisition of a practical and well-grounded knowledge of simple written and spoken French.

FRENCH VERB FORM

By S. T. M. Harmanson, Randolph-Macon Woman's College, Lynchburg, Va.

48 sheets, 35 cents

Each page of Harmanson's " French Verb Form " is a blank chart, the filling out of which gives the student a comprehensive view of the whole verb, arranged according to its parts. There are spaces for every form and tense, including compound tenses, and provision is made for both regular and irregular verbs.

GINN AND COMPANY Publishers